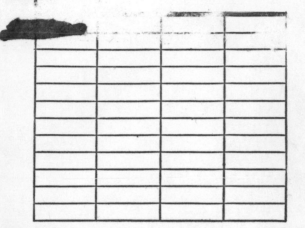

Tobias Smollett

A study in style

For my mother, and in memory of my father

Damian Grant

Tobias Smollett
A study in style

Manchester University Press

Rowman and Littlefield

Published by
Manchester University Press
Oxford Road, Manchester M13 9PL

UK ISBN 0 7190 0607 4

First published in the USA 1977 by
Rowman and Littlefield
Totowa, N.J. 07512

US ISBN 0 87471 926 7

Printed in Great Britain
by Eyre & Spottiswoode Ltd,
Grosvenor Press, Portsmouth

Contents

Preface

When I first became interested in Smollett, about ten years ago, the situation for the student was in many respects very different from that which exists today. To begin with, although one or two popular editions of *Roderick Random* and *Humphry Clinker* were available, Smollett's other works had to be sought either on the library shelves or in second-hand book shops, where they might be found in one or other of the complete editions[1] or in one-volume Victorian monsters (I was grateful enough myself, as a student, to pick up Roscoe's edition in Charing Cross Road for a pound). None of these texts was reliable; indeed, apart from Seccombe's edition of the *Travels Through France and Italy*,[2] which is itself far from being a perfect example, no critical edition of any work of Smollett's had ever appeared. Noyes's edition of the *Letters*[3] was incomplete, and the situation here had been complicated by the publication of Cordasco's supplement to the Noyes collection, which was later proved to include five forgeries.[4]

The interested reader of Smollett did have the advantage already of Lewis M. Knapp's excellent biography,[5] and (if he was lucky enough to live near one of the few libraries that possessed a copy) Fred W. Boege's valuable study of Smollett's reputation,[6] both of which works contain useful critical insights. Seccombe's enthusiasm tended to be catching, as was the genuine regard of occasional critics of Smollett such as Herbert Read, George Orwell and V. S. Pritchett;[7] and there was also A. D. McKillop's chapter on Smollett in his *Early Masters of English Fiction*,[8] which did succeed in providing a critical account of his work that actually coincided with one's experience of reading it.

But apart from these isolated examples there was little critical encouragement. The standard literary histories systematically misunderstood and misrepresented Smollett, which is hardly surprising when we consider the inhibiting precedent of late nineteenth-century criticism. More often than not his Scottish 'crudity' was used to set off the saner and therefore superior art of Fielding—much as Dickens's genius used to be disparaged in comparison with the irony and intelligence of Thackeray. And even the works devoted to Smollett were all restricted either by subject matter[9] or approach[10] from providing any real critical initiative. Smollett had for some reason attracted a good deal of (rather baffling) scholarly attention without stimulating any commensurate critical activity. No one made any audible claims for him as a writer: a situation which seemed absurd as well as unfair, when most readers are immediately struck by Smollett's energy and passion and often carry away a lasting impression of his work. (For what it is worth, my own experience as a university teacher has always been that students respond more readily to Smollett than to any other eighteenth-century writer except Swift and, perhaps, Sterne.)

The situation has now substantially changed. Starting with *Pickle* in 1964, four of Smollett's five novels have now been responsibly edited for the Oxford English Novels series, leaving only *Random* to complete the set.[11] The University of Iowa announced its 'Bicentennial Edition of the Works of Tobias Smollett' in 1967, under the editorship of O. M. Brack, and although none of the volumes has yet appeared this will eventually take its place as the standard edition of Smollett's works.[12] Not least, L. M. Knapp has published his authoritative edition of the *Letters*.[13] And as an index of an increasing readership, well presented paperback editions of Smollett's more popular works have also begun to appear.

There has also been a good deal of renewed critical activity. Five books on Smollett have appeared in the last ten years, including the volume of essays presented to L. M.

Knapp; several other books have included important sections on Smollett; and articles on his work now turn up fairly regularly in the scholarly journals.[14] But has this activity succeeded in making critical reparation after years of neglect, and worse than neglect? Fred W. Boege remarked at the end of his study that a better opinion of Smollett would emerge only 'when critics can convince their readers that Smollett possesses high integrity, a profound satirical intent, and a style of unusual merit'.[15] It is true that we do now see Smollett the man in a more favourable light, with 'high integrity' as the very ground of his character; today's critics are fully prepared to admit Smollett's 'profound satirical intent'; and there has even been some attempt to come to terms with his style.[16] But with the notable exception of one work by a French scholar and critic, these approaches have not been organised into a new view of Smollett; nothing has happened to disturb the indifference his work has usually encountered in the common roads of criticism. Articles on 'Fielding and Smollett' continue to appear,[17] with predictable conclusions as to their relative merit (a relative merit which has not always been conceded);[18] histories of the novel still refer unashamedly to Smollett as Fielding's 'vulgariser';[19] and the dust still rises over academic disputes as to whether or not Smollett can be set down (and left down?) as a picaresque writer.[20] In a review in 1971 G. S. Rousseau reminded us of the 'lamentable fact that no serious book entirely devoted to Smollett's fiction as yet exists':[21] a fact which still obtains, as far as English criticism is concerned.

The book which provides the exception is Paul-Gabriel Boucé's *Les Romans de Smollett*. In what is a formidable piece of research Boucé has digested all the available information about Smollett, and all the relevant information about his times, in order first to present the novelist himself in a more sympathetic light and then to see the novels in context, reflecting as they do a reality which is summoned up in all its moral and physical, social and intellectual aspects. Boucé analyses each of the five novels in great detail in terms of its theme and structure, and concludes his study with an original section on Smollett's style. It is an achievement for which all students of Smollett can be grateful. But Boucé has written exclusively on the novels (in consideration of which he relies heavily on the formal approach with which I take issue in my third chapter); the *Travels* and the *Atom* do not come within his chosen spectrum, whereas for my purposes they are both very important works. And so although Boucé's book is certainly the most important study of Smollett as an artist which has yet appeared, it differs in method, length, and (not least) language from my own. There is sufficient reason to argue that the case for Smollett remains to be made. [22]

The main and obvious cause of Smollett's anomalous position—as an eighteenth-century writer enthusiastically read but not very highly regarded—lies in that conditioned reflex of criticism which can only discuss his work in off-the-peg terminology cut out for other (more regular) shapes. Thus presented, Smollett can only appear like some kind of novelistic vagabond dressed in borrowed robes. Or (to adopt another metaphor) the student sets out with his 'rules and compasses' and comes back from his reading with the information that 'not one of the angles at the four corners was a right angle'. [23]

It is for this reason that I have considered it worthwhile—indeed, necessary—to devote the first part of this study, 'Extrication', to providing a nearer view of the criteria by which Smollett's work is usually judged. The first chapter deals with the implications of the argument about Smollett's fidelity to fact, the second with the question of his moral purpose, and the third with the problems surrounding his consciousness of form and artistic intentions generally.

In the second section, 'Equipment', I work from the basic assumptions of the time with regard to language (in chapter four) and style (in chapter five) towards a recognition of Smollett's distinctive attitude to and employment of both. It is my argument that Smollett writes in a different linguistic tradition from that of his fellow novelists, especially Fielding; and exercises within this tradition a far greater degree of stylistic virtuosity. Although I believe in the value of my earlier chapters, I would still suggest that the reader impatient of theory might begin here to see whether the exercise is going to be worth while.

The first two chapters of the third section 'Exercise' represent a trial of this revised critical approach in a sustained analysis of Smollett's prose style, which I have divided into two contrasting but complementary casts according to the attitude to experience implicit in each: the comic 'style of the circumference' and the passionate 'style of the centre'. (The rationale for this division is proposed at the end of chapter five.) In the last, and shortest, chapter I draw attention to those lyrical qualities in Smollett's style which are the expression of another side of his nature, and which provide further important evidence of his essentially poetic use of language.

In his biography of Smollett David Hannay regretted that the novelist was 'not always quotable' to his fellow Victorians.[24] In contrast, I find Smollett to be an almost irresistibly quotable writer, and I hope that no apology is due for the fact that some pages of this study may read like a critical selection from his work. If I did need to defend myself I could do no better than invoke Smollett's compatriot, David Hume, who maintained that 'no criticism can be very instructive, which descends not to particulars, and is not full of examples and illustrations'.

I would like to express my acknowledgement to Professor Norman Callan, under whose sympathetic supervision I began my work on Smollett at Queen Mary College, University of London;[25] to Professor Lewis Knapp, doyen of Smollett scholars, who has given me personally a good deal of assistance and encouragement; to Paul-Gabriel Boucé, Professor at the Sorbonne, whose dedication to Smollett studies would be quite intimidating were it not for his warm friendship and great good humour; to a former student at Manchester, John Fitzpatrick, whose enthusiasm for Smollett may be measured by his willingness to read parts of this book in typescript; and also to several of my colleagues in the English Department at Manchester. John Anderson and Douglas Brooks both read parts of the work and made useful comments; Alan Shelston and Gerald Hammond helped me with some elusive references; and Helen Maclean drew my diagram.

I must also record my gratitude to the staffs of the British Museum Library, the Senate House Library of London University and the John Rylands University Library of Manchester for generous assistance at all times; and my particular thanks to Mrs Nancy Walsh and Mrs Shelagh Aston, who between them typed the book—parts of it direct from what must unquestionably be (in Smollettian hyperbole) the worst handwriting in the world.

But I am indebted most of all to my wife, Teresa, who (though I blush to recall the fact now) typed my MA thesis, twice, in the first year of our marriage; and has since endured all the stages in the preparation of this book—my frustration, depression, and despair as well as my enthusiasm—with a well judged combination of tolerance where it was fitting, help where it was really required, and, where I needed or deserved it, total disregard.

D.G.

Manchester 1975

Note on texts

I have used first editions of Smollett's works (as listed in the bibliography) except where a reputable modern edition exists, as in the following instances:

The Adventures of Peregrine Pickle (1751), ed. James L. Clifford (1964).
The Adventures of Ferdinand Count Fathom (1753), ed. Damian Grant (1971).
The Adventures of Sir Launcelot Greaves (1762), ed. David Evans (1973).
Travels Through France and Italy (1766), ed. Thomas Seccombe (1907).
The Expedition of Humphry Clinker (1771), ed. Lewis M. Knapp (1966).

Seccombe's text of the *Travels* is not always reliable, and I have on a few occasions silently corrected his reading. (See the preface for a brief account of the situation with regard to the Smollett text in general.)

References are to chapter (or other division) and page; in *Clinker* the letters, which are not numbered, are referred to by date.

Translation of French sources quoted is my own, except where otherwise indicated.

I

Extrication

1 *The facts of the case*

1

In the long and sympathetic introduction which he wrote for his edition of Smollett's *Travels* in 1907 Thomas Seccombe said of the work that 'as a literary record of travel it is distinguished by a very exceptional veracity',[1] and later critics have tended to endorse his claim in respect of this and Smollett's other works.[2] Now one would not set out simply to contradict this view, which does certainly contain a truth about Smollett's work. But one needs to examine the consequences for criticism of a situation where Smollett's 'exceptional veracity' has been allowed to play so significant a role in the assessment of his qualities as a writer. The consequences, I believe, are a general inability on the part of critics to distinguish these qualities (though there is no shortage of readers who enjoy them), and a reluctance to recognise Smollett's art and originality in the exercise of English prose. Once his simple truth or trustworthiness is advanced as a significant criterion of a writer's value he is immediately relegated to a second or third division. This happens as a result of an apparent dishonesty in the consciousness of criticism itself, a kind of doublethink between what it prescribes and what it actually approves of; and according to which the 'fidelity' or 'integrity' for which a writer is applauded entitle him only to recognition on a lower scale of value.

That this is the case may easily be illustrated. When Thackeray said that Smollett 'did not invent much, as I fancy, but had the keenest perceptive faculty, and described what he saw with wonderful relish and delightful broad humour'[3] he sounded a condescending note that has been extensively echoed ever since. C. J. Rawson can still refer to *Clinker* as 'readable and informative as reportage of eighteenth-century life in several parts of Britain'[4] whilst remaining oblivious to its imaginative and stylistic properties. It would seem to be safe to take as a representative critical attitude that expressed by Ian Watt as an afterthought in the last chapter of *The Rise of the Novel*, to the effect that 'Smollett has many merits as a social reporter'.[5] Smollett is damned with faint praise for the truth to which he submits with such apparent servility, and depressed from an artist to a journalist.

II

The requirement of historical truth has always tended to create a distraction in criticism, involving as it does a loss of confidence in the creative imagination and a retreat back into the world itself—the world, with all its pointless prodigality of fact and incident. It is rooted in what Plato called the 'ancient quarrel between philosophy and poetry',[6] the quarrel between different *kinds* of truth, which has a long if not always fruitful history in the evolution of critical ideas.[7] It represents a particularly literal interpretation of the appeal which Johnson believed ought always to be open 'from criticism to nature',[8] from the laws of poetry to the laws of life itself on which these are ultimately founded.

The novel, from its origins and apparent nature, has always laboured under a particular difficulty with regard to its relationship with the real world, which is very often taken to be a matter of simple subservience, of obedient reproduction. (The appeal open from criticism to nature is also open to abuse.) It made its appearance in a context instinctively suspicious of what Johnson called the 'vagrant and licentious faculty' of the imagination, sceptical of the writer's need—or ability—to transform his materials, and generally happier with what Johnson defines elsewhere as 'those relations which are levelled with the general surface of life'.[9]

But it soon became apparent that the 'general surface of life' proved too severe a test for the capacity of the writer and the patience of the reader alike: both were beginning to feel what Henry James described as 'the old burden of the much life and the little art',[10] and so (predictably enough) they rediscovered the point of a compromise—or, better, synthesis—between factual and fictional elements. An Eastern tale was praised in Smollett's *Critical Review* for having 'enough of real incidents to afford the pleasure of instruction, and of the seasoning of fiction, to save the perusal from the tediousness of merely dry historical matter of fact'.[11] And it is surely significant that one aspiring fantasist is advised to 'chasten his imagination, and adhere closely to verisimilitude and probability in his future productions' only, as it were, *faute de mieux*: 'for, though Lucian, Rabelais, and *Swift*, have set nature at defiance, their absurdities are recommended by *exquisite* humour, pregnancy of wit, and well conducted satire'.[12] There is some evidence that this review may have been written for the *Critical* by Smollett himself,[13] and so it is doubly interesting to observe that the appeal to nature is clearly seen here, according to a more demanding critical projection, as evidence of imaginative weakness.

What we need to recognise—especially in the case of a writer like Smollett—is that the imagination ought not to be thought of as somehow at odds with the real world. The truth is that the imagination and reality are mutually dependent; indeed, the concepts can only exist in relation to each other. Reality, so far as we are concerned, is a blank outside the human mind: 'Where man is not, nature is barren' (Blake).[14] And the imagination needs a world to inhabit, a reality to realise, before it can function at all, and begin its characteristic activity of synthesis and transformation: 'No ideas but in things' (William Carlos Williams).[15]

The resolution of this apparent problem is, then, that we can have it both ways; and all great writers have always done so. Let us remember the aphorism of Wallace Stevens: 'The interrelation between reality and the imagination is the basis of the character of literature'.[16] And also the phrase Marianne Moore borrowed from Yeats, which defines the poet's and (surely) every writer's objective most happily. Poets must become, she says, 'literalists of the imagination'.[17]

The reviewer of *Humphry Clinker* in the *Critical* had obviously pondered these problems, in some form, and his account of the novel includes a useful summary of the critical arguments I have outlined.

> Though novels have long since been divested of that extravagance which characterized the earlier productions in Romance, they have, nevertheless, continued, in the hands of meaner writers, to be distinguished by a similarity of fable, which, notwithstanding it is of a different cast, and less unnatural than the former, is still no less unfit for affording agreeable entertainment. From the wild excursions of fancy, invention is brought home to range through the probable occurences of life; but, however it may have improved in point of credibility, it is certainly too often deficient with regard to variety of adventure. With many, an adherence to simplicity has produced the effects of dullness; and, with most, too close an imitation of their predecessors had excluded the pleasure of novelty.
>
> The celebrated author of this production is one of those few writers who have discovered an original genius. His novels are not more distinguished for the natural management of the fable, and a fertility of interesting incidents, than for a strong, lively, and picturesque description of characters. The same vigour that animates his other works, is conspicuous in the present, where we are entertained with a variety of scenes and characters almost unanticipated. Those, in particular, of Mr Bramble, Mrs Tabitha Bramble, and Lieutenant Lismahago, are painted with the highest touches of discriminating humour and expression.[18]

Smollett's realities are 'described in such a manner as to afford a pleasure even superior to what arises from portraits of fancy'; fact and imagination are at last reconciled, with dullness (queen of the *Dunciad*) left as the common enemy.

The same instinct lies behind two later, general criticisms of Smollett which are relevant here. David Herbert's brief 'Life of Smollett' contains some of the best criticism of the novelist, by any standards. In the course of this essay Herbert stands out against what he calls 'a cant use of the word realism in our day' [1870], and proposes that Smollett himself is 'properly understood, the greatest realist in our language. The spirit of truth was the soul of his fancy'.[19] This last sentence contains a fine critical insight, and the whole is a deserved tribute to Smollett's artistic power—what Herbert refers to elsewhere as a 'trinity of energy' charged by Smollett's learning, his industry and his genius.[20] Writing at the turn of the century, J. A. Nicklin may well have been thinking of Herbert's point when he claimed that Smollett was 'by virtue alike of energy and knowledge, a very king among the realists'; and he concludes his own essay with a convincing argument for the reconciliation in Smollett's work of those criteria which so many take to be inevitably opposed:

> In a very prosaic age, he clearly apprehended one kind of poetry—the poetry of action, and he made it apparent to everyone, and glorified it, not by throwing over it a false and extraneous glamour, but by presenting it, with severe precision, as it actually was. With such an intention, and such a method, he deserves to find partisans in the camps of Realism and Romance alike.[21]

III

It is my contention that Smollett was as alert as anyone else to the kinds of claim made alternately for fact and for imaginative freedom in the eighteenth century. Although he never took the trouble to elaborate a systematic theory of fiction (like Fielding) or (like Sterne) to make his work a deliberate exercise in formal possibilities, there are statements dispersed in his letters, in his editorial, critical and historical work, and within the novels and other books themselves, that have a direct bearing on the question. Finally, the character of his imaginative work itself bears witness to his discrimination between the two standards.

It is not difficult to establish Smollett's valuation of the truth of fact where fact is ascertainable and truth required: that is, in private affairs and in all kinds of historical or documentary writing. He took his writing of history very seriously. The *Complete History* was published in 1757–58, and in the latter year he gave his views on the responsibility of the historian in a letter to William Huggins:

I can safely say I had no other view in the Execution of that work than historical Truth, which I have displayed on all occasions to the best of my Knowledge without Fear or affection . . . I look upon the Historian who espouses a Faction, who strains Incidents or wilfully suppresses any Circumstances of Importance that may tend to the Information of the Reader, as the worst of Prostitutes. I pique myself upon being the only Historian of this Country who has had Honesty, Temper and Courage enough to be wholly impartial and disinterested.[22]

Defending himself in *The Briton* against John Wilkes, Smollett says he 'arrogates to himself no authority, but that which is derived from a strict regard to truth and morality'.[23] And he offers a severe personal criticism of the standard historians ancient and modern in an aside in the *Atom*, taking authenticity as his basic criterion:

The whole world has never been able to produce six good historians. Herodotus is fabulous even to a proverb; Thucydides is perplexed, obscure, and unimportant; Polybius is dry and inelegant; Livy superficial; and Tacitus a coxcomb. Guicciardini wants interest; Davila, digestion; and Sarpi, truth. In the whole catalogue of French historians, there is not one of tolerable authenticity. [i, 72]

Smollett declared in the preface to the *Continuation* of his history that he had submitted himself to 'the rigid severity of historical truth' in compiling this work;[24] and in another preface to one of his editorial undertakings, *A Compendium of Authentic and Entertaining Voyages* (the title itself is significant), Smollett felt it appropriate to castigate the current taste for fiction. 'We live in an age of levity and caprice, that can relish little besides works of fancy. . . . But to mix profit with delight should be the aim of all writers'.[25] He would certainly have agreed with Housman's remark that in an historian 'accuracy is a duty, not a virtue'.[26]

The literal truth, then, has its proper value in its proper place, where it does not need 'the resources of Art' (as Hawkesworth intended the phrase)[27] to support it. Obviously in the conduct of our ordinary affairs, where truth is public rather than philosophical, the line between simple truth and an imaginative reworking of the truth needs to be strictly drawn; as Smollett learnt to his cost in 1760, when he was fined £100 and sent to prison for three months for a libel on Admiral Knowles which had been published in the *Critical Review* two years earlier.[28] We find Smollett drawing this line very emphatically himself in a letter to Garrick, to whom he had made reparation in his *History* for the satirical account of the actor which had found its way into the first edition of *Pickle*: 'I thought it was a duty incumbent on me in particular to make a public attonement in a work of truth, for wrongs done him in a work of fiction'.[29]

Smollett shows his conformity to the critical attitudes of his contemporaries in this respect by disparaging the unrestrained fiction of the romances in the synoptic history of the novel which forms part of the preface to *Roderick Random*.

. . . when the minds of men were debauched by the imposition of priest-craft to the most absurd pitch of credulity; the authors of romance arose, and losing sight of probability, filled their performances with the most monstrous hyperboles. If they could not equal the ancient poets in point of genius, they were resolved to excel them in fiction, and apply to the wonder rather than the judgment of their readers.

Smollett goes on to object to the 'extravagance of behaviour' of the typical romance characters, and then turns with relief to Cervantes, who 'reformed the taste of mankind, representing chivalry in the right point of view, and converting romance to purposes far more useful and entertaining, by making it assume the sock, and point out the follies of ordinary life'—that is, by converting the romance into the novel; the terms were distinguished in this way throughout the eighteenth century. We may notice, however, that what Smollett is really getting at here is the incompetence of the writers of romance; it is fiction as a substitute for 'genius', not for fact, that Smollett objects to. The positive terms he prescribes for his own novel imply no restriction on the right of fiction to be fictive: 'Every reader will, at first sight, perceive I have not deviated from nature in the facts, which are all true in the main, although the circumstances are altered and disguised, to avoid personal satire' (i, vi–x).

Smollett obviously recognised, himself, that such an orientation towards the real world does not involve the submission of the imagination. The line drawn between fact and fiction protects each against the danger of coming into competition with the other. In other words, despite Smollett's generous admission to Garrick, the account of the actor David Garrick in the *History* cannot be held to contradict the account of the actor Marmozet in *Peregrine Pickle* (although Smollett did his practical best to achieve this by excising the offending passage from his revised edition of the novel); the two accounts exist on different planes, and cannot be considered as alternatives. Smollett's words to Garrick are evidence not so much of a relegation of fiction as of a delicate social predicament from which he had to extricate himself. (The actor-manager, then at the height of his fame, had accepted Smollett's farce *The Reprisal* for performance at Drury Lane, helped with the rehearsals, and himself performed in *Zara* on Smollett's benefit night.) And in any case, Smollett is not disowning *Pickle*; he is only pointing out that a novel doesn't pretend to the kind of truth that constitutes a slander.

Smollett frequently seizes on the literal outlook which does not recognise these categories as a subject for ridicule. At one point in *Random* Dr Wagtail's 'simplicity' is exposed by an actor and a painter who seek to perfect their talents by direct observation of life. One Bragwell has been boasting of his success in duels:

The player begged this champion to employ him as his second the next time he intended to kill, for he wanted to see a man die of a stab, that he might know how to act such a part the more naturally on the stage.—'Die! (replied the hero) No, by G-d! I know better things than to incur the verdict of a Middlesex jury—I should look upon my fencing-master to be an ignorant son of a b--ch, if he had not taught me to prick any part of my antagonist's body, that I please to disable.'—'Oho! (cried Slyboot) if that be the

case, I have a favour to ask. You must know I am employed to
paint a Jesus on the cross; and my purpose is to represent him at
the point of time, when the spear is thrust into his side.—Now I
should be glad you would, in my presence, pink some impertinent
fellow into convulsions, without endangering his life, that I may
have an opportunity of taking a good clever agony from
nature:—The doctor will direct you where to enter, and how far to
go; but pray let it be as near the left side as possible.'—Wagtail,
who took this proposal seriously, observed, that it would be a very
difficult matter to penetrate into the left side of the thorax, without
hurting the heart, and of consequence killing the patient . . . [46;
ii, 104–5]

(We might see this as a parody before the event of the elaborate preparation of their subjects by some of the pre-
Raphaelite painters.)

Acting provides Smollett with further examples for his
criticism of the shallowly literal interpretation of art. I have
already alluded to the caricature of Garrick's performance in
Pickle. The subject is taken up twice, and each time as part of
a general attack on a false idea of acting. On the first occasion
Peregrine ironically advances 'as a proof of their excellence'
that some of the actors 'fancied themselves the very thing
they represented':

and recounted a story from Lucian, of a certain celebrated pantomime, who in acting the part of Ajax in his frenzy, was transported into a real fit of delirium, during which he tore to pieces the
cloaths of that actor who stalked before him, beating the stage with
iron shoes, in order to increase the noise, snatched an instrument
from one of the musicians, and broke it over the head of him who
represented Ulysses; and running to the consular bench, mistook a
couple of senators for the sheep which were to be slain. [55; p. 277]

(This time it is Stanislavsky's 'Method' which has overtaken
Smollett's ironic intention.) And later it is the literal response
of the audience as well as the absorption of the actor—or
mimic, as he ought in this case to be called—that Peregrine
exposes to ridicule.

I have known a Gascon, whose limbs were as eloquent as his tongue: he never mentioned the word sleep without reclining his head upon his hand; when he had occasion to talk of an horse, he always started up and trotted across the room, except when he was so situated that he could not stir without incommoding the company, and in that case he contented himself with neighing aloud: if a dog happened to be the subject of his conversation, he wagged his tail, and grinned in a most significant manner; and one day he expressed his desire of going backwards with such natural imitation of his purpose, that every body in the room firmly believed he had actually overshot himself, and fortified their nostrils accordingly. [102; p. 654]

Smollett would have subscribed to Johnson's belief that in the theatre 'the spectators are always in their senses, and know, from the first act to the last, that the stage is only a stage, and that the players are only players'; and seconded his challenge to the false assumption (which may be made of other arts besides the theatre) 'that any representation is mistaken for reality'.[30] A true Augustan in this respect, Smollett would have endorsed Brecht's 'alienation effect' as surely as he would have ridiculed Stanislavsky's theories; much as Pope ridiculed Cibber's ability to 'act, and be, a coxcomb with success'.[31] (The implication of Pope's jibe is that Cibber is unable to make any distinction between the two roles.)

Smollett's implicit attitude to the false ideal of illusionism in art is interestingly paralleled by the exposure of the novelists' stock formulas of verisimilitude, which we find especially in the later work. When Tom Clarke, the likable but verbose lawyer's clerk in *Greaves*, prepares to tell Launcelot's story to the eager company in the Black Lion, he prefaces it with exactly the kind of assurance with regard to his 'facts' that Smollett considered irrelevant to fiction:

'Facts are facts, as the saying is.—I shall tell, repeat, and relate a plain story—matters of fact, d'ye see, without rhetoric, oratory, ornament, or embellishment; without repetition, tautology, circumlocution, or going about the bush: facts which I shall aver, partly on the testimony of my own knowledge, and partly from the information of responsible evidences of good repute and credit, any circumstances known to the contrary notwithstanding.' [3; p. 18]

'Facts are facts' is not a bad tautology to start with: but they cannot speak for themselves as Clarke is made to imply here. The most solid of facts cannot survive the context of their happening without the intervention of the imagination, the sponsorship of language, and those strategies of style which the young lawyer affects to despise.

The defensive clichés of the literalists are exposed with delightful humour at the beginning of the *Atom* (I, v–vii), and the prefatory material to *Clinker* also constitutes a sustained irony on the trivial apologia for novels, memoirs and travel books which had been monotonously reiterated since the beginning of the century (and which are likely to surface again at any time even now).[32] The supposed 'onlie begetter' of the letters which compose this novel, Jonathan Dustwich, protests that 'the manner in which I got possession of these letters . . . is a circumstance that concerns my conscience only', though he does express the hope that if he is prosecuted for publishing 'the private correspondence of people still living' he will at least be spared flagellation. The bookseller Henry Davis is able to reassure him on this point: 'If you should be sentenced to the pillory, your fortune is made—As times go, that's a sure step to honour and preferment'; but he himself had already complained of the bad times his trade has to endure:

Writing is all a lottery—I have been a loser by the works of the greatest men of the age—I could mention particulars, and name names; but don't chuse it—The taste of the town is so changeable. Then there have been so many letters upon travels lately published—What between Smollett's, Sharp's, Derrick's, Thickness's, Baltimore's and Baretti's, together with Shandy's Sentimental Travels, the public seems to be cloyed with that kind of entertainment. [pp. 1–3]

The detached humour of this passage tells us much about Smollett; not least it tells us that he dared to call his fiction

fiction. He knew his materials had been fused in the imagination, and that what Kahrl calls the 'heightening' of style[33]
had lifted his work above the ruck of documentation thrown
up in every age.

IV

But what exactly are we meant to conclude from Smollett's
ironic attitude to his materials, as displayed here? Where
does it leave us, from a critical point of view? The situation is
admittedly not clear. Smollett's seven major works, from
Random to *Clinker*, are all in a mixed mode which presents
criticism with the difficult task of reconciling or in some way
combining criteria that bear no necessary relation to each
other—some attempts at which among his contemporaries
we have already observed.

It would be most useful to focus on the *Travels* in an
attempt to answer this question, since this is apparently the
most vulnerable of Smollett's works to the charge that it is
'crude fact'; that there is insufficient evidence of imaginative
transformation to make it a work of literature.

At one level the *Travels* is indeed very factual and
documentary. A considerable part—twelve letters, amounting to nearly a hundred pages—is devoted to a study of Nice
and its environs (13–24; pp. 116–201). Smollett introduces
one letter by saying, 'I had once thoughts of writing a complete natural history of this town and country', until he discovered himself 'altogether unequal to the task', and
apologises for 'such imperfect intelligence' as he is able to
offer (22; pp. 182–3). But this 'imperfect intelligence' includes
a connected study of its history, geography, economy, constitution, agriculture, commerce and contemporary manners. Smollett also kept a register of the weather during his
seventeen-month stay in Nice, the thirty-page record of
which (including readings in two different thermometers,
one mercury and one spirit) he appended to the first edition
of the *Travels*.[34] Johnson's observation that 'ancient travellers
guessed, modern travellers measure'[35] was borne out by
Smollett, who did actually measure the arena at Cemenelion

(now Cimia) with a packthread: though he 'will not answer
for the exactness of the measurement' (16; p. 144). The kind
of question he poses to himself in Italy about the Romans—'I
should be glad to know how the senators of Rome were
lodged' (30; p. 256)—suggests the indefatigable curiosity that
drove Smollett to a minuteness in these matters that is
almost pedantic; and the manuscript corrections he made to
the first edition emphasise his sense of responsibility to the
truth.[36] He had originally written that galleys were still built
in Pisa, but later corrected himself. 'This is a mistake. No
gallies have been built here for a great many years, and the
dock is now converted into stables for the Grand Duke's
Horse Guards' (27; p. 223).

But for all this, the *Travels* is not 'history' as Martz would
have us understand the word; it does not aspire to the condition of 'static synthesis' he describes. Whatever facts it may
include, and however reliable the scientific information
Smollett provides may be, it is not this material that deter-
mines the character of the work. These are static elements in
a higher synthesis—elements that can suddenly be prom-
.oted to another kind of life and relevance. As Kahrl rightly
observes, 'the mass of history, sociology, art criticism,
archaeology, and natural history comprising the factual substance of the *Travels* would be heavy reading were it not
animated by Smollett's own personality'.[37] It is not the facts
but Smollett's account of the facts that establishes its significance; the only projections one can defensibly draw in
attempting to criticise this work converge on Smollett himself.

This does not mean that one is driven back onto biographical criticism, the critically futile search (on Martz's
model) for sources of and parallels between events in the
writing and events in the life, or largely impertinent retrospective analyses of Smollett's character. Because what we
encounter in Smollett's writing is not Smollett's 'empirical
self'—which is the legitimate subject of the biographer—but
his 'poetic self', which should be the exclusive concern of the
critic. This 'poetic self' is composed not of experiences but of
statements; not of facts but of words.

The style of the *Travels* will form part of my subject in chapter seven, and I must leave the main evidence for my argument until then. But it will not be out of place here to invoke one or two examples of how Smollett's personality asserts itself and brings the inanimate facts to life in the most mundane of contexts. It is remarkable that even where Smollett offers practical advice to the 'aftercomer' he cannot do so in a neutral tone; we are always aware of how the harsh reality of his own experience whets the style. 'I mention these circumstances as a warning to other passengers. When a man hires a packet-boat from Dover to Calais or Boulogne, let him remember that the stated price is five guineas; and let him insist upon being carried into the harbour in the ship, without paying the least regard to the representations of the master, *who is generally a little dirty knave*' (1; p. 7: my italics). It is interesting that when this very sentence was incorporated in a guide book published four years after the *Travels* the phrase I have italicised was deleted, for the obvious reason that it identified only too clearly an individual point of view.[38]

Later on, a detailed description of the silkworm industry at Nice is enlivened by Smollett's evident sympathy for the 'acute and delicate sensations' of the unfortunate animal, which seems closely to resemble Smollett himself in its dislike of dirt, crowds and smells (22; pp. 186–7). And Smollett's account of the Roman ruins in Nîmes is rendered distinctive first by a contemptuous aside at modern French building—'Here are likewise ornaments of architecture, which savour much more of French foppery, than of the simplicity and greatness of the ancients'—and then by a more prosaic but also more personal observation:

It must be observed, however, for the honour of French cleanliness, that in the Roman basin, through which this noble stream of water passes, I perceived two washerwomen at work upon children's clouts and dirty linnen. Surprized, and much disgusted at this filthy phaenomenon, I asked by what means, and by whose permission, those dirty hags had got down into the basin, in order to contaminate the water at its fountain-head; and understood they

belonged to the commandant of the place, who had keys of the
subterranean passage. [10; p. 87]

'The observations I made in the course of my Travels thro'
France and Italy I have thrown into a Series of Letters.' This
was how Smollett himself described the *Travels* in a letter to
his friend, John Moore.[39] We should not mistake the sense of
the word 'thrown' here, by which Smollett intends nothing
casual; the observations are 'thrown' as a pot is thrown or
wood is thrown on a lathe, formed and fashioned by art into
something different in character and value. They have suffered what James called 'the sacrament of execution' and
become 'a thing of truth'.[40] This is why he need not 'answer
for the exactness of the measurement' at Cemenelion, nor for
the fairness of the metaphorical measurement to which he
submits the French and Italians. No one would accuse Smollett of the 'temperance and impartiality' with which he no
doubt ironically compliments himself on one occasion (17; p.
155); he would not wish to be considered in the same context
as Keysler and those other commentators who remind him
that 'the German genius lies more in the back than in the
brain' (28; p. 239).

V

The argument I have put forward in defence of the laden
Travels may be repeated, with some adjustment of emphasis,
in respect of all Smollett's works. From *Random* to *Clinker*, all
carry their fraughtage of fact in a vessel of fiction, whose
buoyancy is ensured by Smollett's style. When Jery Melford
writes, in a self-portrait Smollett smuggles into *Clinker*, that
his host 'is one of those few writers of the age that stand
upon their own foundation, without patronage, and above
dependance' (10 June; p. 124) he refers, of course, to his
financial integrity; but I do not think it would be too much of
a distortion to apply the sentence to Smollett's integrity as a
writer, which has its 'own foundation' in his creative imagination and is 'above dependance' of any menial kind on
unworked actuality. Indeed, Jery makes the distinction him-

self in his next letter when he declares to his correspondent, Sir Watkin Phillips, 'I shall grow vain, upon your saying you find entertainment in my letters; barren, as they certainly are, of incident and importance, because your amusement must arise, not from the matter, but from the manner, which you know is all my own' (10 June; p. 136). The manner, not the matter, is what counts; we recognise the terms from the reviewers' debate, and the priority Smollett awards here to style over substance is interesting authority for the critical viewpoint I am trying to establish.

On this authority we can dismiss Francis Vernon's contemporary complaint about the inauthenticity of the picture of the King's Bench prison in *Greaves*. Vernon had derived from another private source 'an account so very opposite to that given by a celebrated Author, in the adventure of Sir Launcelot Greaves, that I cannot avoid embracing this occasion to express my surprise, that a man, who, if I mistake not, was himself a prisoner there, should have drawn a picture so very unlike the original'.[41] Smollett is writing as a novelist, not as inspector of prisons, and is fully entitled to make the kind of selection (described by Knapp) whereby he 'played up the diversions of the prisoners rather than their hardships'.[42]

Johnson cited Smollett's declared antagonist Philip Thicknesse in a well known comment on Smollett's veracity recorded by Boswell. 'All travellers generally mean to tell truth; though Thicknesse observes, upon Smollett's account of his alarming a whole town in France by firing a blunderbuss, and frightening a French nobleman till he made him tie on his portmanteau, that he would be loth to say Smollett had told two lies in one page; but he had found the only town in France where these things could have happened.'[43] But we should react to Thicknesse's scepticism (and Johnson's apparent approval of it) with an appreciation, instead, of Smollett's narrative art: the episode is clearly the work of a novelist who is not seeking at this point to pass himself off as an historian. Similarly, to R. D. Spector's argument that it was in order to 'bring credence' to the Feast in the Manner of the Ancients in *Pickle* that Smollett described 'the revolting details attendant upon its participants—their anal and oral evacuations seem undeniable affirmations of reality',[44] we may reply that no one ever required such an 'affirmation' of the scene before; the reality it creates is the reality of 'a new world in a new orbit',[45] and no mere recension of the 'real'. The writer is not the servant of reality but its sponsor, whose statement enables us to possess more fully, and in greater variety, the atomic hypotheses that compose the solid world.

We do have the intriguing opportunity, in a number of contexts, of witnessing 'manner' at work upon 'matter' in Smollett's work, and I should like to consider one or two examples of this process here; the process whereby the butterfly 'truth' emerges from the chrysalis 'fact', rejoicing (so it appears) in the freedom of its new element. These occur where Smollett has referred back to an historical record written earlier in order to incorporate material in a fictional form; or in the reverse situation, where the later factual record represents a deliberate desiccation of the fictional episode. In either case it is instructive to compare the two versions and observe how the synthesised and stabilised fact contrasts with the animated fiction.

In his 'Account of the Expedition against Carthagene' Smollett relates in a straightforward manner, much after the style of his other historical writing, the events of the campaign against the Spanish in the West Indies of 1740–41 (during which he himself saw service as a surgeon aboard the *Chichester*). Now these same events form part of the hero's adventures in *Random*; but although the chapters (28–34) in which the details of the expedition intrude into the novel are in parts quite as literal as the historical account, Smollett exhibits a tendency, in transposing these events into his narrative, to describe them more imaginatively, more energetically, as if to absolve them as far as possible from dependence upon their original context. Detail is generally streamlined, evidence reduced, and simple facts are cast in a more dramatic form. The impersonality of the record is replaced by Roderick's more immediate first-person story:

— Nor was the eye more agreeably entertained than the

ear . . . ['Account', p. 316]
— . . . but if my sense of hearing was startled before, how must my sight be appalled in beholding the effects of the storm? [*Random*, 28; i, 254–55]

The novel abandons technical language in favour of more descriptive means. A breach is made: in the 'Account' this is 'reported practicable by an engineer' (p. 325), where in *Random* it becomes 'large enough to admit a middle sized baboon' (33; i, 289). A further adaptation is the abandonment of explicit comment for ironic effect. Admiral Vernon's attempt to cover up for his shameful neglect in the assault on the town of Boca-Chica (by sending in one lone ship to demonstrate the futility of a bombardment) is in the 'Account' directly criticised: the action 'seems to have been calculated by Mr Vernon to show the impracticability of attacking that city with ships only' (p. 341); but in *Random* this observation is made more damaging by an ironic presentation. 'This piece of conduct afforded matter of speculation to all the wits, either in the army or the navy, who were at last fain to acknowledge it a stroke of policy above their comprehension' (33; i, 294). In the novel Smollett is using his language more positively, for calculated effect; and the fullest example of this occurs in the description of the wretched food to which the sailors of the time were accustomed. The 'Account' says, with some spirit, that the men were 'fed with putrid beef, rusty pork, and bread swarming with maggots' (p. 329); but Roderick's submission totally surpasses this in vividness:

. . . our provision consisted of putrid salt beef, to which the sailors gave the name of Irish horse; salt pork of New England, which though neither fish nor flesh, savoured of both; bread from the same country, every biscuit whereof, like a piece of clock work, moved by its own internal impulse, occasioned by the myriads of insects that dwelt within it; and butter served out by the gill, that tasted like train-oil thickened with salt. [33; i, 291]

The second version is fuller not because it contains more facts (it does contain one more: the butter) but because it

gives greater imaginative relief to the facts already available.
The articulate wholeness of the passage, its satisfying
rhythm and the lively wit of its descriptive imagery are what
asserts its distinctiveness and contribute to its life. The style,
like the bread it describes, is 'moved by its own internal
impulse', and achieves the kind of imaginative buoyancy
that can afford to dispense with the need for evidence. We
are concerned in literature with the reality of the *descriptions*—how the words strike us—and not the superseded
reality of the thing described.[46]

Let us recall David Herbert's claim for Smollett: that he is,
'properly understood, the greatest realist in our language'.
This proper understanding can be attained only through a
recognition that there is more to realism than simple fidelity
to fact, even where this earns the accolade of 'exceptional
veracity'. Smollett's work contains its truth in the way that
truth is told, in the richness or intensity of a style that 'wakes
the mind to particular attention'. What Knapp says of the
naval episodes in *Random* surely indicates the right critical
perspective on Smollett's work as a whole, and the trouble-
some questions relating to Smollett's use of his own experience: 'More important than just where, when, and with
whom Smollett saw naval service is the fact that he wrote
about it in unforgettable prose'.[47]

2   *The moral of the story*

I

I have tried in the first chapter to expose one reason why criticism of Smollett has been so uninformative, and to suggest that he ought to be revalued as a 'literalist of the imagination'. In this chapter I shall attempt to show how another set of assumptions—this time about the moral value of literature—threatens to distract us from a just appreciation of his work.

For criticism of Smollett has at all times concerned itself with the moral reference; the problem of the moral implication of his work or (more crudely) its possible effects on moral standards and social behaviour. Not always with the same emphasis, or indeed the same conclusions: the argument has shifted its ground, so that where an eighteenth-century critic might reprove Smollett for the moral depravity of his villains, or reproach him for including the scandalous memoirs of Lady Vane in *Pickle*;[1] where a nineteenth-century critic might condemn him for indecency[2] and exclaim (as Thackeray did in the case of Swift) against his 'filth and nastiness', the modern critic has discovered a purifying moral intention and a meaningful moral structure articulated in the novels.[3] As I see it, the reader stands to gain little illumination about the nature of Smollett's writing from any of these approaches. The new fashion of moral endorsement evades the distinctive reality of his work just as efficiently as the earlier reflex of moral dismissal, and (what makes it worse) with a more specious air of reasonableness and apparent demonstration.

A typical version of the moral dismissal is provided by Alexander Chalmers in the preface which he wrote to Smollett's poems, which were included in his *Works of the English*

Poets (1810). Chalmers evidently felt obliged to say something about the novels before passing on to the poetry:

In correct delineation of life and manners, and in drawing characters of the humorous class, he has few equals. But when this praise is bestowed, every critic who values what is more important than genius itself, the interest of morals and decency, must surely stop. It can be of no use to analyse each individual scene, incident, or character in works which, after all, must be pronounced unfit to be read . . . If this be a just representation of his most favourite novels, it is in vain to oppose it by pointing out passages which do credit to his genius, and more vain to attempt to prove that virtue and taste are not directly injured by such productions.[4]

Just how persistent this simplistic view was may be gauged from the fact that it survives without significant alteration in Saintsbury's criticism of the eighteenth-century novel in *The Peace of the Augustans* a century later.

But as I noticed at the beginning of this chapter, critics have switched from defence to attack around Smollett's position on the muddy battlefield of moral influence: though it is doubtful whether they have gained much ground. Many recent critics have committed themselves to demonstrating the 'moral tendency' of Smollett's fiction, and to proving that his novels were

As with a moral View design'd
To cure the Vices of Mankind.[5]

To begin with this means taking Smollett's own (minimal) claims in this regard very literally, accepting the self-conscious prescriptions of the *Random* preface and *Fathom* dedication at their face value; and I shall point out the pitfalls of such an assumption in a moment. Then as far as the consequent criticism itself is concerned, what happens is that the term 'moral' finds itself projected into innumerable unlikely contexts and invited to serve in this dazed state as a crucial term for the discrimination of value. The word is used as a critical shackle to hold the most rickety scaffolding in position; a situation which creates all kinds of falsities.

This is not the place to revive or even to review one of the oldest and most contentious arguments in criticism. But faced with the various attacks on and defences of Smollett that we have been considering here—which tend to be based on similar assumptions, even where their conclusions are different—one might protest that while the relation must obviously *exist* between poetry and morals, art and life, the terms of this relation are by no means easy to determine, and are certainly not subject to categorical prescriptions—from whatever critical chemist's shop. The complex strands and subtle linkages involved may well be invisible to the naked eye of the casual observer, whose ready conclusions tend to make real understanding in this problematical area even more difficult to attain. Of course, there is an unfortunate precedent in Plato. Plato was no casual observer, but the defensive argument developed in the *Republic* on the subject of the poet's influence has always been used in support of simplistic solutions. His notorious decision to exile the poet from the city is a decision that cuts the knot instead of untying it. Plato is not prepared to take the risk a free literature must involve: the risk, ultimately, of a higher consciousness for his citizens; the risk of a more vulnerable if also potentially richer existence.

Indeed, one way of understanding the permanent debate about the moral and social influence of the arts is to see it as a debate between cultural pessimism and cultural optimism. Plato himself adopted the pessimistic stance, but later Platonists (notably Sidney and Shelley) could start with a similar diagnosis and yet end up with a more hopeful account of the function of the free spirit in human affairs. Shelley it was who maintained that 'The great instrument of moral good is the imagination; and poetry administers to the effect by acting upon the cause'.[6] Once we have accepted the necessary obliqueness of all moral influence through art we can attend to the pleasure and leave the profit to take care of itself.

It is not only the romantics who would have agreed with the priority described here. Even Bacon, writing of supposedly didactic poetry in his own time, said, 'I do rather think that the fable was first, and the exposition devised, than that the moral was first, and thereupon the fable framed',[7] an observation which Richard Hurd invoked when presenting Spenser to the eighteenth century as fabulist rather than as moralist.[8] The 'moral aim', according to such a view, is seen as only incidental or ancillary to the fictive impulse; it is an abstraction, a rationalisation and legitimisation of the creative faculty.

The *reductio ad absurdum* of morally oriented criticism is no doubt contained in Taine's notorious judgement on Dickens, that 'the novels of Dickens can all be reduced to one phrase, to wit: Be good, and love'.[9] Reduction indeed; there could be no more comprehensive disparagement of a great imagination than this, the reduction of a life's work, a lifetime's exercise of creative energy, to a moral platitude. And although the evidence is not so extreme, the moral reading of Smollett is exposed in such judgements as that *Pickle* is Smollett's 'most moral novel', and therefore his best, when an unprejudiced reading will convince us that it is for long stretches the least realised of all his works (especially in those places where the 'morality' is supposed to reside); or that *Clinker* is the least interesting of Smollett's novels because in it 'he seems to have nothing really important to say'.[10] As we shall see, not least among the things he does have to say in *Clinker* is that he has no time for moralistic fictions.

II

We must now consider how far we can determine Smollett's own views on the moral value of literature. It is true that Smollett did commit himself to the orthodox moralist position in the Dedication to *Fathom*, which tends to be regarded as Smollett's only interesting pronouncement on the subject of the novel. There he developed an argument to defend his choice of a villain as hero in the following terms:

Almost all the heroes of this kind, who have hitherto succeeded on the English stage, are characters of transcendent worth, conducted through the vicissitudes of fortune, to that goal of happiness, which ever ought to be the repose of extraordinary desert.—Yet the same principle by which we rejoice at the remuneration of merit, will teach us to relish the disgrace and discomfiture of vice, which is always an example of extensive use and influence, because it leaves a deep impression of terror upon the minds of those who were not confirmed in the pursuit of morality and virtue, and while the balance wavers, enables the right scale to preponderate . . . Let me not therefore be condemned for having chosen my principal character from the purlieus of treachery and fraud, when I declare my purpose is to set him up as a beacon for the benefit of the unexperienced and unwary, who from the perusal of these memoirs, may learn to avoid the manifold snares with which they are continually surrounded in the paths of life; while those who hesitate on the brink of iniquity, may be terrified from plunging into that irremeable gulph, by surveying the deplorable fate of FERDINAND Count FATHOM.

He goes on to plead, with a rhetorical flourish,

If I have not succeeded in my endeavours to unfold the mysteries of fraud, to instruct the ignorant, and entertain the vacant; if I have failed in my attempts to subject folly to ridicule, and vice to indignation; to rouse the spirit of mirth, wake the soul of compassion, and touch the secret springs that move the heart; I have at least, adorned virtue with honour and applause; branded iniquity with reproach and shame, and carefully avoided every hint or expression which could give umbrage to the most delicate reader. [pp. 3–4]

The plea is, of course, very conventional. The simple converse of what the neo-classical critic had been saying for a very long time, it is one which had been exploited before (and still does good service) as an excuse for any kind of sensational or unsavoury revelation. If we were 'allured to virtue' by witnessing the 'remuneration of merit', then we might very well be 'deterred from the practice of vice' by reading about (and relishing) its 'disgrace and discomfiture'. But the principle which guarantees the reaction in each case is (as Smollett knew perfectly well) a facile principle, founded in wishful thinking and kept up for convenience. Smollett also knew that it is a writer's function not to 'declare a purpose' but to carry it out in his writing. The novelist who offers to comment on his own work, and spell out his intentions, is like a non-playing captain on the touchline at a game; he may be nearer to what is going on, and his voice may appear to carry more authority, but he has no more real influence over the result than the crowd.

The whole declaration is, as I see it, an expedient Smollett uses to give his novel an appearance of conformity to standards in which he himself did not believe. And if the reader is willing to be so deceived, this proves that it is a legitimate expedient: did not Defoe use a smaller stratagem with respect to the factuality of his stories? But what makes it especially surprising that readers should ever have taken the claims of this dedication at face value is that Smollett deliberately contradicts them within the first few hundred words of the novel. The last three paragraphs of the first chapter are a spirited defence of the novelist's rights against the encroachments of didacticism, and against the limitations entailed by the kind of conformity to moral expectation that the dedication promised to observe. The tone is different, the irony more palpable, as the 'most delicate reader' finds himself (or herself) challenged in a way he had hardly expected:

> And here it will not be amiss to anticipate the remarks of the reader, who, in the chastity and excellency of his conception, may possibly exclaim, 'Good Heaven! will these authors never reform their imaginations, and lift their ideas from the obscene objects of low life?'

The 'anticipation' itself begins as an ironic obeisance to the reader's refinement, only to develop into a direct attack on his hypocrisy:

> Have a little patience, gentle, delicate, sublime, critic; you. I doubt not, are one of those consummate connoisseurs, who in their purifications, let humour evaporate, while they endeavour to preserve decorum, and polish wit, until the edge of it is quite wore off: or, perhaps of that class, who, in the sapience of taste, are disgusted with those very flavours, in the productions of their own country, which have yielded infinite delectation to their faculties, when imported from another clime; and damn an author in despite

of all precedent and prescription; who extol the writings of Petronius Arbiter, read with rapture the amorous sallies of Ovid's pen, and chuckle over the story of Lucian's ass; yet, if a modern author presumes to relate the progress of a simple intrigue, are shocked at the indecency and immorality of the scene.

You are one of those, Smollett continues, 'who eagerly explore the jakes of Rabelais, for amusement, and even extract humour from the dean's description of a lady's dressing-room': the criticism here is not of Rabelais or Swift, but of readers who deceive themselves with a double standard, allowing the status of a writer silently to adjust their response. Smollett moves at this point into that attitude of angry self-justification which he had dramatised so convincingly in the person of Melopoyn in *Random*, and which he was to strike with such consistency in his editorial pronouncements in the *Critical Review*. You are one of those, he says, 'who applaud Catullus, Juvenal, Persius and Lucan, for their spirit in lashing the greatest names in antiquity; yet, when a British satirist, of this generation, has courage enough to call in question the talent of a Pseudo-patron, in power, accuse him of insolence, rancour and scurrility'. Smollett goes so far in his direct attack on the reader; but then returns to the oblique, for a final ironic celebration of that passive, harmless, 'moral' literature, the literature of the repressed imagination, that the reader wants, pretends to want, or feels he ought to want:

If such you be, courteous reader, I say again, have a little patience; for your entertainment we are about to write. Our hero shall, with all convenient dispatch, be gradually sublimed, into those splendid connexions of which you are enamoured; and God forbid, that in the mean time, the nature of his extraction should turn to his prejudice, in a land of freedom like this, where individuals are every day ennobled in consequence of their own qualifications, without the least retrospective regard to the rank or merit of their ancestors. Yes, refined reader, we are hastening to that goal of perfection, where satire dares not shew her face; where nature is castigated, almost even to still life; where humour turns changeling, and slavers in an insipid grin; where wit is volatilized into a meer vapour; where decency, divested of all substance, hovers about like a fantastic shadow; where the salt of genius, escaping,

leaves nothing but pure and simple phlegm; and the inoffensive
pen for ever drops the mild manna of soul-sweetning praise. [1;
pp. 7–8]

Smollett's vigorous imagination and moral honesty could
never submit to the false restraint and false perspectives of
the licensed moralist's fictional presentation. The kind of
care which makes a 'just distribution of good and evil' is not
the right kind of care for a writer to exercise. Such distribution, in fact, denatures the very qualities it pretends to deal
with: 'Active evil is better than passive good'. One would
readily concede that Smollett never explored and illuminated the moral territory of the mind so unremittingly as did
Swift, but what Martin Price says of Swift's deliberate refusal
in his work to compromise the 'right' and the 'good', or to
arrive at the deceptive equilibrium where all moral problems
are resolved, seems to me to apply in Smollett's case too:

> The *Argument* [against Abolishing Christianity], like the *Modest
> Proposal*, is meant to shock men into recognition; not simply recog-
> nition of values they have deserted or duties they have neglected,
> but of the way in which the mind constructs a coherent system as a
> refuge from moral cognition and an asylum from its obligations. To
> do this, he must first denature words—rob them of their meanings,
> make them attractive labels hiding unsavory mixtures, employ
> their force without their restrictions.[11]

The self-deception which expresses itself in the denaturing
of words and the hiding of 'unsavory mixtures' is clearly
what Smollett is seeking to expose in the Dedication to
Fathom, and what the novel itself sets out to dramatise. No
one would suggest that *Fathom* itself is the work of an 'inoffensive pen'; the central theme is by no means calculated to
afford us a comfortable moral sensation. Smollett invests
Fathom's cynical vision with much greater imaginative
power than the facile resolution can contradict. Early in the
book we learn that Fathom 'had formerly imagined, but was
now fully persuaded, that the sons of men preyed upon one
another, and such was the end and condition of their being.
Among the principal figures of life, he observed few or no
characters that did not bear a strong analogy to the savage

tyrants of the wood . . . ' (10; p. 40). This cynicism is reflected in Fathom's behaviour, and Smollett relates the details of his callousness and treachery in a tone of angry compassion—reminiscent of Swift—which cannot be neutralised by any moral reflection. When Fathom deserts Elinor, the young country girl whom he has robbed and seduced on his first arrival in England, she becomes distracted, and is eventually 'conveyed into the hospital of Bethlem, where we shall leave her for the present, happily bereft of her reason' (31; p. 147). Fathom's seduction of another young woman in the house of his benefactor is narrated with unusual detail and particularity, with an inwardness that looks forward to the seduction of Cécile by Valmont in Laclos' *Les liaisons dangereuses*; and Celinda's fate here is if anything more painful than Elinor's, the implications in this final paragraph more grotesque:

. . . she grew every day more and more sensual and degenerate, and contracted an intimacy with one of the footmen, who was kind enough to take her to wife, in hope of obtaining a good settlement from his master; but being disappointed in his aim, he conducted her to London, where he made shift to insinuate himself into another service, leaving to her, the use, and partly the advantage of her own person, which was still uncommonly attractive. [34; p. 165]

Elinor's reason is restored, and she reappears in the last chapter as Fathom's nurse in his eventual distress (though we hear no more of Celinda); but the 'poetic justice' perfunctorily enacted at this late stage in the book is as unsatisfying as Fathom's conversion itself. It is no reassurance for the reader to be told that 'all his vice and ambition was now quite mortified within him, and his whole attention engrossed in atoning for his former crimes, by a sober and penitent life, by which alone he could deserve the uncommon generosity of his patrons' (67; p. 366). It is always a sign of failure, or at least of forced intentions, when the moral point of a novel is made too explicit, comes (usually towards the end) in a detachable capsule. As D. H. Lawrence observed, 'if you try to nail anything down, in the novel, either it kills the novel, or the novel gets up and walks away with the nail'.[12] And the moral point of *Fathom* is nailed down in this way—though the novel as a whole (or in parts) does have the strength to walk away with it. The impossible paragon Renaldo decides to visit Fathom after he has discovered the lifelong deception of his supposed friend, 'not with a view to exult over his misery, but in order to contemplate the catastrophe of such a wicked life, that the moral might be the more deeply engraved on his remembrance' (67; p. 353). This attitude of complacent righteousness is one that Smollett himself detested, and its expression here suggests Smollett's fundamental unease with the exemplary obligations which he acknowledges on the surface of his work. Just how near the surface this obligation lay may be realised from the curious authorial comment Smollett feels driven to make on his hero's moral progress after the 'death' of Monimia (that she is not really dead only increases the artificiality of the exclamation):

Perfidious wretch! thy crimes turn out so atrocious, that I half repent me of having undertaken to record thy memoirs: yet such monsters ought to be exhibited to public view, that mankind may be on their guard against imposture; that the world may see how fraud is apt to overshoot itself; and that, as virtue, though it may suffer for a while, will triumph in the end; so iniquity, though it may prosper for a season, will at last be overtaken by that punishment and disgrace which are its due. [49; p. 242]

We may set beside this spurious consolation Fielding's sober observation in *Tom Jones*: 'There are a set of religious, or rather moral writers, who teach that virtue is the certain road to happiness, and vice to misery, in this world. A very wholesome and comfortable doctrine, and to which we have but one objection, namely, that it is not true.'[13] Celinda's unredeemed misfortune alone should remind us that there is no such consolation available, even within the novel itself; and Smollett certainly knew from his own experience that such a view of life was a falsification. *Et genus, et virtus, nisi cum re, vilior alga est:* the epigraph he used for his first novel bore a truer witness to his understanding of the world.

So the superficial and sentimental conclusion of *Fathom*
('In a word, all parties were as happy as good fortune could
make them', 67, p. 367) compromises the kind of clear-
sighted vision that has operated for most of the book. It
represents (in Price's terms) 'a refuge from moral cognition'.
Only by a simplification can Smollett bring about a 'just distribution of good and evil'. The reversal at the end is no more
convincing—and no more true to Smollett's own
instinct—than the theoretical inversion at the beginning, in
the Dedication: the inversion of the neo-classical exemplum
theory to justify the representation of a villain.

The same argument may easily be demonstrated from the
pages of *Random* and *Pickle*. Smollett is not given to the moral
cliché, to the platitude introduced as a profound discovery
by the author on his characters; in fact he is more likely to
use this kind of thing for ironic effect. The conventional
'moral intention' and 'moral structure' which are current
objects of critical exhumation are insignificant beside the real
radical vision and the real satiric impulse throughout Smollett's work. This is not to deny that Smollett is a moral writer
in the full (I would say truistic) sense of the term; only to
protest that he cannot be comprehended in the limiting
category of moralistic writers, who look along the straight
line of their intention to some determined effect; who write
to endorse a particular set of values, or in defence of a particular ethical standpoint.

Smollett's own ironic attitude to explicit purpose and the
predetermination of response is illustrated very clearly in
Clinker with the story of Tim Cropdale, whose literary career
has suffered a setback from the undue proliferation of moral
novels:

Tim had made shift to live many years by writing novels, at the
rate of five pounds a volume; but that branch of business is now
engrossed by female authors, who publish merely for the propagation of virtue, with so much ease and spirit, and delicacy, and
knowledge of the human heart, and all in the serene tranquillity of
high life, that the reader is not only inchanted by their genius, but
reformed by their morality. [10 June; pp. 127–8]

The terms employed here are directly reminiscent of the *Fathom* Dedication; but Smollett, disdaining the 'propagation of virtue' in these self-cancelling terms, was not the kind of writer to put Tim Cropdale out of business.

Finally in the *Travels* we find a direct statement to confirm this attitude, where Smollett himself complains of the obsessive moralising of the French dramatists. 'Their most favourite dramatic pieces are almost without incident; and the dialogue of their comedies consists of moral, insipid apophthegms, intirely destitute of wit, or repartee' (6; p. 48). The terms 'moral' and 'insipid' are instructively run together here. And to take up the terms from the first chapter of *Fathom* rather than the Dedication, we may suggest that is through the moral intention in these plays that 'nature is castigated, almost even to still life'; that a 'fantastic shadow' of decency is offered as a substitute for action; and that (therefore), the 'salt of genius' has escaped again.

III

It may be argued, however, that Smollett's very pretensions as a satirist must commit him to a moral intention. The poet of *Advice*, after all, boasts of his 'moral rage':

Th' indignant muse to Virtue's aid shall rise,
And fix the brand of infamy on vice[14]

and although the Friend is allowed to put forward another view in *Reproof*:

Sworn foe to good and bad, to great and small,
Thy rankling pen produces nought but gall

the poet again praises 'moral zeal and dauntless truth' and laments that 'vices flourish still, unprun'd by me'.[15] Then in the preface to *Random* Smollett makes several allusions to the satirical character of the novel which critics have been quick (or slow) to use as evidence of its author's high seriousness. Smollett begins by asserting that 'Of all kinds of satire, there is none so entertaining, and universally improving, as that which is introduced, as it were, occasionally, in the course of an interesting story, which brings every incident home to life'; for as the reader is persuaded to sympathise with the hero 'his indignation is heated against the authors of his calamity; the humane passions are inflamed; the contrast between dejected virtue and insulting vice, appears with greater aggravation, and every impression having a double force on the imagination, the memory retains the circumstance, and the heart improves by the example'. Smollett also specifies that he intends to arouse 'that generous indignation which ought to animate the reader, against the sordid and vicious disposition of the world' (i, iii–viii).

This is a clear acknowledgement of the satirist's traditional function: that of criticising and correcting vice. But of all kinds of writer, we might retort, the satirist has always been the most unrelentingly misunderstood and systematically misrepresented—not least by himself; and his traditional function has been dangerously oversimplified.[16] The fundamental mistake is the tendency to think of him in ethical rather than artistic terms, in terms more of his moral disposition, consistency, and perhaps even his apparent 'results', than of the coherence of his vision and the intensity of his statement. The satirist, that is to say, has been taken too literally. When Denis Donoghue says of the *Drapier's Letters* that 'the sole declared object is to get something done'[17] he has failed to look beyond the *declared* object and consider the very relevant question of what happens to satire when its object (as in this instance) has been achieved. More significant than the fact that Swift prevented the publication of the last letter when he heard that Wood's notorious patent was to be cancelled is the fact that we continue to read the *Drapier's Letters* today—having meanwhile succumbed to a cupro-nickel currency.

It is true that Dryden wrote in the address to the reader with *Absalom and Achitophel* that 'the true end of Satyre, is the amendment of Vices by correction',[18] it is true that Swift declared his works were

As with a moral view of design'd
To cure the Vices of Mankind,[19]

and it is true that Pope wrote to Swift before the publication

of *The Dunciad*, 'As the obtaining the love of valuable men is
the happiest end I know of this life, so the next felicity is to
get rid of fools and scoundrels.'[20] But none of them was
deceived about the possibility of realising his objectives.
'Mankind is unamendable', wrote Pope to Swift later[21]
(when the *Dunciad* had already had a year to do its work);
and Swift prefaced *Gulliver's Travels* with Gulliver's trans-
parently ironic complaint to his cousin Sympson:

. . . after above six Months Warning, I cannot learn that my Book
hath produced one single Effect according to mine Intentions . . . These, and a Thousand other Reformations, I firmly
counted on by your Encouragement; as indeed they were plainly
deducible from the Precepts delivered in my Book.[22]

This is not to deny the moral impetus behind satire
altogether; only to remind ourselves that this is overlaid in
the front of the writer's mind by the technical concern of
expressing what he feels. Moral sense, heightened and disturbed, there must always be at the root of satire, but this is
(as Stravinsky says of sincerity in art in general) 'the *sine qua
non* which yet guarantees nothing'; many a genuine root can
rot in the ground. Where a writer is susceptible to spasms of
moral outrage—as Juvenal was, and Swift, and Smol-
lett—then *difficile est satiram non scribere*; but the writing itself
is a more intimately aesthetic than moral activity, which
need not (and probably will not) operate on the cause at all.
A man may temporarily cauterise his indignation if he articulates it, just as he may derive some satisfaction from achieving a love poem; but the world remains corrupt, and the
mistress remains inconstant. A writer in the *World* in 1756
thought that among the ancients satire 'was considered only
as an ingenious piece of invention', and (though he did not
approve) supposed that 'men of wit never satirize with any
offensive design, but purely for the sake of displaying their
abilities'.[23] This is in truth a more satisfactory diagnosis of
the satirist's case, one which seems to be endorsed by Martin
Price: 'A man may write satire because he is indignant, but
he may also cultivate his indignation in order to write
satire'.[24]

This introduces a new perspective into the discussion; we have to take account of the satirist's delight in the exercise of his expressive faculty, the satisfaction he obtains from the successful articulation of what he feels. The only intolerable feelings, perhaps, are those we cannot compass with words: once objectified in this way they are to a certain extent mastered, and become part of the ritual with which we worship 'the God within the Mind'. For all his dislike of fools and knaves as a man, as an artist Pope rejoiced in them as material. 'Fools (in one Sense) are the Salt of the Earth', he confessed to Robert Digby; and again, 'when a stale cold Fool is well heated, and hashed by a Satyrical Cooke, he may be tost up into a Kickshaw not disagreeable'.[25] The beginning of the Sporus portrait betrays Pope's eagerness to bind Hervey in his couplets:

> Let *Sporus* tremble—'What? that Thing of silk,
> *Sporus*, that mere white Curd of Ass's milk?
> Satire or Sense, alas! can *Sporus* feel?
> Who breaks a Butterfly upon a Wheel?'
> —Yet let me flap this Bug with gilded wings,
> This painted Child of Dirt that stinks and stings . . .[26]

The impatient 'Yet let me . . . ' is a more straightforward answer to Arbuthnot's caution against satire on individuals than that Pope offered in his letters.[27] We may well argue that Pope's feelings were justified, but this does not make the attack any more *morally* constructive. Steele's belief that satire should originate in good nature is wishful thinking. The satirist is rarely able (as Steele requires) to keep *'himself* quite out of the question';[28] for every temperate Boileau there will be a dozen malignant lampooners. D. H. Lawrence has a character in his last novel remark 'It is a curious thing that the mental life seems to flourish with its roots in spite, ineffable and fathomless spite'.[29] We could no doubt refer this ultimately to the idea that there is an intrinsic resentment in our consciousness to other consciousness; but here let us simply confirm that this resentment and even 'spite' will be an important spur to the satirist, as he seeks to bring the 'ineffable' to adequate expression.

And finally one has to admit the pleasure that the reader, too, takes in this exercise. Both Dryden and Pope use the metaphor 'tickling' to describe the effect of satire. Dryden says 'there's a sweetness in good Verse, which Tickles even while it Hurts';[30] but the possibility of being 'hurt' by *Absalom and Achitophel* is eliminated for us, and so our pleasure is unmixed. When Swift writes to Pope, 'the chief end I propose to myself in all my labours is to vex the world rather than divert it',[31] he knows full well that the world is resolved to be diverted despite him; and predictably Pope assures him that *Gulliver's Travels* 'will be in future the admiration of all men'[32].

Having established this deeper perspective on satire, and qualified the obvious but also deceptive assumptions that set criticism off on the wrong tack, we may now return to see how this applies to Smollett's satire, and his own understanding of satiric technique. We have already remarked how the conventional attitude is expressed in the *Random* preface ('the memory retains the circumstance, and the heart improves by the example'), where the optimistic assertion simply avoids the question, declining to see it as a question at all. But Smollett did consider the question, and gave a very full answer to it. In the *Atom* there occurs a very clear-sighted, not to say cynical, recognition of what use human nature does in fact make of the satirical writings intended for its improvement.

> While the constitution of human nature remains unchanged, satire will be always better received than panegyric, in those popular harangues. The Athenians and Romans were better pleased with the Philippics of Demosthenes and Tully, than they would have been with all the praise those two orators could have culled from the stores of their eloquence. A man feels a secret satisfaction in seeing his neighbour treated as a rascal. If he be a knave himself, (which ten to one is the case) he rejoices to see a character brought down to the level of his own, and a new member added to his society; if he be one degree removed from actual roguery, (which is the case with nine-tenths of those who enjoy the reputation of virtue) he indulges himself with the Pharisaical consolation of thanking God he is not like that publican. [i, 108–9]

So much for the reforming power of satire, as Smollett saw it from the cockpit of his only totally satirical work. The fact that this passage resembles very closely Swift's observations on the effects of satire in the Author's Preface to *A Tale of a Tub* underlines what I see as Smollett's unusually realistic assessment of the moral value of his medium; and surely allows us to qualify Elkin's view that Swift alone of the major writers of the eighteenth century 'entertained serious doubts about the reformative effects of satire'.[33] One need not deduce from these negative findings that satire actually tends to make men worse (though Smollett does seem to have that in mind here), but simply that it cannot seriously be expected to make us better; it has not that kind of efficacy. Satire addresses itself to the understanding: like poetry, it 'ends in speculation'. It is interesting that J. B. Heidler says of the *Atom* that 'Smollett's novel . . . was purely splenetic . . . The author . . . made no attempt at reform'.[34] But reform can be carried out only by the legislature; the writer has public access only to men's minds and imaginations, no private audience (whatever his pretensions) in the recesses of their moral sense.

In a relevant analysis of Peregrine's temperament Smollett provides what might be seen as an image of the writer's situation:

Had the executive power of the legislature been vested in him, he would have doubtless devised strange species of punishment for all offenders against humanity and decorum; but, restricted as he was, he employed his invention in subjecting them to the ridicule and contempt of their fellow-subjects. [93; p. 576]

The satirist is similarly 'restricted' from acting directly on his circumstances, and so his influence has to operate (if at all) indirectly, through the fiction he invents to express his 'ridicule and contempt'.[35]

But this is not a restriction Smollett (or any writer) necessarily laments; it is in fact a confirmation of his freedom in the only realm he is really responsible to. The friend in *Advice* urged the poet ironically to 'enjoy that petulance of stile',[36] and Smollett *does* enjoy it, like any other satirist—enjoys it in that it fulfils a need. The kind of need, and the kind of fulfilment obtained, Smollett dramatises very fully in the character of Matthew Bramble in *Clinker*. V. S. Naipaul suggests that modern satire tends often to take the form of 'a dramatisation of the self',[37] and his observation could justifiably be applied to Smollett in retrospect, in that (as Professor Knapp has shown)[38] Bramble is a *persona*, very closely modelled on Smollett himself, who conducts himself on his travels about England and Scotland much as Smollett conducted himself on his travels through France and Italy: with superlatively articulate discontent. Bramble is described by his nephew Jery as a 'misanthrope', albeit 'the most risible misanthrope I ever met with', and his temper thus: 'He is splenetic with his familiars only; and not even with them, while they keep his attention employed; but when his spirits are not exerted externally, they seem to recoil and prey upon himself' (30 April; pp. 49–50). It is made clear that Bramble needs to exercise his satirical faculty: 'he goes in person to the pump, the rooms, and the coffee-houses; where he picks up continual food for ridicule and satire' (24 April; p. 33). And he himself admits this to his doctor correspondent:

If I did not know that the exercise of your profession has habituated you to the hearing of complaints, I should make a conscience of troubling you with my correspondence, which may be truly called *the lamentations of Matthew Bramble*. Yet I cannot help thinking, I have some right to discharge the overflowings of my spleen upon you, whose province it is to remove those disorders that occasioned it; and let me tell you, it is no small alleviation of my grievances, that I have a sensible friend, to whom I can communicate my crusty humours, which, by retention, would grow intolerably acrimonious. [23 April; p. 33]

In the *Atom*, too, Smollett observes that the spirit of Taycho (Pitt) was 'so corrosive, that it would have preyed upon himself, if he could not have found external food for it to devour' (ii, 106). Arthur Calder-Marshall brings home the relevance of these examples to Bramble's creator when he says that Smollett himself 'was, I think, one of those writers to whom writing is a condition of health, a means of achieving in art the balance lacking in life'.[39]

Smollett would not have claimed that the assuaging of this need by the communication of his crusty humours, and in the external exertion of satire, deserved to be singled out as a 'moral' activity from the many other activites of the civilised mind which do not happen to involve reference to (it can never be the substance of) moral behaviour; nor that it was any more likely to involve moral behaviour in its consequences. And in this he would show—he does show—a better understanding of the moral element in literature than many of his critics.

Once we divert our attention from the moral intention to the satiric statement as such we forfeit the traditional moral excuse for the satirist and his satire; but this fits in with my whole argument in this chapter, which is that such reasoning is in any case equivocal and may as easily (and as rationally) be used to attack a work as to defend it. Jeremy Collier insisted that Juvenal 'teaches those Vices he would correct, and writes more like a Pimp than a *Poet*'.[40] We are reduced to a peculiarly pointless game of critical snakes and ladders. Paul Fussell has recently remarked that 'justifications of Pope's character no longer seem very interesting, for what has come to matter is the poetry, that is, the adequacy with which the satiric rhetoric succeeds in realizing the moral contempt which is the indispensable attribute of the genre'.[41] And Smollett's biographer David Hannay anticipated this shift of emphasis, pointing out that we have to provide a different kind of excuse altogether:

. . . the satirist must justify his work to posterity by his workmanship, if he is to be excused for disgorging into the general world all the 'embossed sores and headed evils', which he has been at the trouble of collecting.[42]

Smollett's work is justified by his 'workmanship', but this is not merely an excuse. It is a reason; the very good reason why he is still read with delight today, when those ladies who wrote 'merely for the propagation of virtue' have been long forgotten.

3   *A matter of form*

There is a third critical approach which has tended to divert attention from Smollett's work as it is, to what it might be, or ought to be; and this is the approach through form. Again the arguments are conflicting. Some critics have argued that Smollett has no sense of form at all, that his works are law-less, ill considered productions;[1] others (more recently) that Smollett does in fact exercise a marked degree of formal control that contributes largely to the novels' meaning.[2] But it is assumed in each case that the question is important, even decisive: Smollett must be either cried down for his lack of form, or cried up when it is discovered that he does have form after all. The formal question has to be dealt with, it seems, because it is 'there'. I intend to argue that it is not 'there' nearly so obviously, or so obtrusively, as critics have supposed; that it is in fact a pseudo-problem, and may be circumvented or otherwise ignored at no cost to the discussion of Smollett's merits as a writer.

The main impulse behind formal description is the need to discover unity, 'that unity upon which', Paulson suggests, 'all good art depends for its verisimilitude'.[3] Character, theme and point of view all become elements of a 'rhythm'; satire is endowed with a 'rhythmic function'; everything must be perceived in relation to everything else, so that the precious characteristic of unity may be discovered in a work. Critics look for unity in Chaucer's *Canterbury Tales* and Byron's *Don Juan*. Yeats maintained that Shakespeare's plays were 'only a mass of magnificent fragments' beside the Greek drama.[4] More flexible than Yeats in this respect, Dr Johnson, we know, challenged the concept in his *Preface* to Shakespeare, remarking of the neo-classic 'unities' of time, place and action that 'perhaps a nearer view of the principles on which they stand will diminish their value'.[5]

The concept of unity itself has been subjected to a 'nearer view' by W. K. Wimsatt in a valuable essay[6] which underlines the real difficulties it involves for the critic, and the falsities it is likely to commit him to. 'One of the most persistent implications of holism and explicationism', he says, 'is that the parts do have value only as interacting and making the whole'. But 'extreme holism is obviously contrary to our experience of literature': in Johnsonian spirit, Wimsatt submits the 'merely positive' valuation of unity to his own 'daily experience' of reading, and finds that the criterion simply does not operate with the purity, the absoluteness and the convenience that critics often imply. (Wimsatt suggests as an example that *The Rape of the Lock* would not come off were not the couplets witty'.) Satisfaction in the structure cannot outweigh disappointment in the parts; though this can work in reverse, as Longinus argued, and as the Longinian voice in criticism has always sought to reiterate. And so Wimsatt concludes that 'the validity of partial value as a general principle in tension with holism seems obvious. The whole with which explication is concerned is something elastic and approximate'.[7] This must always be particularly true of the novel, whose very length precludes the kind of organisation a rigorous unity would seem to require. And even were such organisation possible one wonders how much of it could actually be perceived by the reader.[8]

The characteristic vice of formal criticism is its tendency to generalise, to substitute for the verbal particularity of the given work some ghostly paradigm. It draws maps without contour; offers to deal in plane geometry with a three-dimensional world. This is exactly the vice of F. W. Hilles's representative analysis in his essay 'Art and Artifice in *Tom Jones*'.[9] Hilles takes up Dorothy van Ghent's hint about *Tom Jones* being shaped like a Palladian mansion, and compares the book systematically to the ground plan of an actual house (Prior Park), discovering that the novel 'reflects the same mathematical exactitude'.[10] Everything is literally flattened out; every book becomes like every other book—or

as meaninglessly unlike—when treated to this facile
geometry of forms.[11] Works of art become simply the raw
material for factitious theses:

So Architects do square and hew,
Green Trees that in the Forest grew.[12]

Threatened by this creeping paralysis of criticism, the very
language of discrimination degenerates to a generalised
notation of structures, totally inclusive and utterly meaning-
less. Blake's note on Reynolds will serve as a just reproach in
this context. 'To Generalize is to be an Idiot. To Particularize
is the Alone Distinction of Merit. General Knowledges are
those Knowledges that Idiots possess.'[13]

In the end the only meaningful structure, for the novel, is
the structure of words; the only meaningful whole, the
whole of language. R. A. Donovan makes this point in connection with *Tristram Shandy*. 'The novel's deepest meaning,' he suggests, 'as well as its principle of organization,
may be sought in the commentary it offers on its own
medium'; and therefore 'the inner form of the novel may be
said to be objectified in the most public of all systems—language'. Donovan has already explained that 'Literary criticism, obviously, must begin with the linguistic surface of
any work it proposes to examine'; however, 'in dealing with
most novels, the critic can, indeed must, pass very quickly to
the things which language signifies, specifically, thought,
character, events'. To this rule he rightly considers *Tristram
Shandy* an exception: 'Sterne is deliberately holding our
attention on the surface of the novel, so to speak, on the
words which compose it'.[14] I would simply argue that Sterne
is not, after all, so very exceptional in this—though it is
perhaps only the exceptional reader who recognises the fact.
Most of us are too inattentive and precipitate when we read
novels (as some are, no doubt, when they write them): too
ready to pass very quickly from the local to the general, from
the linguistic surface to the formal projection. It is my main
argument in this study that criticism of Smollett should

begin to concern itself with the varied details of the terrain itself, rather than devising what projections can be raised upon it.

'To Particularize is the Alone distinction of Merit.' A brief description of each of Smollett's original works will itself demonstrate how unamenable they are to the vocabulary of forms, and prepare the way for my own criticism of style in the third section this study.

II

Smollett wrote his first novel in the space of eight months in 1747; it was published in January of the next year. *Roderick Random* is a first-person narrative which describes, at varying levels of intensity, and in sharply contrasting stylistic stances, the miscellaneous adventures of the hero. Having endured an unfortunate childhood, a mismanaged education (from which he is rescued by his seafaring Uncle Bowling) and an abortive apprenticeship to a surgeon, Roderick makes his way—and it is an eventful journey—to London, accompanied by his faithful servant, Strap. Here he is variously cheated, assaulted and deceived whilst trying for his surgeon's examination (this is his introduction to 'the artifice and wickedness of mankind': 15; i, 115), before being pressed finally aboard a man-of-war. He serves as a ship's surgeon on the Carthagena expedition, enduring shipboard tyranny as well as the stress of the fighting itself; returns to England, where he skulks under an assumed name as a footman and, having made the acquaintance of his eventual wife, Narcissa, is once again abducted, this time by smugglers, and dumped in France. He rescues his destitute uncle, joins the French army, and after various private quarrels fights at the battle of Dettingen. He meets up with Strap (metamorphosed as 'Monsieur d'Estrapes'), who secures his release from the army, and the two return to England. In London again, Roderick goes through a round of riots, interspersed with amatory adventures and curious debates on subjects ranging from politics to etymology, and takes on the disreputable character of a fortune hunter. He meets

Narcissa again, but she disappears and Roderick shortly
ends up in prison for debt. It is Bowling's turn to relieve him
once more, and Roderick goes to sea with his uncle. The
hero meets his long-lost father in South America; and
accounts are squared, marriages performed and estates pur-
chased on their final return to England.

Interspersed are two stories told by characters Roderick
encounters by chance: the 'History of Miss Williams', a
woman of the town (chapters 22 and 23), who later turns up
as Narcissa's maid, and marries Strap; and the story of
Melopoyn, a failed tragedian (chapters 62 and 63), based on
Smollett's own experiences with *The Regicide* at the hands of
the London theatre managers.

But even this variety of incident is less remarkable than the
curious mixture of styles Smollett uses in relating his story.
Defoe is as prodigal of incident as Smollett, but his style is all
on the same level; and although he assures his reader, in the
preface to *Moll Flanders*, of the 'infinite variety' of the book's
contents,[15] this variety is to be understood in only a very
narrow sense—the sense in which one incident 'varies' from
another in not being identical to it in all respects; the sense in
which cutting a purse in the city differs from stealing a
bracelet in Mile End. Now Smollett's narrative style has been
consistently praised by all critics from his own day down to
the present; even the most determined of his detractors have
not been able to deny him this. But the significant fact, for
my argument, is that Smollett does not choose to restrict
himself to the exercise of this style alone. The style in *Random*
sometimes accelerates in energetic dialogue, or flowers in
fantastic caricature; it can attend to small details, provide
inventories, or concentrate in a sustained description; pause
to reflect, poise to ridicule, or gather to a head to excoriate
some grotesque absurdity.

I shall consider examples of this stylistic variety later; for
the present I wish to argue that it is a mistake to look for a
formal focus in the novel. Certainly Roderick himself does
not provide one. It is worth insisting on this point here
because of the way in which critics tend to treat the hero as
an effective principle of organisation in the book; here, and

also in *Pickle, Fathom* and *Greaves* (*Clinker*, of course, offers a
different situation). The materials in each case are supposed
to be 'held together' by the hero's development (or degeneration), and his every action is consequently burdened by
moral and structural significance. Now although it may be
true that Roderick begins in ignorance and poverty and ends
up with some experience and a fortune, this doesn't alter the
fact that there is no moral centre to Roderick's character at
all, nothing on which his experiences can valuably print
themselves; and this applies to the main characters in the
later novels too. Roderick describes himself as 'capable of
reflection', and refers to what 'my misfortunes had taught
me' (6, 7; i, 30, 45); he even recalls how on one occasion 'I
found myself involved in doubts and perplexities, that kept
me awake the greatest part of the night' (47; ii, 120). But his
reflections are ludicrously superficial. 'We travelled half a
mile without exchanging one word,' the hero relates, 'my
thoughts being engrossed by the knavery of the world' (11; i,
73); at another time we find him 'musing upon the unhappi-
ness of my fate' (21; i, 182). But something always happens
to distract Roderick from his unwelcome thoughts (here, 'I
was alarmed by a groan than issued from a chamber contiguous to mine . . .'). The following passage, occasioned by
his being left on shore, stripped and unconscious, by the
crew of the *Lizard* is typical of his response to adverse circumstances:

I cursed the hour of my birth, the parents that gave me being,
the sea that did not swallow me up, the poignard of the enemy,
which could not find the way to my heart, the villany of those who
had left me in that miserable condition, and in the exstacy of
despair, resolved to lie still where I was and perish. [37; ii, 7]

The easy syntactical arrangement here contains no suggestion of a disturbed state of mind; Roderick's catalogue of his
misfortunes is more remarkable for its cheerful lack of dif-
ferentiation than for any personal or dramatic quality.
Roderick never learns from the worldly-wise Banter, who
conducts him through his metropolitan vicissitudes.

Roderick's resentment is a reflex: 'It was happy for me that I
had a good deal of resentment in my constitution, which
animated me on such occasions against the villainy of mankind, and enabled me to bear misfortunes otherwise intolerable' (43; ii, 57), and his emotions are realised in reflex
action. 'To this inuendo I made no reply but by a kick on the
breech, which overturned him in an instant' (44; ii, 68). This
is the style of Roderick's encounters with his fellow men.

Roderick is more acted upon than acting. His capture by
the press gang is an extreme instance of this. Roderick is
about to throw himself on a friend's charity: 'But my destiny
prevented this abject piece of behaviour; for as I crossed
Tower-wharf, a squat tawny fellow, with a hanger by his
side, and a cudgel in his hand, came up to me, calling, "Yo,
ho! brother, you must come along with me" ' (24; i, 219).
Roderick has as little influence as Gulliver over what happens to him in his successive adventures. When he is
released from the Marshalsea by Bowling, Roderick
describes himself as 'utterly confounded at this sudden
transition' (64; ii, 306): he acts simply as a switch, which
connects and completes a circuit to release energy.

A close acquaintance with Roderick—in so far as that is
possible—reveals a hero who is both unwilling and unable to
mediate the kind of moral and structural intention often
attributed to the novel as a whole. It is pointless, then, to
complain that Roderick is a blackguard, or to lament his
typical ingratitude to Strap. We are dealing not with a
human personality but with an excuse, a simple formal
stratagem that permits the stringing together of certain
episodes themselves very different in character and—for the
most part—causally unrelated. There is no critical purpose to
be served, then, in talking about the novel's structure. What
the novel is will only be appreciated by a direct experience of
its verbal power. The language of forms is inappropriate; the
descriptive mesh it uses is too large, and lets the details of
Smollett's execution fall back into the sea. Before comparing
Smollett blandly with Le Sage we should remember that
although Smollett acknowledged *Random* was 'modelled on
his plan' he also reserved the right to 'differ from him in the

execution': and this, of course, is the real determining factor.

Peregrine Pickle (1751) is a much longer novel than *Random* and, considering its bulk, a much less rewarding experience for the reader. Smollett travelled abroad to gather materials for his second novel, but for all this there is less variety in the incidents (which I shall not recapitulate) and less vitality in their narration. But the principle of disorganisation is still active, in Smollett's inability to create a consistent (one does not ask for a credible) hero. His author simply cannot make up his mind about Peregrine. He is a 'child of passion' (94; p. 594), a compound of 'vanity and pride' (27; p. 360), and derives endless entertainment from the discomfiture of his fellow beings. His lust is selfish and brutal; on one occasion he whips a companion like a dog for unwittingly impeding his progress in an affair (61; p. 301). Yet we are at the same time asked to believe that 'there was a fund of good nature and generosity in his composition' (12; p. 57). But the occasional benefaction to a hospital out of winnings at the gaming table can hardly be expected to increase his credit with us. When Smollett offers us at the end 'a man of honour, sensibility, and politeness' (113; p. 771) we can only conclude he has given up all pretence of creating an integrated character, and expects us to recognise the fact in the perfunctoriness of his efforts on Peregrine's behalf. Smollett faces this problem early in the book, when he begins a chapter with the following lame defence: 'Howsoever preposterous and unaccountable that passion may be, which prompts persons, otherwise generous and sympathising, to afflict and perplex their fellow-creatures, certain it is our confederates entertained . . . a large portion of it' (16; p. 72).

Smollett makes repeated attempts to assure us of Peregrine's moral resources; there are several instances where 'his reflection was called to a serious deliberation upon the posture of affairs' (99; p. 627). But these are only assurances, and the reader becomes progressively sceptical of them. Facing imprisonment for debt, Peregrine is 'waked to all the horrors of reflection' (105; p. 678); but Smollett has earlier observed, with something of an equivocation,

No man was more capable of moralizing upon Peregrine's misconduct than himself; his reflections were extremely just and sagacious, and attended with no other disadvantage, but that of occurring too late. He projected a thousand salutary schemes of deportment, but like other projectors, he never had interest enough with the ministry of his passions to bring any one of them to bear. [45; p. 217]

This absolves Smollett from showing any development in Peregrine's character, or any modification of his behaviour; and true enough, Peregrine rages just as extravagantly in the last chapter (when Emilia shows some reluctance to marry him immediately) as at any other time in the novel. By the end we are more likely to believe (if we are disposed to believe anything) that Peregrine still takes 'no great pleasure in conversing with his own thoughts' (105; p. 684), that his 'stock of experience' (112; p. 766) amounts to nothing, and that there is no reason to expect that his second inheritance will be any better disposed of than the first.

Peregrine's adventures have no more significance than the fortunes of a counter in a game of snakes and ladders; and, if we are relying on his consciousness of it, his experience in the Fleet prison is as meaningful as confinement in jail on a Monopoly board. One has to admit that all the moral abuse heaped on Peregrine's character is therefore critically redundant: 'our hero' is merely an unconvincing hypothesis; his actions, grotesque though many of them are in isolation, never converge on a discussable centre. But then so too are the arguments for a plan in *Pickle*, based on Peregrine's developing moral sense. Life, for Peregrine, is a practical joke (this is all his 'practical satire' amounts to), endlessly and tediously repeated. And besides the imaginative prostration to which Smollett is reduced in devising a career for its hero the novel is further burdened by the indigestible details of the interpolated 'Memoirs of a Lady of Quality' (chapter 88: 108 pages), which created a scandal at the time but which make dull reading now, and the equally redundant 'Memoirs of a Prisoner' (chapter 106: forty-four pages), in which Smollett attempted to give publicity to what he saw as injustices in the Annesley case.

At the same time one must recognise that there are many excellent things in this novel that survive the collapse of its structure and stand out amidst the general inferiority of its materials. There is much brilliant comedy that exists independent of Peregrine's stratagems, and much measured statement of great power that proceeds obviously from Smollett himself and does not intersect with his fictional scheme. With these qualities I shall deal in chapters six and seven; for the present I must simply reiterate my argument that the value of this novel is not to be discovered by a 'scheme' but lies available to all who will see it on the outward surface.

But it is in *Ferdinand Count Fathom* (1753) that the problems entailed in determining Smollett's form are most clearly exposed. It is in the Dedication, after all, that Smollett offers his only systematic definition of the novel, in very conventional terms:

A Novel is a large diffused picture, comprehending the characters of life, disposed in different groupes and exhibited in various attitudes, for the purposes of an uniform plan, and general occurrence, to which every individual figure is subservient. But this plan cannot be executed with propriety, probability or success, without a principal personage to attract the attention, unite the incidents, unwind the clue of the labyrinth, and at last close the scene by virtue of his own importance. [pp. 2–3]

One might observe at the outset that Aristotle protested this was a trivial idea of 'unity': 'A plot does not possess unity, as some people suppose, merely because it is about one man. Many things, countless things indeed, may happen to one man, and some of them will not contribute to any kind of unity; and similarly he may carry out many actions from which no single unified action will emerge'.[16] But even this mechanical 'unity' is very ill maintained in the person of Fathom, whose 'importance' does not submit this work to any more discipline than the earlier two. The centrifugal tendency, running counter to these intentions, throws out the 'occasional incidents of a different nature' which Smol-

lett also allowed for in his Dedication; and it is these that
capture the reader's attention—as they draw most certainly
on Smollett's creative energy—rather than the exemplary villain Fathom or the impossible stage hero Renaldo that Smollett has 'raised up . . . in opposition to the adventurer'.

Fathom is shouldered aside by each successive comic
apparition in the novel. He cultivates the English baronet,
Sir Giles Squirrel, whom he meets in Paris, but on very
unequal terms (chapters 22–3), as is emphasised when Sir
Giles is joined by Sir Stentor Stile, 'habited in the exact
uniform of an English jockey', and these two divide the conversation between them (chapter 24). Fathom is 'transported
with joy at the sight of this curiosity' and seizes an opportunity of 'insinuating himself into his favour'—only to lose heavily to him at cards, before he vanishes as suddenly as he had
appeared at the end of the chapter (pp. 102–6). Smollett has
made some attempt to relate Fathom to these phenomena,
albeit in a subordinate role; but he is reduced to the capacity
of passive spectator—or listener—in the coach on his first
arrival in England. Fathom finds himself wedged 'between a
corpulent quaker and a fat Wapping landlady, in which
attitude he stuck fast, like a thin quarto between two voluminous dictionaries on a bookseller's shelf'; and there
Smollett leaves him for the rest of the chapter, sitting 'in
silent astonishment of the manners of his fellow-travellers',
the dramatisation of which engrosses Smollett's interest (28;
pp. 130–3). This order of priority is repeated when Ferdinand finds himself confined for the space of three chapters
in the Fleet prison. Smollett uses him simply as a set of
senses ('his ears were invaded . . .', 'he could not help taking notice . . .', 'This was the most remarkable object which
had hitherto presented itself to the eyes of Fathom': 39, 40;
pp. 181–2, 189) to provide a vantage point on the extravagant
comedy kept up by Captain Minikin, Major MacLeaver, Sir
Mungo Barebones, the French knight, and Theodore King of
Corsica—himself an incongruous participant in such a scene.

When we consider how Ferdinand's own career is marked
by a series of sudden transitions;[17] when we recall that he is
dismissed from the novel for a hundred pages while Smollett

unravels the romantic complications surrounding Renaldo and Monimia; and when we have attempted to recognise in the abject creature who is summoned in the last chapter to 'give a *relief* to the moral' the Fathom who has previously infected the narrative, then we must disallow any serious argument for the form or moral coherence of this work. Smollett described himself in a more relevant part of the Dedication to *Fathom* as 'impatient of caution or controul', and we must be prepared to find evidence in the novel of both this impatience and the 'looseness of thought' which he also acknowledges (p. 2).

We should be prepared to adopt a more positive attitude to the change of tone which signalises Smollett's intrusions in his own person in *Fathom*, and the juxtaposition in the narrative itself of discordant stylistic attitudes. An example of Smollett's intrusion is where, in the middle of the extravagant gaiety of the gaol scenes, Smollett suddenly recalls that the imprisoned king of Corsica (whom he has already introduced into his comedy: 'instead of a crown, his majesty wore a woollen night-cap') is the victim of the English nation's gross ingratitude: and he drops the comic tone to observe with sudden, savage irony that 'their posterity of this refined age, feel no compunction at seeing an unfortunate monarch, their former friend, ally and partizan, languish amidst the miseries of a loathsome gaol, for a paultry debt contracted in their own service' (40; p. 188). The convivial Fleet suddenly reverts to being a 'loathsome gaol', in what is a dramatic collision between two alternative points of view.

It is not unreasonable to conclude that Ralph Griffiths's account of *Fathom* in the *Monthly Review* offers a more genuine and critical description of the book than does Smollett's own Dedication. Smollett proposed what the novel might be; Griffiths saw what it was.

On the whole, the history of count *Fathom* is a work of a mixed character, compounded of various and unequal parts. It abounds on the one hand with affecting incidents, with animated descriptions, and alternate scenes of melting grief, tenderness and joy;

diversified with some few exhibitions of a humorous kind. On the other hand (exclusive of the objections we have hinted at, with respect to the character of the principal personage) there are some extravagant excursions of the author's fancy, with certain improbable stories, (from which, indeed, none of the novels we have ever read are free) marvelous adventures, and little incongruities; all of which seem to be indications of the performance being hastily, nay and carelessly composed. Yet, with whatever crudities it may be chargeable,—with all its imperfections, we may venture to pronounce that the work has still merit enough to compensate with the discerning reader for its defects: it carries with it strong marks of genius in the author, and demonstrations of his great proficiency in the study of mankind.[18]

Despite Griffiths's fair criticism, *Fathom* was not well received, and seven years elapsed—seven years during which Smollett burdened himself with such labours of compiling, editing and reviewing that he came to 'loathe the sight of Paper'[19]—before he took up the novel again with the serialisation of *Sir Launcelot Greaves* in the *British Magazine* (1760–61). Smollett needed to adapt his manner very little to suit the requirements of serial publication; he was naturally equipped to provide the self-contained episodes, the scenic chapters, of which this (his shortest novel) consists. Smollett's lack of concern with structure, or formal integrity, is palpable in his ostensible subject: a baronet, his head turned by love and misfortune, rides about the countryside armed 'cap a pee' on a horse named Bronzomarte, attended by a grotesque squire, seeking to redress grievances. The plot reveals itself as an uncompromising pattern of convenient accident and fortunate coincidence, culminating at 'that point of happiness to which, as the north pole, the course of these adventures hath been invariably directed' (chapter the last; p. 205). We can detect in this novel, more than in any of the others (though traces of it are always apparent), Smollett's fundamentally ironic attitude to the contrivances of fiction as such. One critic goes so far as to propose *Greaves* as a parody of the novel form,[20] but this would attribute to its author a degree of concern with the problems and possibilities of fictional form which I believe was foreign to his nature. *Tristram Shandy* is a genuine anti-novel, because it represents a deliberate critique and revision of fictional procedure; but *Greaves* is simply a reversion to some pre- or non-novelistic form of writing, 'fiction' in the unspecialised sense, which makes only perfunctory use of the conventions of the novel. Smollett invests little imaginative energy in relating the romantic misadventures experienced by Sir Launcelot and the 'all-accomplished' Aurelia Darnel. The details of their cross-country itinerary, the missed meetings, overheard voices, and abductions are too obviously imitated from *Tom Jones*.

But what makes the novel worth reading is the series of brilliant scenes this frail structure allows; the magnificently externalised characters of Crabshaw, Captain Crowe and the misanthrope Ferret, the vigorous exercise of language in the many arguments that brew up in the novel, and the sudden authority of Smollett's own voice intervening in the fiction. I shall deal with these distinctive features later; here I simply state my belief that they create the value of *Greaves*; that the book will be better enjoyed as the 'agreeable medley of mirth and madness, sense and absurdity' promised in the exordium to chapter 16 than as the investigation of illusion and reality described by some of its critics.

Smollett's manner of proceeding as a writer of fiction is not unlike the conversation of Dick Distich, the 'poet and satirist' whom Launcelot encounters in the asylum: 'So saying, he flew off at a tangent, and our knight could not help smiling at the peculiar virulence of his disposition' (23; p. 189). And again there is an excellent contemporary account of the novel to support this view; one that appeared in the *Critical Review* in 1762, during the time of Smollett's own active involvement, no doubt with his understanding and approval. In the common run of novels, the reviewer argues,

It is the suspense merely, with respect to the issue, that engages the reader's interest. Characters are distinguished merely by their opposition to some other characters; remove the contrast, and you annihilate the personages, just as little wits in conversation are reduced to mere inanimate figures, when you have taken away the

fool who drew forth their talents. How different from this is the
ridiculous simplicity of Adams, the absurd vehemence of Western,
the boisterous generosity of Bowling, the native humour of Trunnion, and the laughable solemnity of uncle Toby! Each of these
characters singly is complete; without relation to any other object
they excite mirth; we dip with the highest delight into a chapter,
and enjoy it without reflecting upon the contrivance of the piece,
or once casting an eye towards the catastrophe. Every sentence,
and every action, diverts by its peculiarity; and hence it is that the
novels in which these characters are to be found, will furnish perpetual amusement, while others, which entertain merely from the
nature of the incidents, and the conduct of the fable, are for ever
laid aside after a single perusal.[21]

What is remarkable about this passage is its pointed rebuttal
of formal criteria. Formal tension is considered irrelevant to
the qualities described. We enjoy Smollett's writing 'without
reflecting upon the contrivance of the piece, or once casting
an eye towards the catastrophe'; and we read him, we may
be sure, as he wrote. It is especially true in Smollett's case
that each of his characters 'singly is complete'; the concept of
completeness must in consequence be scaled down to the
chapter, the episode, the paragraph, the sentence, if it is to
remain at all relevant—for it is here that we find our satisfaction. The passage which 'diverts by its peculiarity' need not
await the authorisation of a general 'contrivance' to make its
point.

The devolutionary idea of form towards which I am working
will allow me to take account of the *Travels through France and
Italy* (1766) and *Adventures of an Atom* (1769) at this
point—works which are usually left in the margin of Smollett's achievement (if indeed they are admitted at all)—before
passing on to his last novel, *Humphry Clinker*, which was
published posthumously in 1771.

I have already considered the formal properties of the
Travels in chapter one, where I argued that its firm basis in
observation and record cannot be said to determine the literary value of the work. But a few points remain to be made
here, relating to the originality of Smollett's enterprise in

narrating his adventures abroad with such unabashed indulgence of his own prejudices and quirks of character. It was not mere loyalty that prompted the *Critical* reviewer to claim that the *Travels* was 'formed upon no hypothesis, but experiment';[22] for although the writing of travels was a common enough literary exercise at the time, and often in letter form, Smollett was not the man to fall in with a prevailing fashion. It is the unusual perspective Smollett attains from his own distinctive personality that establishes the 'experimental' nature of the work and enables us to recognise its innovatory quality. (Ian Jack has conceded that 'Smollett's book helped Sterne to define a *persona* for himself, as a traveller'; it is a pity that Sterne could repay 'the learned Smelfungus' only with abuse.[23])

There is a paragraph in one of the letters from Rome that contains a perfectly adequate prospectus to the *Travels*.

I do not pretend to give a methodical detail of the curiosities of Rome: they have been already described by different authors, who were much better qualified than I am for the task: but you shall have what observations I made on the most remarkable objects, without method, just as they occur to my remembrance; and I protest the remarks are all my own: so that if they deserve any commendation, I claim all the merit; and if they are impertinent, I must be contented to bear all the blame. [31; p. 264]

No wonder Smollett made enemies. In this aggressive statement he guarantees the value of his work by his own personality—which betrays a high degree of confidence in his own judgement and (though it is not specifically mentioned here) his style: the means through which he is able actually to project his personality. 'A Frenchman lays out his whole revenue upon tawdry suits of cloaths, or in furnishing a magnificent *repas* of fifty or a hundred dishes, one half of which are not eatable nor intended to be eaten. His wardrobe goes to the *fripier*; his dishes to the dogs, and himself to the devil, and after his decease no vestige of him remains' (26; pp. 213–14). The violence of his reaction to the French and Italians is justified, artistically, by the energy with which he records it: it is no mere diffused discontent but a sharply focused and systematically articulated statement which supports itself by its own internal strength of style. I shall develop this argument in a later chapter; for the present I will only remark that just as the *Travels* offers the most positive argument for a valuation of Smollett's work according to qualities of style, so its almost totally accidental form reminds us how incidental Smollett evidently considered the question of larger organisation, and the problems posed by conceiving a work as a whole.

The *History and Adventures of an Atom* requires the allowance of such a critical approach even more obviously. The *Atom* is one of Smollett's most distinctive and personal works, and contains some of his most powerful writing, but it has been almost entirely neglected by his critics. This is partly due, no doubt, to continuing uncertainty about Smollett's authorship of the book—an uncertainty which relates to the irritating lack of conclusive external evidence but which ignores, it seems to me, even more conclusive internal evidence, in terms of both particular parallels and very clear general characteristics.[24]

If in the *Travels* Smollett took us on a physical tour, in the *Atom* he conducts us with equal forthrightness on an intellectual tour of political England during the Seven Years' War. Smollett had been restricted in his writings on contemporary affairs for over ten years before the *Atom*, first by reason of his adoptive role as historian and then as a political journalist publicly defending the Duke of Newcastle's Ministry in *The Briton*. The judicial function he exercised as editor of the *Critical Review*, and the responsibilities involved in the edition of Voltaire, hardly offered much opportunity for the expression of his impatient individuality (although we can see this breaking through in occasional defiant addresses to the reader); nor, one can be sure, did the labour of compilation which he undertook in these same years, the *Compendium of Voyages* (1756) and the *Present State of All Nations* (1768–69).

Smollett wrote the *Atom*, it is reasonable to conclude,

partly as a release for his passionate and pent-up feelings; he adopted the fictional framework simply because it offered him an opportunity to present, with some degree of immunity, his private opinions on the controversial public issues of the immediate past. (It is no accident that he went abroad before the book was published in March 1769—with the deliberately misleading '1749' on the title page). Smollett derived the idea of his transmigratory atom from a number of sources, including Voltaire's *Micromégas*—which Smollett himself translated into English—and Charles Johnstone's *Chrysal; or, the Adventures of a Guinea*; while the transparent stratagem of referring to England as Japan and inventing mock-Japanese names for all the characters is also borrowed, this time from Swift's *History of the Court and Empire of Japan*. But the fictional structure does not promote, order or otherwise impart significance; it simply provides the occasion for the powerful excursions that give the work its character. The more memorable of these either provide unrestrained portraits of the principal actors or give derisive accounts of the politics and campaigns of the Seven Years' War. We have the two Georges; the two Prime Ministers involved, Newcastle (a 'half-witted original . . . so ignorant of geography, that he did not know that his native country was surrounded by the sea': i, 24–5) and the maligned Bute, whom Smollett defends; Frederick the Great of Prussia; the 'great commoner' Pitt, seen by Smollett as an 'egregious demagogue' (i, 221); lesser lights such as Hardwicke, Anson, Fox, Bedford and Grenville—all identified with some decisive image or pungent phrase; and the detested Cumberland.

Smollett does, in the course of his narrative, occasionally recall his fiction, in the 'conversation' between the Atom and the supposed narrator Nathaniel Peacock: as when the Atom on two occasions gives Peacock precise details of his whereabouts (in George II's toe, and later in Mansfield's lungs); and it is the fiction that provides the excuse for the various eccentric digressions. The Atom regales Peacock, at intervals, with a defence of the Pythagorean transmigration of souls, a short view of historians, 'a dissertation on trousers' (i, 90), a digression on satire, an advocacy of magic, a dis-

quisition on surnames, a theory of music, and a study of the
questions of punctilio raised by the receiving of kicks in the
breech or boxes on the ear. From each of these he returns
abruptly to his narrative. But the form—even this
form—degenerates, and is completely forgotten towards the
end of the book (which seems in any case to be incomplete),
as neither the Atom nor Peacock is mentioned for fifty pages.
The urgency of the political satire has taken over from the
requirements of the narrative; we are reminded once again
that 'the satiric impulse is not at all a narrative one'.[25]

Contemporary tributes to the virtuosity of the *Atom* are
again very instructive. The *Critical* said, 'This satire unites
the happy extravagance of Rabelais to the splendid humour
of Swift . . . ridicule and reality are here blended together
with inimitable art and originality.' The reference to Rabelais
and Swift is very appropriate in this context, and the idea of
a 'blend' in the materials of the work—extravagance and
humour, ridicule and reality—a further tribute to Smollett's
power of imaginative synthesis. The account of the London
mob, this reviewer claimed, 'exceeds all description, both for
humour and justness': again it is the reconciliation of the
thing of fact (in life) with the thing of truth (in art) that has
caught his attention. He also appreciates the author's 'high
style of recognizable caricature'.[26] Of course it is Smollett's
verbal genius that enables him to perform so much more
than the menial duties of description; and the *Atom* certainly
deserves to survive its political context for the same reasons
as do *Gulliver's Travels* or *The Dunciad*. The important point
about the essentially verbal character of Smollett's art, as
seen in this work, was well made by Hawkesworth in the
course of a fairly casual review in the *Monthly*. He declined
to go about the almost universal critical practice of providing
a summary of the *Atom*, observing that 'nothing . . . could
bear less resemblance to it, than a concise epitome of the
events, taken out of the terms in which they are related'.[27]
Hawkesworth had clearly seen what many critics continue to
ignore, that a 'concise epitome' of a book's contents,
abstracted from its verbal texture, need have very little to do
with the book's essential qualities as experienced by the

reader.

Especially when considered after Smollett's last two loosely knit productions, it must be allowed that *Humphry Clinker* represents by contrast a minor triumph of form. And the reason why we must take account of formal characteristics on this occasion is simple: this is the only one of Smollett's works in which the form is in meaningful alignment with the diverse energies of his prose style. This energy, which has asserted itself quite capriciously throughout Smollett's writing, to the destruction of any formal principle, finds itself in this last novel actually exploited by the simple but satisfying contrivance of the epistolary form. Those qualities of style which jar in the earlier work function here in deliberate and productive contrast as they are allocated to the different correspondents. Albrecht Strauss is certainly right to conclude that '*Humphry Clinker* is Smollett's finest work because the epistolary method as he has molded it to his use legitimized a variety of styles and moods that was more congenial to his restless temperament than anything he had ever tried before'.[28]

It is as if Smollett had come to understand himself better as an artist, and developed (or adopted) a form which was naturally accommodated to what I have called the centrifugal energy of his imagination. Five correspondents share eighty-two of the eighty-three letters. Jery Melford provides the basic narrative; his letters (which amount to about half the total) take us from place to place and perform introductions. His point of view is typically external, runs round the circumference of experience. As he writes to his friend at Oxford of the social incongruities observable in Bath, 'I cannot account for my being pleased with these incidents, any other way than by saying, they are truly ridiculous in their own nature, and serve to heighten the humour in the farce of life, which I am determined to enjoy as long as I can' (30 April; p. 49). For Jery life is farce; and so most of the comic scenes, and many of the caricatures, turn up appropriately in his letters.

But his uncle Matthew Bramble's perceptions are on

another level. As Jery confesses in this same letter, 'he is as
tender as a man without a skin; who cannot bear the slightest touch without flinching' (p. 49). And on Bramble's disposition the enormities of Bath have a different effect: 'every
day teems with fresh absurdities, which are too gross to
make a thinking man merry' (5 May; p. 57). Bramble's heightened sensitivity involves an aggravated consciousness of his
physical circumstances and moral confrontations which is
rendered with a passionate precision rare in eighteenth-
century prose—or, indeed, in prose of any period. And so if
Jery's letters provide the narrative and the comedy, Bramble's letters provide the intensity and contour. Jery's operate
at the circumference, Bramble's at the centre. (I shall develop
this distinction later.) Bramble's letters represent something
under half the total; the remainder, far from being 'padding',
is further invigorated and diversified. On the one hand we
have the impressionable Lydia betraying her conventional
enthusiasms, and on the other the orthographically impressionistic Win Jenkins and Tabitha Bramble revealing, very
intriguingly, Smollett's almost anarchic delight in the properties of language itself.

So the book is beautifully ordered (if not exactly flawless: it
is true, for example, that Bramble seems false to his own
voice in Scotland, where his enthusiastic appreciation of
Smollett's homeland is scarcely distinguishable from
Lydia's). But this is not to concede that form is of primary or
even particular significance in *Clinker*. It is still true that efficiency of organisation is more a mechanic than an artistic
function; the art lies in creating the style that justifies this
preparatory patterning; in creating the substance that
realises the possibilities allowed by the form. The form of
Clinker is only significant at all because it displays Smollett's
style to better advantage; it is indeed a *dimension* of style. It is
absurd, then, to reverse the critical priorities, to winnow the
wheat and keep the chaff. The form of *Clinker* does not ask to
be admired for its own sake, for its own symmetry, as does
that of *Tom Jones*. We shall get things into perspective if we
remember that for all its effectiveness the structure of this
novel is very simple. The plot is frail, and very conventional,

as Jery comes near to confessing at the opening of his last letter: 'The comedy is near a close; and the curtain is ready to drop' (8 November; p. 346). It is the different voices that compose the form, rather than any complexity of organisation; and the form works only because Smollett was capable of differentiating the voices so resourcefully.[29]

III

What such material requires of a critic, obviously, is a reductive theory of form. And although criticism always tends to favour formal qualities (discovered or devised), it is certainly possible to find critics who are prepared to resist this formal bias—in the spirit of the Wimsatt essay to which I have already referred. Johnson himself conceded that the 'resistless vicissitudes' of Shakespeare's work 'may sometimes be more properly ascribed to the vigour of the writer than the justness of the design';[30] and he pursues this positive idea in another *Rambler* essay, recognising the tendency of the creative impulse to render rules obsolete:

Definitions have been no less difficult or uncertain in criticism than in law. Imagination, a licentious and vagrant faculty, unsusceptible of limitations, and impatient of restraint, has always endeavoured to baffle the logician, to perplex the confines of distinction, and burst the enclosures of regularity. There is, therefore, scarcely any species of writing, of which we can tell what is its essence, and what are its constituents; every new genius produces some innovation, which, when invented and approved, subverts the rules which the practice of foregoing authors had established.[31]

The 'constituents' here I take to be the formal requirements, the structure, whilst the 'essence' is the literary character or quality these order but cannot provide. Once again Johnson casts doubt on the necessary dependence of one upon the other.

The atmosphere of formal declension abroad in the eighteenth century is thoroughly documented by A. O. Lovejoy in his important article '*Nature* as aesthetic norm',[32] where he connects the diversity of forms with the philosophical

idea of plenitude. Central to the thought of the time, this
conception of the goodness of God expressed in the infinite
variety of created things had eventually begun to influence
the forms as well as the subject matter of literature. The
irregularity, the lack of design, the contrasts, the mixture of
genres and styles identified by Lovejoy are all characteristic
of Smollett. This was perceived by many of the early reviewers of his novels, who set a very good critical example in this
respect which has not always been followed. Griffiths on
Fathom, Hawkesworth on the *Atom* and the *Critical* reviewer
of *Greaves*, the *Travels* and the *Atom* all saw through the
'constituents' to the essence of Smollett's achievement. And
since then it is always the critics who have been prepared to
enjoy Smollett's 'happy extravagance' whilst tolerating its
occasional less happy consequences who have given the
most reliable account of his qualities as a writer. Scott quotes
Lord Woodhouselee's observation that Smollett had 'a
happy versatility of talent, by which he could accommodate
his style to almost every species of writing. He could adopt
alternately the solemn, the lively, the sarcastic, the burles-
que, and the vulgar'.[33] (This recalls are of the grounds on
which Smollett defended himself in the *Critical* against
Grainger's intemperate attack: that he had 'generally succeeded in many different kinds of writing'[34]). And Scott
himself was prepared to appreciate how Smollett 'never
shows the least desire to make the most either of a character,
or a situation, or an adventure, but throws them together
with a carelessness which argues unlimited confidence in his
own powers'.[35] Any doubts which Hazlitt may have had
about Smollett's intentions in *Fathom* are outweighed by his
belief that 'there is more power of writing occasionally
shewn in it than in any of his works':

I need only refer to the fine and bitter irony of the Count's
address to the country of his ancestors on his landing in England;
to the robber scene in the forest, which has never been surpassed;
to the Parisian swindler who personates a raw English country
squire (Western is tame in comparison); and to the story of the
seduction in the west of England. It would be difficult to point out,

in any author, passages written with more force and mastery than these.[36]

But even beside these observations, and beside the occasional recognition by other recent critics of what Paul Boucé justly calls Smollett's protean genius, one of the most profoundly understanding and significantly appreciative judgements on Smollett remains that offered by William Godwin in *The Enquirer* at the very end of the eighteenth century. Godwin's testimony regarding the extreme variety of Smollett's works includes a most generous attribution of the highest powers to their author:

[Smollett] has published more volumes, upon more subjects, than perhaps any other author of modern date; and, in all, he has left marks of his genius. The greater part of his novels are peculiarly excellent. He is nevertheless a hasty writer; when he affects us most, we are aware that he might have done more. In all his works of invention, we find the stamp of a mighty mind. In his lightest sketches, there is nothing frivolous, trifling and effeminate. In his most glowing portraits, we acknowledge a mind at ease, rather essaying its powers, than tasking them. We applaud his works; but it is with a profounder sentiment that we meditate his capacity.[37]

What is particularly intriguing is that Godwin betrays a genuine sense of frustration here at the thought that Smollett may not have realised his full capacity as a writer; which, considering his busy life and relatively early death, is very probably the case. But this does not deter him from maintaining a very positive position towards his works. The formal strictures reserved by Godwin and the other critics cited here did not interfere in any significant way with their enjoyment of Smollett, and their enthusiastic attempt to communicate this enjoyment to others.

IV

I will conclude this chapter with an attempt to interpret Smollett's own understanding of form. Because a definite sense of the more flexible attitude to form which I have advocated is discoverable, with a little discrimination, in Smollett's own criticism as we find it dispersed through his work. This may be seen to provide a kind of apology for the formal qualities of his novels, travels and satires as I have already described them.

Towards the end of *Random* the poet Melopoyn (Smollett's first critical mouthpiece) astonishes Roderick in prison by delivering to the assemblage of felons, 'with great significance of voice and gesture, a very elegant and ingenious discourse upon the difference between genius and taste' (61; ii, 270). It is unfortunate that Smollett includes no paraphrase of this lecture; for the two terms contrasted here refer to those two faculties in the artist the intricate relation between which, in terms of effects sought and achieved, has been my real subject in this chapter. Genius is the fundamental expressive faculty, the artistic identity, which is to be recognised by qualities of spirit, energy and expression; and taste the self-critical faculty that trains these qualities along particular lines, submitting them to a formal discipline in order to achieve unity, symmetry and proportion. Now what we find in Smollett's criticism is a superficial acceptance of the traditional value attaching to the classic formal properties associated with 'taste', but severely qualified (if not actually contradicted) by the further evidence of Smollett's personal sympathies, which tend—especially in his criticism of literature—to work in the other direction, in favour of unrestrained genius and Longinean ideal of 'brave disorder'.

I acknowledged earlier in this chapter that the *Fathom* dedication contains Smollett's most straightforward statement of the classical priority of form (however misleading this may be with regard to the novel that follows). The subservience of parts to the unity of the whole was a fundamental axiom of classical criticism, and it is this criterion that informs most of the criticism of art and architecture that occurs in the pages of Smollett's *Travels*. Throughout this work we find Smollett appealing to 'the principles of the Greek architecture' to criticise modern French and Italian building (31; p. 266).[38] The following passage contains a fair summary of his views:

I am disgusted by the modern taste of architecture, though I am no judge of the art. The churches and palaces of these days are crowded with petty ornaments, which distract the eye, and by breaking the design into a variety of little parts, destroy the effect of the whole. Every door and window has its separate ornaments, its moulding, frize, cornice, and tympanum; then there is such an assemblage of useless festoons, pillars, pilasters, with their architraves, entablatures, and I know not what, that nothing great or uniform remains to fill the view; and we in vain look for that simplicity of grandeur, those large masses of light and shadow, and the inexpressible ΕΥΣΥΝΟΠΤΟΝ, which characterise the edifices of the antients. [30; p. 257]

When we come to painting and sculpture we find that Smollett's attitude is rather more tolerant—or, should one say, more adventurous. The formal rigour is still there, but tempered by a sensitivity to qualities which may exist independent of the form. His reaction to Raphael's 'Transfiguration' is a good example of this tempered criticism. True, Smollett suggested that the painting should be cut in two because

The three figures in the air attract the eye so strongly, that little or no attention is payed to those below on the mountain. I apprehend that the nature of the subject does not admit of that keeping and dependence, which ought to be maintained in the disposition of the lights and shadows in a picture. The groupes seem to be intirely independent of each other.

But he then went on to insist on the 'extraordinary merit of this piece', which 'consists, not only in the expression of divinity on the face of Christ; but also in the surprising lightness of the figure, that hovers like a beautiful exhalation in the air' (33; p. 288). Expression is similarly allowed to make up for formal defects in the *Campo Santo* frescoes in Pisa: 'Though the manner is dry, the drawing incorrect, the design generally lame, and the colouring unnatural; yet there is merit in the expression' (27; p. 225); and the lack of it cannot redeem the Venus de Medicis in Smollett's eyes, for all that 'the limbs and proportions of this statue are elegantly formed, and accurately designed, according to the nicest rules of symmetry and proportion' (28; p. 235).

But it is when Smollett comes to write of his response to literature that the classical ideals suddenly find themselves relegated to a position of very subordinate value. In the section on English Literature in the *Present State* Smollett remarks of the poets that 'they have generally more genius than taste, more spirit than art, more strength than beauty', and concedes that 'some of their most admired pieces are replete with impurity, absurdity, and extravagance'. The pairs of alternatives summarise conveniently the recurrent contrast between artistic ideals as I have alluded to them in this chapter; and there is no doubt where Smollett's own sympathies lie. The positive terms 'spirit', 'strength', and 'genius' apply, of course, to himself as well; and this self-justification is even more apparent in Smollett's emphatic defence of the English dramatists, who 'have made amends for the want of regularity, by the amazing force of their genius, their fire, character, passion, poetry, incident, wit, and humour'.[39] The requirement of 'regularity' is completely superfluous to the 'minor forms' (of which Smollett lists seven here, very warmly) that can do without such structuring. There could be no truer indication of the qualities Smollett valued in his own work.

Smollett relies upon the same terms in the introduction or 'Advertisement' he wrote to the English edition of the works of Voltaire. The French author is positively appropriated by him, and directly on account of his formal negligence: 'how much soever he may be admired in other countries, he seems to be peculiarly adapted by nature, for the entertainment of the English people, distinguished as he is by that impetuosity of genius, that luxuriancy of imagination and freedom of spirit, which have characterized the most eminent poets of the British nation'. Voltaire's imagination, Smollett goes on, 'is so warm and impetuous, that it often transports him from image to image, and from sentiment to sentiment, with such rapidity as obliges him to leave the picture half disclosed, and the connexion unexplained'.[40] So much for the 'uniform plan' of the *Fathom* formula, when the greatest writers can be applauded for dispensing with the need for it.

It is safe to conclude, then, that Smollett was on the same side of the formal fence as his more sympathetic critics have always been in resisting the depredations of taste on the natural province of genius.[41] Towards the end of *Fathom* Renaldo dreams of his departed Monimia; 'he beheld her faded lips, her pale cheek, and her inanimated features, the symmetry of which, not death itself was able to destroy' (60; p. 306). The observation is significant. 'Symmetry' is of no value by itself; it can be readily enough simulated by 'inanimated features', and can coexist even with the death of the imagination. The 'salt of genius' is the only essential ingredient: the salt which cannot lose its savour.

'Improvement makes strait roads; but the crooked roads without Improvement are the roads of Genius.'[42] Every writer, in the end, must echo the fundamental appeal made by Blake at the beginning of his last great work, *Jerusalem*: 'Therefore, *dear* Reader, *forgive* what you do not approve, & *love* me for this energetic exertion of my talent'.[43] Smollett could not be quite as forthright, but the attitude Blake requires of his reader is no less requisite in his case—the case of a novelist given to crooked roads and to excess; to the overflowing of the imaginative fountain rather than the cistern's conventional containment.

II   Equipment

4   *Language*

One of the most unexpected things about Smollett when
considered in the context of his age is his attitude to language. Only if we recognise certain important differences
between his views on the subject and those generally held by
his contemporaries will we be prepared for some of the most
distinctive features of his work. His relation to his medium
will obviously be of extreme significance for a writer, and our
criticism must, so far as is possible, take account of it.

The eighteenth century was suspicious of language.
'When men desired stability in politics and society, they
advocated stability in language,' writes A. S. Collins, who
estimates that 'from about 1660 there developed a conscious
anxiety about the stability of the language and a sense of the
need both to reform and fix it'.[1] Dryden had confessed in his
Discourse Concerning the Original and Progress of Satire (1693)
that 'I rather fear a declination of the language than hope an
advancement of it in the present age',[2] and this was nearly
thirty years after Thomas Sprat had applauded the Royal
Society for doing its best to reform the writing of English by
demanding 'from all their members, a close, naked, natural
way of speaking, positive expressions, clear sense, a native
easiness, bringing all things as near the mathematical plainness as they can, and preferring the language of artisans,
countrymen and merchants before that of wits and scholars'.[3] Paul Fussell has warned, wisely, against taking the
Royal Society's programme as an adequate introduction to
eighteenth-century prose—'seeking is one thing, succeeding
another'[4]—but even though the declared ideal is often
ignored and contradicted the ideal itself is significant,

and was based after all on more formidable authority than Sprat's.

The mistrust of the properties of language—the language of artisans, countrymen and merchants as well as that of wits and scholars—is best exemplified, as it is most authoritatively contained, in Locke's *Essay Concerning Human Understanding*, published a decade before the turn of the century. The influence of Locke's account of language on succeeding generations of thinkers and writers can hardly be overestimated; and although I have no space to include a full account of his ideas here, I must at least refer to Locke's attack on what might be called the 'creative' use of language. All empiricist theories of language dicount figurative expression, and what Locke has to say on the subject is predictably severe:

. . . if we would speak of things as they are, we must allow, that all the Art of Rhetorick, besides Order and Clearness, all the artificial and figurative application of Words Eloquence hath invented, are nothing else, but to insinuate wrong *Ideas*, move the Passions, and thereby mislead the Judgment; and so indeed are perfect cheat: And therefore however laudable or allowable Oratory may render them in Harangues and popular Addresses, they are certainly, in all Discourses that pretend to inform and instruct, wholly to be avoided; and where Truth and Knowledge are concerned, cannot but be thought a great fault, either of the Language or Person that makes use of them. [X, p. 34][5]

Language for Locke is quite simply 'the great Conduit' men use to convey Knowledge, and 'he that makes an ill use of it, though he does not corrupt the Fountains of Knowledge, which are in Things themselves, yet he does, as much as in him lies, break or stop the Pipes whereby it is distributed to the public use and advantage of Mankind' (IX, 5).

Were his own ideas for the reform of language to be carried into effect, discourse would be greatly simplified, and 'many of the Books extant, as Poets Works, might be contained in a Nut-shell' (XI, 26). But Locke does not deceive himself about the possibility of this happening, and the *Essay* is memorable not so much as a plea for the reform of language as a statement of dissatisfaction with language; a dissatisfaction that leads Locke to doubt 'whether Language, as it has been employ'd, has contributed more to the improvement or hinderance of Knowledge amongst Mankind' (XI, 4).

There were writers who expressed their impatience with this state of affairs by conceiving symbolic systems which would dispense with language altogether; parodied by Swift in the 'Scheme for entirely abolishing all Words whatsoever' proposed by the language professors in the Grand Academy of Lagado. One needs to remember, in this context, that parody inevitably contains a vestigial confirmation of the very idea it seeks to expose, and Swift's comedy at the expense of the empirical version of language indicates how firmly rooted this was in the eighteenth-century mind.

But more in the spirit of Locke's rules was the developing feeling that since language was naturally unstable it ought to be regulated by positive (and where necessary restrictive) action for the benefit of the community at large. This was the programme followed by the prescriptive grammarians and lexicographers through the greater part of the eighteenth century. Such is the view expressed by a more sober Swift in his *Proposal for Correcting, Improving, and Ascertaining the English Tongue* (1712). Some idea of the seriousness of the concern for language is suggested by Defoe in his *Essay upon Projects* (1697), where he urges that if only there were an Academy to regulate the language then its corrupters could be officially reprimanded, and 'twould be as Criminal to Coin Words, as Money'.[6]

Acting on the well founded conviction that effective government depended upon the consistent use of words, the mandarin class in China, we are told, used to take an annual inventory of words so as to maintain control of their meanings—and hence of civil order. This precaution would have been as well understood in the eighteenth century as it is in our own day. The political advantages of controlling language, the 'great Conduit' of human consciousness and communication, were recognised well before George Orwell spelt them out with the example of the State language Newspeak in *1984*.

II

But the independence of Smollett's position on language will be more effectively demonstrated by contrast with his immediate contemporaries, and so before passing on to my author I shall consider briefly the linguistic temper of both Johnson and Fielding, one a professional and representative figure and the other a fellow novelist with a declared interest in the ways of words.

As one might expect, Johnson inclines to neither of the extremes I have described. He confesses in the preface to his Dictionary that he flattered himself for a while that his work might 'fix our language, and put a stop to those alterations which time and chance have hitherto been suffered to make in it without opposition', but he also makes it clear that he found out the vanity of this particular human wish. The 'vigilance and activity' of academics established for the purpose have been in vain; 'sounds are too volatile and subtle for legal restraints; to enchain syllables, and to lash the wind, are equally the undertakings of pride'.[7]

But although Johnson was careful to treat language as a human creation which must inevitably reflect human imperfection—particularly in this matter of its instability—he was not wholly reconciled to the fact. He could not consider the deliquescence of language without regret. He confesses that 'Language is only the instrument of science, and words are but the signs of ideas'; but his reaction is significant: 'I wish, however, that the instrument might be less apt to decay, and that signs might be permanent, like the things which they denote'. And in the observation that 'our language is yet living, and variable by the caprice of every one that speaks it'[8] one hears the echo of Pope's lament:

> Our Sons their Fathers' *failing Language* see,
> And such as *Chaucer* is, shall *Dryden* be.[9]

Johnson observed in his *Plan of a Dictionary*:

To our language may be with great justness applied the observation of *Quintilian*, that speech was not formed by an analogy sent from heaven. It did not descend to us in a state of uniformity and perfection, but was produced by necessity and enlarged by accident, and is therefore composed of dissimilar parts, thrown together by negligence, by affectation, by learning, or by ignorance.[10]

But it is precisely this free interplay of contradictory influences, which we would see now as a condition not only of the origin but also of the continuing vitality of language, that Johnson is himself disposed to inhibit. (We can recognise the continuing influence of Locke here.) The constant implication of his own writings on language is that the time for 'accident' is over. Learning should wage war on ignorance and other disruptive elements affecting language. 'Tongues, like governments, have a natural tendency to degeneration; we have long preserved our constitution, let us make some struggles for our language'.[11] The practical confirmation of his linguistic theory lies in the fact that Johnson, like most of his contemporaries, was an uneasy guest at the 'great feast of languages' provided by Shakespeare; the diet proved too rich for an Augustan stomach.[12]

One may conclude, then, that Johnson's stance towards language was characteristically defensive. For all his awareness that the fact was otherwise, his instinct was to see language as something static. He saw words naturally in isolation, as objects of etymological curiosity; as a theorist he shows little sense of their expressive possibilities. Johnson was amused to relate in his 'Life of Pope' how the poet, challenged with the authority of the lexicographer Patrick, replied that he *would allow the publisher of a Dictionary to know the meaning of a single word, but not of two words put together*;[13] however, the anecdote does contain a valid comment on Johnson's own limited sense of the way words actually behave.

Fielding was influenced by Locke's philosophy of language in a more immediate way than was Johnson; or perhaps it would be better to say that there was an affinity of intellectual temper that drew Fielding inevitably to Locke's

ideas. Glenn W. Hatfield (to whose penetrating study of
Fielding's language I am much indebted) suggests that what
Fielding took from Locke was 'not a systematic philosophy
of words so much as a working rationale of his own intuitive
concerns about language', concerns 'directed to the practical
questions of its imperfections and abuse'.[14]

Now Fielding's criticism of language is worked out (or
worked at) in the numerous periodical essays he wrote on
the subject during the ten years or so preceding the publication of *Tom Jones*; on which material Hatfield's book provides
an excellent commentary. But for my own purposes it will be
sufficient to consider *Tom Jones* itself, since the novel treats
language as part of its subject matter (almost as part of the
plot) and provides sufficient evidence of Fielding's theory
and practice in this direction. It takes only one reading of
Tom Jones to alert the reader to this fact, and increasing familiarity enables us to appreciate that Fielding's unremitting
consciousness of the words he is using—and which he lets
his characters use—implies a very deliberate criticism of language, conducted at various levels.

There is an excellent paragraph later in the novel which
characterises the tone (and substance) of much of Fielding's
attention to the state of English:

Jones now declared that they must certainly have lost their way:
but this the guide insisted upon was impossible; a word which, in
common conversation, is often used not only to signify improbable, but often what is really very likely, and, sometimes, what hath
certainly happened: an hyperbolical violence like that which is so
frequently offered to the words infinite and eternal; by the former
of which it is usual to express a distance of half a yard, and by the
latter, a duration of five minutes.[15]

The lessons of this commentary are embedded in Fielding's own technique of expression, and result in that 'language of irony' which is generally recognised as the hallmark
of his style. Sensitive to what Ian Watt has called the
'ironigenic' tendency of eighteenth-century language,[16]
Fielding mistrusts the corruptible word 'conscience' and
writes instead: 'Mr Jones had somewhat about him, which,

though I think writers are not thoroughly agreed in its name, doth certainly inhabit some human breasts; whose use is not so properly to distinguish right from wrong, as to prompt and incite them to the former, and to restrain and with-hold them from the latter'.[17] Fielding keeps one step ahead of the decay of language with his own continuous vigilance, in which the reader is invited to share.

But the most persistent evidence of Fielding's scrupulous linguistic hygiene in *Tom Jones* is the repeated use of phrases like 'in truth', 'in reality', 'in short', 'in plain English', either to undermine inflated language (many of the mock-heroic passages are brought to an abrupt conclusion in this way) or to underline some other kind of ironic stratagem. ' "For my own part," confesses Mrs Fitzpatrick of her husband, "I made no doubt but that his designs were strictly honourable, as the phrase is; that is, to rob a lady of her fortune by way of marriage" '.[18] Fielding uses such phrases literally hundreds of times throughout his novel to maintain a cautious distance from the dangerous encroachments of his medium. It is Hatfield's argument that Fielding's verbal irony absolves him from the original sin of language: its tendency to renegue its original meaning. 'For "the language of irony" . . . is for Fielding a way of at once exposing the corruption of words and rescuing them from the debased condition into which they have fallen. It is a way of speaking truth in a corrupt medium.' But one effect of what Hatfield calls Fielding's 'sheer sensitivity to language'[19] is paradoxically that Fielding becomes progressively less able to use language at all. And perhaps this is not even a paradox, when we consider the nature of that sensitivity: an inhibiting sensitivity to imperfection, a negative guard which nowhere promises or provides a positive consequence.

It can only be a lack of confidence in language that leads Fielding to write: 'Sophia then retired to her chamber of mourning, where she indulged herself (if the phrase may be allowed me) in all the luxury of tender grief', or 'Allworthy having left her a little while to chew the cud (if I may use that expression) . . .', or ' . . . to speak truly, this was one of those houses where gentlemen, to use the language of advertisements, meet with civil treatment for their money'.[20] The writing is clogged with hesitations and uncertainties; as if Fielding feels obliged to apologise for offering to write at all. It is hard to know what to make of the traditional claims for his subtlety, self-consciousness and 'sheer sensitivity' when we see him grasping clumsily at the handrails of his intention in this manner.

Fielding has to make a positive effort to be able actually to say something; an effort which is evident when he introduces a paragraph on ways of reducing the slaughter of war by saying 'I would avoid, if possible, treating this matter ludicrously'.[21] If possible. He is no longer in control of his medium; language has 'sunk under him' in a sense rather different from that Addison intended when he used the phrase of Milton.[22] At one point in the novel Tom confesses to the company that '"tho' I have been a very wild young fellow, still in my most serious moments, and at the bottom, I am really a Christian"'.[23] The trouble with Tom's creator is that in *his* most serious moments he has nothing left to say; at the bottom of all his levels of irony there is no language left to use.

'We are but critics, or but half create':[24] the dilemma of the artist who is distracted by his own critical consciousness was already a dilemma for Fielding. His critical faculty bears on his creative impulse so immediately as almost to stifle it. He fights a losing battle throughout *Tom Jones* with the reluctance of language to mean anything—a reluctance which is the direct result of his own subversive criticism. This is the crucial factor that distinguishes Fielding's irony from Swift's or Smollett's, and makes it in the end self-defeating. Irony has been described as 'language mocking itself',[25] and it is as if in *Tom Jones* language has succumbed to the mockery. Verbal irony as Fielding employs it is 'the green-eyed monster, that doth mock / The meat it feeds on', or the sow that consumes its own farrow. These metaphors seem to me to . offer an appropriate description of what happens in what is taken to be Fielding's greatest work. Language cannot survive such treatment; the effort to speak truth in a corrupt medium is too exhausting.

One might even suggest that 'verbal irony' in this sense is the myopia of true ironic vision, since it exhausts its effect on individual words and phrases rather than retaining its strength, which must always be deployed *in* language, for the exposure of that 'refuge from moral cognition' which cannot be charged on language itself. The ironigenic tendency of eighteenth-century language may be seen in the end as a perverse and desperate rhetoric, the result of a misguided attempt to purify language of its natural weakness at the cost of its natural strength: an exercise which goes against its very nature.

The analysis I have attempted here will help to explain why I find myself in total agreement with the criticism of Fielding's style in *Tom Jones* which was made by William Godwin in *The Examiner* at the end of the eighteenth century. Godwin found the style 'glaringly inferior to the constituent parts of the work. It is feeble, costive, and slow . . . The general turn of the work is intended to be sarcastic and ironical; but the irony is hard, pedantic, and unnatural'.[26] Other adjectives Godwin uses ('hide-bound', 'jejune', and 'puerile') are severe but not I think unjust to this very defective classic of Augustan prose.[27]

III

Now what has gone for too long unrecognised—and at a cost to our understanding of Smollett's genius—is that there was another attitude to language discoverable in some eighteenth-century writers; one which was not so much upheld against the Augustan norm as implicit in another tradition of linguistic usage. One might suggest the spirit of it by converting Conrad's phrase to read: 'in the linguistic element immerse'.[28] This was the attitude which looked on language positively as the prime agent of the human imagination and regarded the material of language as a maze of infinite possibilities—not a set of obstructions—which it was the writer's delight as well as his duty to explore. The tradition to which this attitude belongs reaches back to Lucian and Apuleius; its modern fountainhead is unquestionably

Rabelais, as its most recent master is evidently James Joyce.

All these writers, and those others who may be related to this alternative verbal tradition, have sought to emphasise the wonderful, obtrusive fact of language itself; and they have written for the most part in an atmosphere of linguistic luxuriousness—which of course includes depravity. Lucian's *Ass* and his *True History* contain many examples of anarchic humour of a purely verbal kind which are as outrageous as the stories themselves. The Elizabethan translator of Apuleius's *Golden Ass*, William Adlington, remarked that his author wrote 'in so dark and high a style, in so strange and absurd words and in such new invented phrases, as he seemed rather to set it forth to show his magnificent prose than to participate his doings to others'.[29] All Locke's categories of linguistic abuse would not have been comprehensive enough to include the liberties taken with language by Rabelais: the Rabelais who detonated his great work under the complacent classical assumptions about *res* and *verba*, delighting in catalogues, curses, travesties and mock etymologies that completely subvert the sober function of language as envisaged by the empiricists. And in our own time James Joyce has turned language inside out, complicating the levels of meaning in what he called 'the kink's English' until it could serve as the adequate statement, or extension, of a reality that refused to be simplified.

It is to this tradition, despite his superficial Augustanism, that Smollett really belongs as a writer, and where he has his natural temperamental and artistic affinities. All the elements are there, unashamedly discordant: the implicit narrative gift to start with, then the startling expressive facility, the parody, the travesty, the distinctive rhythm or 'melos' that Northrop Frye sees as proper to writers of this kind;[30] the simple collocations of words; the verbal caricature, the brilliant stylised dialogue, the spurious etymology that makes a circus of the 'pale of words'; the pun cultivated to the complication and destruction of all simple meaning. These features taken together amount to an interest in language for its own sake, beyond its function as a precise instrument of communication: or 'conduit'.

But before developing this point further I must take account of an important passage in the *Atom* that might at first seem to contradict what I am saying here. This is an exposure of Pitt's style of oratory, and a study of its effect on those at whom it is directed, which occurs—fully dramatised—towards the middle of the work. Smollett observes that Pitt assailed the mob 'in the way of paradox, which never fails to produce a wonderful effect upon a heated imagination and a shallow understanding':

Having, in his exordium, artfully fascinated their faculties, like a juggler in Bartholomew-fair, by means of an assemblage of words without meaning or import; he proceeded to demonstrate, that a wise and good man ought to discard his maxims the moment he finds they are certainly established on the foundation of eternal truth. That the people of Japan ought to preserve the farm of Yesso, as the apple of their eye, because nature has disjoined it from their empire; and the maintenance of it would involve them in all the quarrels of Tartary: that it was to be preserved at all hazards, because it was not worth preserving: that all the power and opulence of Japan ought to be exerted and employed in its defence, because, by the nature of its situation, it could not possibly be defended . . .

Pitt succeeds, for reasons which Smollett then enlarges upon. 'After a weak mind has been duly prepared, and turned as it were, by opening a sluice or torrrent of high-sounding words, the greater the contradiction proposed the stronger impression it makes, because it increases the puzzle, and lays fast hold on the admiration.' But the best is yet to come, as Smollett goes on to give some contemptuous examples of Pitt's perversion of language:

. . . he was perfectly well acquainted with all the equivocal or synonimous words in his own language, and could ring the changes on them with great dexterity. He knew perfectly well how to express the same ideas by words that literally implied opposition:—for example, a valuable conquest or an invaluable conquest; a shameful rascal or shameless villain;[31] a hard head or a soft head; a large conscience or no conscience; immensely great or immensely little; damned high or damned low; damned bitter, damned sweet; damned severe, damned insipid; and damned fulsome. .

Smollett concludes with an extended analogy which identifies what Kenneth MacLean justly calls the 'completely Lockian'[32] assumptions that lie behind it:

He knew when to distract its weak brain with a tumult of incongruous and contradictory ideas: he knew when to overwhelm its feeble faculty of thinking, by pouring in a torrent of words without any ideas annexed. These throng in like city-milliners to a Mile-end assembly, while it happens to be under the direction of a conductor without strength and authority. Those that have ideas annexed may be compared to the females provided with partners, which, though they may croud the place, do not absolutely destroy all regulation and decorum. But those that are uncoupled, press in promiscuously with such impetuosity and in such numbers, that the puny master of the ceremonies is unable to withstand the irruption; far less, to distinguish their quality, or accommodate them with partners: thus they fall into the dance without order, and immediately anarchy ensues [i, 165–72]

Now what I want to suggest is that this passage, though apparently Lockian in its assumptions, is not so in its effect; and therefore operates less cogently as the Augustan defence of rational language than at first appears. For two reasons. The first is less significant, but has not, I believe, been noticed before: that the most lucid (and Lockian) part of this analysis—the image of the unaccompanied dancers—is in fact borrowed from one of Fielding's early *Champion* essays.[33] As such the image can hardly be said to have the authority of Smollett's own thinking behind it; it is simply turned to account. But more important, we should notice that the whole passage is an exercise of style rather than a criticism of style; as is so often the case with Swift, it operates through destructive imitation rather than by analysis. The best description of Pitt's technique is contained in Smollett's own passionate parody of it; Smollett is himself using to excellent effect the very faculty which he sets out to castigate in another. (And demonstrating, incidentally, a rather

more intimate sense of the workings of words than Locke
betrays in his *Essay*.) It is a perfect case of pot and kettle; for
it is certainly true that the *Atom* from which this passage
comes is the most unrestrained and virulent of Smollett's
works, where he himself disdains no manipulation of language (or of principle, one might almost add) in the overrid-
ing compulsion to make his point. Pitt has himself been
introduced earlier as 'this mountebank in patriotism, this
juggler in politics, this cat in pan, or cake in pan, or κατα παν
in principle' (i, 128); which is itself a rather more rhetorical
than objective description, and evidently calculated to have a
particular effect on the reader. The whole context reminds
us, in other words, that Smollett is himself immersed in the
linguistic element; it is not his intention (like some critical
Canute) to repel its tides.

The fact I wish to establish is one which this passage
would seem to corroborate: that Smollett's creativity exists in
a different relation to language from that of Fielding, and the
other Augustan writers who share Fielding's scepticism.
Fielding mistrusts language, insures himself by strategic
irony against its deception, where Smollett relies upon language, takes it into his confidence. Fielding insulates himself
against the treachery of words; Smollett is at home among
words, and is more prepared to trust himself to their depths
and running currents. Virginia Woolf provides an image, in
a suggestive essay on the writer's relation to words, which
will serve to clarify the distinction I am trying to make.
Words, she reminds us, 'do not live in dictionaries; they live
in the mind':

All we can say about them, as we peer at them over the edge of
that deep, dark and fitfully illuminated cavern in which they
live—the mind—all we can say about them is that they seem to like
people to think and to feel before they use them, but to think and
to feel not about them, but about something different. They are
highly sensitive, easily made self-conscious. They do not like to
have their purity or their impurity discussed. If you start a Society
for Pure English, they will show their resentment by starting
another for impure English—hence the unnatural violence of much
modern speech; it is a protest against the puritans. They are highly

democratic, too; they believe that one word is as good as another; uneducated words are as good as educated words, uncultivated words as cultivated words, there are no ranks or titles in their society. Nor do they like being lifted out on the point of a pen and examined separately. They hang together, in sentences, in paragraphs, sometimes for whole pages at a time.[34]

Now Fielding is the perfect example of the writer who offends against words in the way Virginia Woolf describes here. He thinks about them obsessively; he makes them abnormally self-conscious; their 'purity or impurity' is his constant theme; and he holds them out on the point of his critical pen for prolonged examination. He is the veriest verbal puritan. Whereas Smollett is much happier to listen to the sounds which come from the 'fitfully illuminated cavern' of the mind, and sees no threat to his own security in the grouping or ganging of words in sentences, paragraphs or 'whole pages at a time'. There is a distance between Fielding and his medium of expression; Smollett's identification with the language he uses is total, his attitude is seamless. Fielding uses language like a fine instrument; but it is a glove on Smollett's hand.

In considering the elements that go to make up what Boucé calls Smollett's 'linguistic sensitivity'[35] one should not forget the fact of his Scottish nationality. The Scots have always been renowned for their hospitality to words, their love of dense and complicated verbal surfaces, and have reaped the benefit of this attitude in their rich, resolute and uncompromising articulateness. It was probably no accident that it was a Scot who first offered to translate Rabelais into English: Sir Thomas Urquhart of Cromarty, of whom Hugh MacDiarmid (a convincing if not unbiased witness) has said he 'showed a verbal resource and range of vocabulary that in many instances went beyond that of Rabelais himself'.[36] Smollett shared this range and resource, even if the circumstances of his own work did not allow him to explore it so freely; there is enough evidence for us to conclude that he had the same kind of appetite for the raw material of language that led the Russian poet Mayakovsky to advise the

poet-aspirant 'Fill your storehouse constantly, fill the
granaries of your skull with all kinds of words, necessary,
expressive, rare, invented, renovated and manufactured'.[37]

Now the distinctive attitude to language that I am trying to
identify here is, as I have said, largely implicit; we must not
look for a formal apologist, and I do not pretend to be able to
offer Smollett himself as one. The nearest we come to a
methodical contradiction of Locke in the eighteenth century
is the very deliberate parody of his ideas on language in
Tristram Shandy; but this certainly did not represent—or at
least, did not operate as—a counter-initiative. No; we have
to read the contrary argument in the books that show us
what can be achieved when language is used according to
very different assumptions. And the evidence which contradicts the very English and very Augustan Locke, Fielding
and Johnson may be found in the style of the un-English and
(in their different ways) non-Augustan Swift, Smollett and
Sterne.

Since I mean to appeal to a wide range of Smollett's work
to establish this, many of my examples must inevitably find
their place in my next chapter on Smollett's style, and in the
later chapters of stylistic analysis. There is, however, some
evidence of a purely linguistic nature, and some stylistic evidence with an essential linguistic element to it, that I shall
make use of here.

One very immediate way in which Smollett confesses his
interest in the stuff of language is his tendency to
'etymologise', to explore (often in an eccentric, and sometimes in a deliberately ludicrous, manner) the surprising
semantic adventures of certain words. In the same essay to
which I have referred above (on Sidney Goodsir Smith)
Hugh MacDiarmid claims that 'philology has always been
one of the main concerns of great Scots';[38] and it is clear (in
this context) that MacDiarmid does not mean the sober
philology of the scholar but the obsessive and inventive
philology of the creative writer, engrossed in his feast of
languages. It is the kind of philology, in other words, of
which Johnson expressed his disdain when castigating the
lexicographer Junius in his *Plan of a Dictionary*: 'it can be no

criminal degree of censoriousness to charge that etymologist with want of judgment, who can seriously derive *dream* from *drama*, because *life is a drama, and a drama is a dream*; and who declares with a tone of defiance, that no man can fail to derive *moan* from μόνος *monos, single* or solitary, who considers that grief naturally loves to be *alone*'.[39]

Examples of Smollett's philological self-indulgence are likely to turn up anywhere, from *Random* onwards. When Roderick first meets Dr Wagtail the coffee they are drinking sets the pedant off on a philological wild-goose chase:

He let me know, that it was utterly unknown to the ancients; and derived its name from an Arabian word, which I might easily perceive by the sound and termination. From this topic he transferred his disquisitions to the verb *drink* . . . to drink a vast quantity, or, as the vulgar express it, to drink an ocean of liquor, was in Latin *potare*, and in Greek *poteein*; and on the other hand, to use it moderately, was *bibere* and *pinein*;—that this was only a conjecture of his own, which, however, seemed to be supported by the word *bibulous*, which is particularly applied to the pores of the skin, that can only drink a very small quantity of the circumambient moisture, by reason of the smallness of their diameters;—whereas, from the verb *poteein*, is derived the substantive *potamos*, which signifies a river, or vast quantity of liquor.

Roderick 'could not help smiling at this learned and important investigation', and goes on to contradict the doctor's theory with references to Horace, Homer and Anacreon (45; ii, 97–8). On another occasion Roderick comes upon Wagtail and his friend Medlar 'disputing upon the word Custard, which the physician affirmed should be spelled with a G, because it was derived from the Latin verb *gustare*, "to taste" '; this time Roderick decides in favour of the doctor, for purely mischievous reasons (48; ii, 126).

Smollett takes up the subject in his own person in the *Travels*. In the third letter he suggests with respect to the name of the bird 'wheat-ears' that 'this is a pleasant corruption of *white-a—se*, the translation of their French name *cul blanc*, taken from their colour; for they are actually white towards the tail'; and then, faced with the word 'samphire',

he becomes more frankly inventive. 'The French call it
passe-pierre; and I suspect its English name is a corruption of
sang-pierre . . . As it grew upon a naked rock, without any
appearance of soil, it might be naturally enough called *sang
du pierre*, or *sang-pierre*, blood of the rock; and hence the
name *samphire*' (3; pp. 18–19). But the most extreme examples occur in that curious, unclassifiable work the *Atom*,
where Smollett pauses from his narrative on several occasions to make surprising digressions of this kind. First he
fills four pages with a plan for 'a dissertation on trousers or
trunk breeches', examining the names for this article in
Greek, Latin, Spanish, Italian, French, Saxon, Swedish,
Irish, Celtic and Japanese, and citing the authority of Persius, Jamblychus, Abaris, Linschot and Dr Kempfer for his
researches, which, if completed, 'would have unveiled the
mysteries that now conceal the origin, migration, supersti-
tion, language, laws, and connections of different
nations—*sed nunc non erit his locus*' (i, 90–3). A little later he
fills ten pages with an astonishingly and absurdly erudite
account of some key words from witchcraft and magic (i,
194–205)—one is left to wonder what Johnson would have
made of this exercise—and then caps this with a fantastic
fifteen-page excursion in the incongruity of the meanings
which lie embedded in *cognomina* or family names (ii, 13–28).

In fact Smollett's sense of the value of names is highly
developed, and this is a small but significant indication of
how he responded to linguistic phenomena in general. Pat
Rogers has demonstrated in his recent study of eighteenth-
century London sub-culture how the names of certain streets
and areas in the vicinity of Grub Street—and elsewhere—assumed a particular descriptive significance.
'People of the age still saw symbolic meanings in a name,
which in any case was held to be of divine origin and hence
magical in quality'.[40] Rogers does not use Smollett as a
quarry for names, but he might well have done, for Smollett
was characteristically alert to the semantic suggestion of
such names as 'Crutched Friars' or 'Butcher Row' and used
them regularly as part of his energetic verbal delineation of
character or context.

Roderick Random overlooks a *billet-doux* sent to a friend from Vinegar Yard, Drury Lane—or 'Vingar-yard Droory-lane' as the girl subscribes it (16; i, 128). As his fortunes falter in London he takes an apartment 'in a garret near St Giles's, at the rate of ninepence per week', and later 'became so mean as to go down toward Wapping' in the hope of a job on a coastal vessel (21, i 181; 24, i 218–9). The place names punctuate Roderick's decline purposefully here; while for his acquaintance Miss Williams, as she plies her trade between Charing Cross and Ludgate Hill, the names Bridewell and Newgate hold their appropriate terrors. There is a pertinent example in *Greaves* where Crowe secures Launcelot some lodgings 'hard by St Catherine's in Wapping' (again), offering a view across the river to 'the oozy docks and cabbage-gardens of Rotherhithe' (20; pp. 161–2): it is as if Smollett has developed the unpleasant suggestions of the name, through a kind of verbal impressionism, in the additional details he provides.

But the use of place names is even more pointed and aggressive in the later works. The Atom accuses Peacock of dealings with one 'goody Thrusk at Camberwell', and 'an intrigue with the tripe-woman in Thieving-Lane' (i, 195–6); later on he insults Peacock's ear for music by exclaiming 'thou mightest be justly ranked among the braying tribe that graze along the ditches of Tottenham-court or Hockley-i'-the-hole' (ii, 63–4). These names, we may notice, are not 'encoded' like the rest of the names in this work; Smollett needs to preserve their debased associations to ensure the maximum charge of disparagement. And disparagement is certainly Bramble's objective when he inveighs against those 'delicate creatures from Bedfordbury, Butcher-row, Crutched-Friers, and Botolph-lane' who destroy the social order of Bath, and derisively identifies 'an eminent tinman from the borough of Southwark', 'a broken-winded Wapping landlady' and 'a paralytic attorney of Shoe-lane' among the select company at a ball in the town (23 April, p. 37; 30 April, p. 49). Bramble even seems to detest his sister's dog Chowder—'a filthy cur from Newfoundland, which she had in a present from the wife of a skipper in Swansey'—as

much for where it came from as on account of its own hateful
qualities (6 May; p. 62).

It is also true, of course, that Smollett used language in an
imaginative, free-associative way in devising names for his
characters. (In this respect he resembles Dickens, who kept a
list of names that might come in useful for his fiction: extraordinary names like Tuzzen, Bantinck, and Chinkible.[41])
Names are an example of the material of language in an
unusually pure form, sounds whose sense is completely
arbitrary, and freely available to serve the writer's intentions. For this reason a writer's use of names is particularly
interesting. Whether he lets this material remain inert (as in
the name 'Tom Jones') or whether he provokes it into action
('Roderick Random') can be evidence of a writer's fundamental feel for words. Some of Smollett's names are simply
descriptive, and his practice in this respect is not very different from Fielding's, who, although he went to some pains to
use as plain a name as possible for the eponymous hero of
Tom Jones, nevertheless embedded a description in the
names of other characters such as Allworthy and Thwack-
um. Thus the heroes of Smollett's first two novels are
alliteratively labelled: Roderick Random is evidently
destined for the miscellaneous adventures that befall him,
and Peregrine Pickle for the travels and ignoble complications of his own career. Ferdinand Fathom offers a definite
promise of deviousness and black treachery (a villain by any
other name would not be quite as meet), and Launcelot
Greaves confesses plainly enough his consecration to the
ideals of chivalry. A whole concourse of minor characters
receive their names on this principle. *Random* provides
Squire Gawky and Miss Snapper, Mr Cringer and Mr
Staytape; the London crowd of Medlar and Doctor Wagtail,
Banter and Bragwell, Strutwell and Straddle. Miss Grizzle's
moods threaten the early pages of *Pickle*; and we soon meet
Peregrine's tutors Jumble and Jolter, the first of whom
endures a lampoon which plays on his name, whilst the
second is certainly more jolted than jolting in his supervision
of Peregrine abroad.

Other characters assume their names more by association

than direct description, and this procedure offers more possibilities; it is more fully poetic, in that more elements are persuaded to interact. *Random* is rich in such inventions; the good-hearted sailors Bowling and Rattlin (to be joined later by Trunnion, Hatchway, Tom Pipes and Captain Crowe); the tyrannical midshipman Crampley and the affected Captain Whiffle; the apothecaries Potion, Crab and Lavement; the schoolmaster Concordance, the highwayman Rifle, the hunting squire Thicket, and of course the barber Strap. *Pickle* provides the painter Pallet, the abused Mr Hornbeck, the misanthrope Crabtree (compare Ferret from *Greaves*, and indeed Matthew—more appropriately Matt—Bramble from *Clinker*; all these names contain the relevant suggestions of temperamental contortion and contracted energy); while Lyttleton and Fielding appear as Gosling Scrag and Mr Spondy. In Paris Fathom is fooled by Sir Stentor Stile and Sir Giles Squirrel; during his stay in the King's Bench prison he is entertained by Bess Beetle, Major Macleaver, Sir Mungo Barebones and Captain Goliah Minikin. (Minikin's behaviour dramatises the paradox announced in his name.) Besides Crowe and Ferret *Greaves* assembles such characters as Fillet the surgeon, Justice Gobble, Launcelot's squire Crabshaw; the Whig Isaac Vanderpelft and the Tory Valentine Quickset; and a crowd of rustics, 'Geoffrey Prickle, Hodge Dolt, Richard Bumpkin, Mary Fang, Catherine Rubble, and Margery Litter', whose spokesman is one Farmer Stake (17; p. 141). The Bramble menage regularly encounters people who rejoice in names like Frogmore, Buzzard, Griskin and McCorkindale; and Bramble's own name is amiably converted by the Duke of Newcastle to Brambleberry— which suggests a different sort of character altogether (5 June; p. 113).

But many of Smollett's names—especially in *Clinker*—are either more complex or more extravagant than this. A good example of a complex name is provided by Humphry Clinker himself, whose surname works as a net of associations encapsulating the themes of the novel. The first sense of 'clinker' in the later eighteenth century was (as it is now) the fused ore left by materials burnt in a fire or furnace. This gave the slang sense of excreta, relating the name to the theme of constipation and flux in the novel—which is supported by the word 'expedition' (the full title of the novel is *The Expedition of Humphry Clinker*), meaning an act of freeing as well as a purposeful voyage out into the world. 'Clinker' also refers onomatopoeically to the function of a smith, which Humphry temporarily usurps in the novel; and was used besides to signify a prisoner, or one who clinks the chains a smith has forged. (Humphry, of course, descends to this condition too.) Paul Boucé points out that another sense, 'he who or that which clinches' (*OED*)—a term taken not inappropriately from boat-building—alludes to Humphry's agency in bringing the characters in the novel together at the end; and there is a further sense recorded by Partridge, 'a crafty, designing fellow', which allows for the view of Clinker held by some of the characters for some of the time.[42]

One could conduct a similar if not quite so extensive analysis of other names in this novel; but I am more concerned to make than labour the point here that Smollett's linguistic alertness and inventiveness are particularly apparent in this direction. We can certainly concur with Philip Stevick when he observes that 'Smollett's world, first of all, is peopled with characters whose very naming is an act of rhetorical excess'.[43]

However, the writer who feels the impulse to explore the possibilities of language is not restricted to etymology or nomenclature for his entertainment. There is the living language, language in people's mouths—and in people's writing—that offers possibilities of a literally limitless range and variety. And Smollett worked on the living language with a natural delight and unceasing inventiveness from his first novel to his last. Indeed, we may apply to him what Randolph Quirk says of Dickens, that his 'abiding interest was in the act of expression, in whatever aspect and of whatever kind'.[44]

Smollett effects his successive transformations of language through his characters, and as part of their characterisation;

both through their dialogue and in their corruption of the written word. Linguistic distortion is easily displayed in dialogue, where language is at the mercy of the idiom of the speaker. The Augustan image which equated the corruption of language with intellectual and moral degeneracy—the image with whose authority Dryden sentenced Shadwell:

> A Double Noose thou on thy Neck does pull,
> For Writing Treason, and for Writing Dull[45]

and which lies at the heart of the *Dunciad*—was well adapted to dialogue, as many a poet and dramatist had discovered; and Fielding, one-time dramatist himself, took it over into the novel. Smollett himself certainly uses this convention. Consider his presentation of the grotesque Justice Gobble and his wife in *Greaves*, whose corruption of language (particularly legal language) serves as an appropriate image for their combined abuse of the magistrate's office.

The laws of this land has provided—I says, as how provision is made by the laws of this here land, in reverence to delinquems and manefactors, whereby the king's peace is upholden by we magistrates, who represents his majesty's person, better than in e'er a contagious nation under the sun: but, howsoemever, that there king's peace, and this here magistrate's authority, cannot be adequably and identically upheld, if so be as how criminals escapes unpunished. Now, friend, you must be confidentious in your own mind, as you are a notorious criminal, who have trespassed again the laws on divers occasions and importunities; if I had a mind to exercise the rigour of the law, according to the authority wherewith I am wested, you and your companions in iniquity would be sewerely punished by the statue: but we magistrates has a power to litigate the sewerity of justice, and so I am contented that you shoulds be mercifully dealt withal, and even dismissed. [11; p. 93]

Gobble's vocabulary and syntax are equally garbled in this ludicrous harangue. Ten years before Sheridan popularised the formula we have a litter of malapropisms, such as 'importunities' for 'opportunities', 'litigate' for 'mitigate', and—one of Mrs Malaprop's own favourites—'contagious' for 'contiguous'. The redundant idioms 'this here' and 'that there' are several times repeated as part of Gobble's slovenly syntax, in which all relation between the singular and plural of noun and verb has been obliterated. And Gobble provides the perfect implicit comment on his performance with the inspired phrase 'sewerity of justice': an example of the cross-grained, counter-logical play of language which Smollett was to develop so effectively in his last novel.

But more typically, in Smollett's dialogue, distortion of dialogue is freed from such menial moral duties—or performs them only incidentally—and becomes simply one of the elements that go into the creation of an idiom which he indulges more for delight than for any formal purpose, and as part of that 'verbal and stylistic play'[46] which Boucé describes as the most original and richest aspect of Smollett's comedy, part of the 'filigrane', or filigree work, which gives his writing its life and distinctiveness. *Random* is a brilliant virtuoso work in this respect. The vivid rhythms and peculiar jargon of squires, schoolmasters; soldiers, sailors; rich men, poor men, beggars and thieves are jostled together with the affected diction of physicians, peers, pedants and homosexuals; the persuasive idiom of wits and poets (both male and female); lawyers, innkeepers, and priests; the cant of chemists, fiddlers, statesmen and buffoons.

Smollett had declared his intention to expose the absurdity of such language in the preface to his novel. 'That the delicate reader may not be offended at the unmeaning oaths which proceed from the mouths of some persons in these memoirs, I beg leave to premise, that I imagined nothing could more effectually expose the absurdity of such miserable expletives, than a natural and verbal representation of the discourse in which they are commonly interlarded' (i, x–xi). But it is obvious that he seeks to exhibit rather than expose this language. Such is the vigour and inventiveness of these 'natural and verbal representations' (which are, of course, not natural representations at all, but deliberately heightened versions made out of the diffuse material of such idiom) that we are in no doubt that Smollett conducts his exposure in much the same spirit that Sterne exposes the jargon of military historians, lawyers and scholastic philosophers in *Tristam Shandy*—or Rabelais the special language of innumerable other groups in the *Gargantua*; that is, in a spirit of collaboration; following language beyond the potentially into the actually absurd, and taking delight all the time, himself, in the linguistic elaboration involved.

Smollett shared this delight with the early dramatists, and like them he was able to adapt many different idioms to his purpose. Most idiosyncratic among all these is the naval jargon which had obviously made an indelible impression on his sensitive ear during his experience at sea, the extensive use of which throughout his novels was a source for imitation by many later writers. Bowling and Morgan in *Random*, Pipes, Hatchway and Trunnion in *Pickle*, are each given a distinctive personal variation of this idiom, in conforming to the other elements in their personalities. And there is an interesting development in the 'discourse' of Captain Crowe in *Greaves* which I will consider here. Smollett offers his own description of this in advance: 'when he himself attempted to speak, he never finished his period; but made such a number of abrupt transitions, that his discourse seemed to be an unconnected series of unfinished sentences, the meaning of which it was not easy to decypher'; and when Crowe opens his mouth we are not disappointed.

"Belay, Tom, belay:—prithee, don't veer out such a deal of jaw. Clap a stopper upon thy cable, and bring thyself up, my lad.—What a deal of stuff thou hast pumped up concerning bursting, and starting, and pulling ships, Laud have mercy on us!—Look ye here, brother—look ye here—mind these poor crippled joints: two fingers on the starboard, and three on the larboard hand: crooked, d'ye see, like the knees of a bilander.—I'll tell you what, brother, you seem to be a—ship deep laden—rich cargoe—current setting into the bay—hard gale—lee-shore—all hands in the boat—tow round the headland—self pulling for dear blood, against the whole crew.—Snap go the finger-braces—crack went the eye-blocks.—Bounce daylight—flash starlight—down I foundered, dark as hell—whizz went my ears, and my head spun like a whirligig. [1; pp. 2,4]

Here standard syntax has gone the way of standard vocabulary in what must be one of the earliest attempts to render—or to create in a stylised form, for such material is never simply imitated—the actual patterns of speech. For once we escape the almost exclusive convention of organised conversation; that conversation of Johnsonian regularity which few people attain to in life but which most characters habitually employ in fiction. Crowe relies upon the vigour of his own delivery to make his dislocated details intelligible; we could not really say he 'blunders round about a meaning' because in Crowe's speech, in a peculiarly symbolic way, passion and energy supply the place of ordinary grammatical connection, which is less crucial in spoken than in written language.

It is clear that Dickens had Captain Crowe in mind when he devised Mr Jingle's manner of speech in *Pickwick Papers*. Just as Smollett was directly indebted to the Elizabethan and Jacobean dramatists (and prose writers) in arriving at the exuberance and originality of his own style, so Dickens was obviously indebted to Smollett in discovering his. The influence of Smollett on Dickens generally deserves more attention than it has received,[47] but here I simply wish to draw attention to the natural affinity between the two writers in their attitude to language—and particularly that most perishable but endlessly interesting province of language, the spoken word. What critics have said about Dickens in this respect will, therefore, be relevant to Smollett also. I am thinking again of the essay by Randolph Quirk in which he argues that Dickens was first of all a brilliant individualist student of language: 'he proceeded to make himself master of a language that was sensitively appropriate and responsive to a thousand occasions, and proceeded to operate selectively a linguistic range that few users of our tongue can ever have exceeded'.[48] If Smollett does not equal Dickens's linguistic range in this respect he does, I think, anticipate and in some sense provide for it; and the frequent irruption of the play of language for its own sake is even more remarkable a feature in the earlier novelist.

Smollett's distortion of language in dialogue has been

pushed beyond the point where it has any significant moral implications, into the sphere of pure linguistic virtuosity.[49] This is why I prefer to use 'distortion' rather than 'corruption' to describe the process: the latter word bears too strong traces of the eighteenth-century distaste for linguistic experiment. The effects to be achieved by dialogue are, however, limited, both linguistically and by the convention (in a novel, unlike a play, people are not always talking), and Smollett may reasonably be supposed to have exhausted them by the time he reached mid-career—which is roughly where *Greaves* brings him. It is certainly true that Smollett devotes less attention to the spoken word in his later work. The form of both the *Travels* and *Humphry Clinker*, and the satiric density of the *Atom* are all unreceptive to dialogue. But this is not to say that Smollett's indulgent interest in the bad behaviour of language had ceased. The *Travels* and the *Atom*, we have already seen, contain their own distinctive evidence of this; and it was in his last novel that he pursued his highly personal exploration one stage further, with what is for the time a surprising persistence and originality. Responding to the possibility made open to him by the epistolary form he had chosen for this novel, Smollett turned his attention to variations on the written word; his implicit objective being the complication and destruction of simple meaning. I want to argue that what we have in the letters of Win Jenkins and Tabitha Bramble—which are sixteen in number, getting progressively longer and more interesting, and forming indeed no inconsiderable part of the novel[50]—is a significant testimony to the wilfulness of words, and a spirited exposure of the simple model of language proposed by the empirical tradition.

The experiment with language is conducted, in the letters of these two ladies, at various levels. First one has what one must anachronistically call 'malapropisms'. Thus Win complains of 'odorous falsehoods' uttered against her, and writes of 'common manufactors'; Tabitha declaims against an 'impotent rascal', and describes how Win herself has become a new creature from the 'ammunition' (= admonition) of Humphry Clinker (pp. 71, 155; 78, 274). Simple misspellings one need take no notice of; but Smollett makes frequent use of a technique where a word is so purposefully misspelt as to become in fact another word—as when Tabitha writes of 'the litel box with my jowls' and Win is 'taken with asterisks' (pp. 6, 7). This is capable of more subtle effect than malapropism. At one level there is the simple incongruity: infidel becomes 'impfiddle', bible 'pyebill', pious 'pyehouse' (pp. 306, 155, 109). Already there is some suggestion that a subversive element is being deliberately introduced here, destroying the simple equivalence of word and idea; and this is indisputably the case where grace appears as 'grease', church as 'crutch', and matrimony 'mattermoney'; where the eyes of affection Tabitha casts on Lismahago are recorded as 'the heys of infection', where Mrs Baynard's woman dresses 'like a parson of distinkson' and dines with the 'valley de shambles' (pp. 155, 261, 352, 306).

It is when individual words are grouped in phrases and deployed in sentences that we can see how Smollett's imagination has gone to work, picking at the seams of language, revealing the abyss that opens (or is ordinarily concealed) under our everyday handling of words. Tabitha chastises Dr Lewis for putting her affairs 'in composition with the refuge and skim of the hearth'. Win enjoys living among 'the very squintasense of satiety' (quintessence of society) in Bath, and writes that the vet has 'subscribed a repository' for Tabitha's dog Chowder; at the news of her mistress's engagement to Lismahago she wonders that Tabitha should 'disporridge herself for such a nubjack' (pp. 78; 43, 7, 306). Language is rocking at its moorings. Win resolves to 'deify the devil and all his works'; Smollett works in a contradiction against the grain of the phrase here as deftly as he inserts a semantic endorsement on another occasion, when Tabitha commands 'let none of the men have excess to the strong beer' (pp. 306, 6).

Although Johnson might have scorned to notice the fact, its readiness to lend itself to coprophilic or bawdy suggestion is surely one of the most human characteristics of language (one that Shakespeare, Jonson and the early dramatists in general cannot be accused of having neglected); and much of the verbal play in *Humphry Clinker* tends in one of these directions. Smollett channels different words in the same inevitable direction: Tabitha reminds her housekeeper to 'have the gate shit every evening before dark', and vows she will never write to Dr Lewis again 'though he beshits me on his bended knees'; Win deduces that the men have caught colds 'by lying in damp shits at sir Tummas Ballfart's' (pp. 6, 156, 307). Win confides that 'if I was given to tail-baring, I have my own secrets to discover', and excites Mary Jones's interest in Clinker in what may be felt to be a dubious manner:

O Mary Jones, pray without seizing for grease to prepare you for the operations of this wonderful instrument, which, I hope, will be exorcised this winter upon you and others at Brambleton-hall. [pp. 220, 156]

Mary Jones is again the recipient of Win's protestation that 'my parents were marred according to the rights of holy mother crutch, in the face of men and angles' (p. 338). It seems to work out that Tabitha is guilty of the more blatant lapses, as she protests 'Roger gets this, and Roger gets that; but I'd have you to know, I won't be rogered at this rate by any ragmatical fellow in the kingdom' (we know the sense of 'roger' here from Boswell's *London Journal*) and advises Mrs Gwyllim to 'keep accunt of Roger's purseeding in reverence to the butter milk' (pp. 78, 274). It is wholly consistent with Freud's theory of unconscious ambiguities that Tabitha, who as Jery says 'has left no stone unturned to avoid the reproachful epithet of old maid', should betray her obsession with the idea of a sexual partner in this way. There is a particularly explicit example of this self-betrayal when she instructs her maid to have 'the father-bed and matrosses well haired' against her return (pp. 60, 274). Of course Win's slips have the same logic behind them. Giorgio Melchiori points out the indecent innuendoes from the Italian in Win's version of Lismahago, 'Kismycago', and her word 'minchioned' for mentioned (pp. 220, 261)—remarking that 'even Joyce's trick of availing himself of foreign words to compli-

cate the polysignificance of his new vocabulary is found in
Smollett'.[51]

The most developed examples of systematic counterpoint
to the surface meaning occur in the last letter—as if Smollett
was warming to his task. The newly married Win Lloyd (*née*
Jenkins) informs us that 'Providinch hath bin pleased to
make a great halteration in the pasture of our
affairs'—besides the slang allusion to marriage in 'halteration', the logic of association between 'halter' and 'pasture'
supplies a gratuitous piece of wit. And where she expresses
the wish that she will live 'upon dissent terms of civility'
with her neighbours the accidental replacement of the adjective 'decent' by the noun 'dissent' amusingly subverts Win's
intention. But the most memorable effect is provided by her
version of 'our society is to separate', which becomes 'our
satiety is to suppurate'. Melchiori describes this phrase as 'a
masterpiece of grim humour: that courting of decay which,
beyond Joyce, has been popularised by the easy surrealism
of Salvador Dali', and he goes on to wonder whether one
could transfer to *Humphry Clinker* what another critic has
said of *Finnegan's Wake*: that 'it expresses a malady of the
spirit through a corruption of the language'.[52] One notices
that 'corruption of language' is here understood positively,
as a legitimate component of a viable total meaning, rather
than in any negative sense, as some kind of betrayal of the
verbal medium.

William Empson has remarked that 'eighteenth-century
ambiguity was easy and colloquial; it was concerned to exploit, as from a rational and sensible mental state, the normal
resources of the spoken language'.[53] But it should be obvious by now that Smollett goes quite beyond the simple exploitation envisaged by Empson, and also beyond what C. J.
Rawson refers to as 'that coy eighteenth-century genre, the
misspelt, malapropist letter'.[54] There is nothing easy or colloquial about the calculated linguistic complications of
Clinker, in consideration of which we are indeed taken
beyond Dickens to Joyce: the Joyce who 'capitalising upon
the fact that the imagination delights in running beyond
nature . . . set words loose';[55] the Joyce of *Finnegan's Wake* in

which, as Hugh Kenner has observed, 'the mind is detached from responsibility towards things, cut loose in the nowhere—the not quite trackless nowhere in which words remain'.[56]

Language thrives on impurity: it is an impure element, the characteristic product of human imperfection, as well as of human freedom. We try to trap language in a cistern, but its nature is that of a fountain. 'The cistern contains: the fountain overflows', and it is the overflowing of language, the *excess* of language, that bears witness to the vitality as well as the vagrancy of the human imagination. Blake also wrote that 'Poetry Fetter'd Fetters the Human Race';[57] it is similarly true that language fettered fetters the human mind, and the restriction which men from the Restoration onwards sought to put on language undoubtedly formed one of the links in the 'mind-forg'd manacles' Blake abominated.

Smollett knew the value of sound in language as well as the Pitt he portrayed so contemptuously in the *Atom*, and at least as well as Captain Weazel, who sustained his courage with his voice and was (as Smollett describes him) *'vox & preterea nihil'* (*Random*, 11; i, 78). He would never have disqualified any one element of language from its place in the total effect; such selectivity would be part of what Lieutenant Lismahago dismisses as the pursuit of 'false refinement' by which we have 'impaired the energy of our language' (*Clinker*, 13 July; p. 200).

In the linguistic element immerse. I hope that the evidence I have assembled in this chapter—selective as it is—will help to replace the conventional idea of Smollett as narrator, journalist, or whatever other inferior category, with a truer idea which will represent him as sharing in the same linguistic element with Jonson and Shakespeare, with Swift and Sterne, with Dickens and Joyce; with all those writers who have been glad guests at the 'feast of languages', all those who have lived long, and luxuriously, on the 'alms-basket of words'.[58]

5   *Style*

I

The common assumptions about style in the eighteenth century were inevitably related to contemporary ideas on language, and in this chapter I propose to show, first, how
Smollett's theory and practice of style depart once again
from these recognised norms. This will be preliminary to a
description of the essential characteristics of Smollett's
style—what I see as two complementary planes of expression—in the later part of the chapter.

It is fair to say that since the common prejudices about the
purity of language relied upon popular and practical rather
than philosophic or genuinely linguistic considerations[1] they
were at least as much concerned with 'that assemblage of
words which is called a style'[2] as with the words themselves
in isolation. Pride of style is the necessary accompaniment to
pride of words, and the inflated period was just as distaste-
ful as the 'hard word' or contraction to the linguistic
puritanism of the time. The very phrase 'figurative language'
applies at the intersection of words and style, where the
word surrenders its primary meaning in a new context, and
undergoes a process of semantic extension. The language
could not be refined without some attention being paid to
syntax and rhetoric as well as to semantics.

The ideal of plainness and perspicuity therefore includes
style, the compound, as well the component words. Swift
warned his Young Gentleman against stylistic as well as verbal impropriety: 'obscure Terms' and *'Hard Words'* go along
with 'a quaint, terse, florid Style, rounded into Periods and
Cadencies, commonly without either Propriety or Meaning';
and his celebratedly simple definition of a style as 'Proper
Words in proper Places' covers both categories. 'When a

Man's Thoughts are clear, the properest Words will generally offer themselves first, and his own Judgment will direct him in what Order to place them, so as they may be best understood.'³

A situation where its complicated requirements can be summarised as only a matter of the order of words implies a reductive theory of style; a theory that is in sharp contrast both to what preceded it (among the Elizabethan and early seventeenth-century rhetoricians) and what followed in the nineteenth century, with the developing attentiveness on the part of critics to the 'other harmony' of prose. (The styles of Browne and Taylor beforehand and Burke and Carlyle afterwards contain their own implicit comment on eighteenth-century theory and practice.)

The reduction of the significance of style was an inevitable consequence of the normative attitudes of the time. It was a hundred times repeated that a style could be learnt by reading and practice. John Hughes recommended 'a diligent and careful perusal of the most correct writers of the language in their various kinds', and Lord Chesterfield urged his son that it required 'nothing but application' to achieve 'a pure and elegant English style'.⁴ Johnson himself liked to identify the ingredients of his own style—though he did not deceive Boswell, who recognised that 'Johnson's comprehension of mind was the mould of his language'.⁵ And so there developed that competent but colourless common form which is often castigated as the standard of eighteenth-century prose. At the time this was complacently regarded as a collective achievement. 'There is now an elegance of style universally diffused,' claimed Johnson; and again, 'nobody now talks much of style: everybody composes pretty well'.⁶ Nobody now talks much of style. And so the criticism of style atrophied; the very consciousness of style became attentuated in people's minds. Fielding complained that 'there is no Branch of Criticism, in which Learning, as well as Good-sense is more required, than to the forming an accurate Judgment of Style, tho' there is none, I believe, in which every trifling Reader is more ready to give his Decision';⁷ but for all his criticism of language and theorising about the novel at the formal level Fielding himself never paid much attention to style, and in a preface written for his sister Sarah's novel *David Simple* deliberately relegated it to a position of very minor importance.

> The Diction I shall say no more of, than as it is the last, and lowest Perfection in a Writer, and one which many of great Genius seem to have little regarded; so I must allow my Author to have the least Merit on this Head . . . but Experience and Habit will most certainly remove this Objection; for a good Style, as well as a good Hand in Writing, is chiefly learn'd by Practice.[8]

We have reached an extreme in the disparagement of style where it can be compared to handwriting—and by one of the foremost writers of the age; but Fielding's attitude is, as I have suggested, by no means unrepresentative.

II

Smollett himself took the question of style more seriously. This seriousness is most clearly to be seen in his actual exercise of style, but may also be glimpsed in a few stray statements to be found in his voluminous journalism—which are at least sufficient to qualify Boucé's belief that Smollett's subtle sense of language did not include any original idea of style.[9]

In the preface to his *Present State of all Nations* Smollett offers a definition of style which explicitly contradicts some of the assumptions we have already considered. Style, he says, is 'an art, which may be truly stiled the gift of heaven, inasmuch as it never yet was acquired by dint of meer industry and application' (i, iv). Both the attitude and the terms in which it is expressed here might well take us by surprise, since by emphasising natural aptitude and minimising acquired ability Smollett is standing out against a whole tradition of thought about style. But more interesting is the fact that this brief definition echoes a longer commentary on style introducing a review of a collection of essays on literary topics which had appeared in the *Critical Review* eight years earlier. This was at the height of Smollett's active connection

with the review, and although unfortunately there is no way
of being quite certain, the close verbal parallels, and the
consonance of the whole article with Smollett's views as
expressed elsewhere, amount to a strong probability that he
was responsible for it. [10]

To write well, something more than learning, and even taste and
sentiment, is wanting. The happy art of expressing one's self with
facility and elegance, is born with the writer, and the gift of heaven
as much as genius: it is improved, but not attained by habit; it often
accompanies, but is not essential to genius; it cannot soar to its
highest pitch, but it may exist with a slender proportion of fancy,
invention, and erudition. Like a graceful air of the body, it
heightens every other quality, conceals trivial defects, bespeaks
regard and applause, implies a variety of talents, and yet is, in fact,
but a single talent, which we vainly sweat and toil, and study, to
acquire.

The *absolute* valuation of style in this passage contrasts very
emphatically with what we have seen of the views of Smollett's contemporaries. In the first place style cannot be
'learned by practice' as Fielding representatively argued; it is
a 'gift of heaven' which may be improved, but (significantly)
not 'attained by habit'; no amount of 'sweat and toil, and
study' will bring what is not born in a writer.

Equally significant is Smollett's contention that the 'happy
art of expressing one's self with facility' does not relate to
other qualities—learning, taste, sentiment, genius; fancy,
invention or erudition. He is prepared to contemplate a more
fundamental separation between subject and style than
would have satisfied Aristotle. The image of bodily grace
(itself gracefully turned) identifies the nature of the gift as
something inherent, demonstrable but not definable; and
intimates, it is not too much to suggest, one of the fundamental beliefs of romantic theory.

At this point in the review Smollett gives his impressions
of the prose styles of recent and contemporary writers, and
the pre-eminence awarded to Swift—who 'had [the gift of
style] from nature' and who 'is, perhaps, the single author in

our language who is easy, manly, and copious, without labour'—again contradicts Johnson's standard of judgement. Of Johnson himself Smollett says that he 'has dignity, but it is the artificial dignity of an actor, and not that natural importance which accompanies majesty'. The preference for the 'natural' properties of style over the 'artificial' embellishments of the ornamentalist tradition is consistent with Smollett's other progressive attitudes. He goes on to remark upon the minute particulars of prose style in a way that offers a further contrast to the habitual inattention of other critics. 'The least transposition of a syllable gives an aukward stiffness; and even the pointing, which is deemed arbitrary, offends both the ear and the eye, if done injudiciously'. If his general valuation of style suggested Flaubert, Smollett's concern with the small details of rhythm and punctuation finds a parallel in James, who insisted that in the achieving of his effects 'no humblest question involved, even to that of the shade of a cadence or the position of a comma, is not richly pertinent'.[11]

The independence of outlook exhibited in this review article confirms what we have been able to discover about Smollett's views elsewhere, which amount to a significant revision of the Augustan values with which he is usually (and not so much falsely as inadequately) associated. The revision is always in the direction of the developing expressive and affective theories of the later eighteenth century, and away from the 'rules of pedants'. In another review, which we know to be his, of Thomas Warton's *Essay on the Genius and Writings of Mr. Pope*,[12] for example, Smollett challenged Warton for his inadequacy in dealing with 'the merits of versification' (which 'has not yet been considered in a proper point of view'). He rejects the ornamentalist theory, extending the sense of 'versification' to include stylistic as well as metrical considerations:

Versification not only includes the colouring of poetry, but even the drawing that gives energy and warmth, and the attitude which bestows elegance upon the figure.—Let two writers, for example, produce the same image upon paper, in verse; the one shall be aukward, lifeless, and insipid, tho' exhibited in proper language and studied cadence; while the other shall strike the imagination with all the force of expression and all the fire of enthusiasm.

I would recall to the reader at this point Smollett's valuation of the intrinsic qualities of style above the extrinsic properties of form, which I considered in chapter three. Implicit in all Smollett's criticism is the criterion that becomes explicit here: the romantic criterion of *energeia*. 'Energy and warmth . . . force of expression and fire of enthusiasm'—these are all qualities which cannot be prescribed for or anticipated in formal terms but only directly created in the exercise of style.

But despite what I have managed to extract from Smollett's fragmentary theory it is still true that the evidence of the prose itself is likely to be of more use than the dictates of art in determining what were the qualities he most valued in his medium. A theory will always be too abstract to detain a style, which is not an idea at all and can be described only very approximately even according to its strategic devices. The very fact that 'the evidence of his theoretical pronouncements is more explicit and clearer than that of his practice', as Wimsatt says of Johnson, is proof enough of their unreliability as critical insights into the prose itself. 'It is not to be expected that any man should be able to define his own style adequately, even if we make the rash assumption that he is fully aware of it.'[13]

So the only reliable 'theory' is that derived retrospectively from the practice itself; and the more attentive to detail this is, the more it will take the form of description. But as no critic can hope to describe any style exhaustively—a complete description would take the form of a complete recitation of a writer's work—we shall be reduced to using representative examples, suggesting comparisons and contrasts, and proposing categories in something of a 'geometrical and systematical spirit': the necessary evil courses of criticism. It is my intention, however, and belief, that these courses will in the end illuminate rather than obscure the natural powers of Smollett's prose.

III

What I mean to do in this section is to describe what I see as
two basic directions or tendencies in Smollett's style, which I
can then use as a structure for my analysis of this style in the
concluding chapters. And one must work towards this division through Smollett's own temperament; through some
understanding of the creative energy which can express
itself in such divergent ways.

'The style is the man.' Even our present techniques of
analysis—stylistic and psychological—are not yet competent
to follow up the implications of Buffon's celebrated axiom;
perhaps no techniques of analysis will ever be adequate to
do so. Perhaps we have to accept Jung's view that there is a
mystery at the heart of artistic creation that we can never
hope to penetrate.[14] We will never fully understand the process simply described by Conrad as 'the conversion of nervous force into phrases';[15] but it is still worth while paying
some attention to the precise nature of the 'nervous force' in
a writer whose work lays hold of us.

The basic fact we have to remember is that Smollett was a
passionate Scotsman, not a moderate Englishman like the
Fielding whom I have taken throughout this study as the
representative of another tradition. The purely linguistic
implications of this I have dealt with in the last chapter; but
the circumstance has a larger and more continuous significance. It has been claimed that the contrasts between
England and Scotland in the eighteenth century were
extreme, even extraordinary. Whereas the guiding principle
of equilibrium underlay the philosophy, culture and even
political events in the southern part of the kingdom, 'the
philosophy of equilibrium was unable to cross the Tweed';
and whereas the Englishman might think of the eighteenth
century in terms of order, duty and Dr Johnson, to the Scot
'it is the century of Rob Roy and Prince Charlie—an unstable, adventurous, even heroic century, full of bitter-sweet
memories. It was in fact an era that, far from being static,
was marked by violent and bewildering change'.[16] Modern
studies of Smollett, newly alert to this context, provide a

much fuller and more sympathetic account of him than did earlier writers—and there is an ironic justice in George Orwell's suggestion that his 'outstanding intellectual honesty may have been connected with the fact that he was not an Englishman'.[17] Through Knapp's biography and the recent study of the novels by Boucé we are now acquainted with a rich and complex personality whose writings bear all the traces of the varied experience out of which they were composed. The energy required to sustain a distinct individuality is convertible, for a writer, into a distinctive style. (Even Hannay had conceded Smollett this: 'No man can confound his style with any other, and as Sainte-Beuve has said, it is no small thing to have a style of your own'.)[18]

Knapp returns more than once to the unresolved conflicts at the centre of Smollett's sensibility.

There were in Smollett, as in many other dynamic and complex personalities, two powerful forces, at times mutually antagonistic, but, in the long run, essentially interlocking and complementary. In many respects Smollett aspired to be, and was, a typical rationalist, a typical satirist, and a conventionally aristocratic gentleman of the mid-eighteenth century. At the same time, he was, in many respects, a man of ebullient and violent feelings which often escaped from the leash of reason; a person repeatedly unconventional for his time in romantic self-confession; and a very generous humanitarian.

Recalling that he was 'passionate in speech, explosive in action, highly irascible in sarcasm and invective', Knapp concludes: 'There were in Smollett violent emotional tensions impossible wholly to account for or to analyse'.[19] It may be true that we cannot account for them; but we can recognise in them, more practically, the source of Smollett's stylistic energy. Paul Boucé too, in his full and fair analysis of Smollett's personality, balances his aggressiveness, violence and irritability with his generosity and fellow-feeling; his 'acute sensibility' with his ceaseless activity and lifelong intellectual passion.[20] And he draws on this analysis in his chapter on Smollett's style, where he says that 'Smollett's style is evidence of his passionate nature', identifying this with what Henri Morier classifies as the 'truculent' style—a style whose master, significantly, is Rabelais.[21]

Now Smollett's personality permeates *Humphry Clinker* in a way that offers us both the most intriguing access to the springs of his style and also a possible structure for the description and analysis of that style—not simply within this novel itself, but as it has been employed right from the beginning of his literary career. Because here, for the first time, we can observe how the different strands of Smollett's personality have been, as it were, 'separated out' and allocated to different characters, who then express this trait at the appropriate stylistic level. This literary process, the pathological version of which is known by psychologists as 'decomposition', was lucidly described by Freud in his paper 'Creative writers and daydreaming':

> The psychological novel in general no doubt owes its special nature to the inclination of the modern writer to split up his ego, by self-observation, into many part-egos, and, in consequence, to personify the conflicting currents of his mental life in several heroes.[22]

The way this process is carried out in *Clinker* is complex, and hinges on the presentation of Matthew Bramble. As Knapp has demonstrated, the Bramble of the novel is 'very true to the psychology of the novelist in his declining years';[23] he is compassionate, generous and occasionally enthusiastic as well as offended, outraged and often disillusioned. He is a contradictory figure; certainly a plausible version of Smollett himself. His moral energy, converted into words, is the core of the novel; the imaginative gravity pulls decisively in his direction.

Some simplification has, however, taken place. Those extremes of aggressiveness and perversity to which Smollett was liable are vested in Lieutenant Lismahago. Jery affirms in the letter where Lismahago first makes his appearance that 'this Caledonian is a self-conceited pedant, aukward, rude, and disputatious . . . he is so addicted to wrangling, that he will cavil at the clearest truths, and, in the pride of argumentation, attempt to reconcile contradictions', and remarks later that he had 'become so polemical that every time he opened his mouth out flew a paradox, which he maintained with all the enthusiasm of altercation' (10 July, p. 190; 13 July, p. 201). Bramble himself notices that

The spirit of contradiction is naturally so strong in Lismahago, that I believe in my conscience he has rummaged, and read, and studied with indefatigable attention, in order to qualify himself to refute established maxims, and thus raise trophies for the gratification of polemical pride.—Such is the asperity of his self-conceit, that he will not even acquiesce in a transient compliment made to his own individual in particular, or to his country in general. [15 July; p. 203]

Smollett's own uneasiness in the face of compliment, or indeed the outward demonstration of any kind of sympathetic feeling, is reflected in this last trait of Lismahago's; and there is an instructive passage later in this letter where Bramble as it were 'offloads' on to Lismahago a ragbag of political ideas—some reactionary, some radical, but all extreme—which one can readily recognise (from comparison with ideas expressed in the *Critical*, the *History*, the *Atom* and elsewhere) as in some sense Smollett's own.

Lydia meanwhile takes over the sympathetic emotions. She it is who enthuses over Clifton as 'a charming romantic place', who wonders at Bath as 'an earthly paradise':

The Square, the Circus, and the Parades, put you in mind of the sumptuous palaces represented in prints and pictures; and the new buildings, such as Princes-row, Harlequin's-row, Bladud's-row, and twenty other rows, look like so many enchanted castles, raised on hanging terraces. [21 April, p. 27; 26 April, p. 39]

Hers is the innocent 'maze of admiration' for London which contrasts so sharply with the reaction of Bramble himself; as she aptly observes, 'People of experience and infirmity, my dear Letty, see with very different eyes from those that such as you and I make use of' (31 May; pp. 91, 93).
But the quality that is most significantly separated out

from Bramble is laughter: the capacity for amusement at 'the farce of life' which was a redeeming and no doubt consoling feature of Smollett's own personality. Jery does, it is true, describe Bramble as a 'risible misanthrope': 'A lucky joke, or any ludicrous incident, will set him a-laughing immoderately, even in one of his most gloomy paroxysms; and, when the laugh is over, he will curse his own imbecillity' (30 April; p. 49). But in Bramble's own letters—on his own level of style—there is little allowance for the comic attitude; the 'gloomy paroxysm' predominates, to be replaced towards the end by quiet satisfaction rather than amusement.

The detached, amused response to the spectacle of experience is reserved for Jery himself. 'Notwithstanding the gravity of the occasion, it was impossible to behold this scene without being seized with an inclination to laugh' (3 October; p. 299). Jery identifies this attitude, appropriately enough, by the frequent use of theatrical metaphors in his letters. 'The farce is finished, and another piece of a graver cast brought upon the stage'; 'The comedy is near a close; and the curtain ready to drop: but, the later scenes of this act I shall recapitulate in order' (11 June, p. 146; 8 November, p. 346).

Now the real function of the epistolary form in *Clinker* becomes clear. The separating out of his own reactions, impulses and even ideas into appropriately differentiated characters (or correspondents) enables Smollett to give his complete attention to each in turn; and therefore to maximise his stylistic range, exploiting all the advantages of his natural talent (his 'gift of heaven') to the full. Instead of their being reduced to a norm, or contained within one disciplined sensibility that would find adequate expression in a cool meridian of prose (like Fielding's), we find that the emotions in *Clinker* are deliberately polarised by the vigour of Smollett's personality and the force of his style. Smollett's 'generous abandonment to one point of view',[24] his ability to throw his formidable expressive energy behind a number of different attitudes, is comparable to—indeed, part of—that voluntary immersion in the element of language which I described in my last chapter.

'And I must borrow every changing shape / to find expression':[25] through the changing shapes he 'borrows' in *Clinker* Smollett finds expression for a whole range of vivid emotions; pride, anger, indignation; aversion, disgust; admiration and affection; nostalgia; love, sympathy and amusement. This is what makes the novel the absolute antithesis, stylistically, of *Tom Jones*, where all the emotions are subdued in one style, and relative intensities of feeling disguised in one ironic posture.

What I wish to emphasise, then, is the polarity that exists between Bramble and Jery in particular; a polarity which is sustained by their very different technique and intensity of expression. The reason being that this reflects a tension rooted in Smollett's own temperament, which is in evidence throughout his work; so that what we can discover of their propensities will offer us a genuine 'section' of Smollett's style.

In the following passage Jery describes the incongruous scene at a ball in the Assembly Rooms in Bath, and concludes by identifying his own reaction to it.

I was extremely diverted, last ball-night, to see the Master of the Ceremonies leading, with great solemnity, to the upper end of the room, an antiquated Abigail, dressed in her lady's cast-clothes; whom he (I suppose) mistook for some countess just arrived at the Bath. The ball was opened by a Scotch lord, with a mulatto heiress from St. Christopher's; and the gay colonel Tinsel danced all the evening with the daughter of an eminent tinman from the borough of Southwark—Yesterday morning, at the Pump-room, I saw a broken-winded Wapping landlady squeeze through a circle of peers, to salute her brandy-merchant, who stood by the window, prop'd upon crutches; and a paralytic attorney of Shoe-lane, in shuffling up to the bar, kicked the shins of the chancellor of England, while his lordship, in a cut bob, drank a glass of water at the pump. I cannot account for my being pleased with these incidents, any other way than by saying, they are truly ridiculous in their own nature, and serve to heighten the humour in the farce of life, which I am determined to enjoy as long as I can. [30 April; p. 49]

What Smollett gives us here is at once an example and a

description of the comic attitude. Comedy, Maynard Mack has admirably formulated, 'presents us with life apprehended in the form of spectacle rather than in the form of experience',[26] and in this passage we see Jery both exercising and insisting upon his role as spectator. He not only enjoys but is 'determined to enjoy' the 'farce of life' which is played before him; and he maintains his detachment both through the language ('an eminent tinman'), the detail ('a paralytic attorney of Shoe-lane . . . kicked the shins of the chancellor of England'), and not least by the syntax, which helps to perform the function of running these people incongruously together. The minimal use of punctuation and the absence of any form of grammatical subordination ('while' functions more as a simple conjunction here than to introduce a temporal clause) enacts the lack of any social subordination in the scene itself, and Smollett obviously relishes the opportunity to make the parallel.

The humour of this 'truly ridiculous' scene depends partly upon what Fielding defined as 'the only Source of the true Ridiculous', namely affectation:[27] the affectation of gentility on the part of the tradespeople, and the affectation of civility among the people of rank. But more obviously it has to do with the physical circumstances as Jery perceives them, the essential incongruity which is the fruit of this social complication.

Jery himself suggests the contrast between Bramble's views on such circumstances and his own. 'This is what my uncle reprobates, as a monstrous jumble of heterogeneous principles; a vile mob of noise and impertinence, without decency or subordination. But this chaos is to me a source of infinite amusement.' And in the next letter Bramble is allowed to develop this argument on his own account, in a style which is significantly different from that allocated to his nephew.

About a dozen years ago, many decent families, restricted to small fortunes, besides those that came hither on the score of health, were tempted to settle at Bath, where they could then live comfortably, and even make a genteel appearance, at a small

expence: but the madness of the times has made the place too hot
for them, and they are now obliged to think of other migra-
tions—Some have already fled to the mountains of Wales, and
others have retired to Exeter. Thither, no doubt, they will be followed by the flood of luxury and extravagance, which will drive
them from place to place to the very Land's End; and there, I
suppose, they will be obliged to ship themselves to some other
country. Bath is become a mere sink of profligacy and extortion.
Every article of housekeeping is raised to an enormous price; a
circumstance no longer to be wondered at, when we know that
every petty retainer of fortune piques himself upon keeping a
table, and thinks 'tis for the honour of his character to wink at the
knavery of his servants, who are in a confederacy with the
market-people; and, of consequence, pay whatever they demand.
Here is now a mushroom of opulence, who pays a cook seventy
guineas a week for furnishing him with one meal a day. This portentous frenzy is become so contagious, that the very rabble and
refuse of mankind are infected. I have known a negro-driver, from
Jamaica, pay over-night to the master of one of the rooms, sixty-
five guineas for tea and coffee to the company, and leave Bath next
morning, in such obscurity, that not one of his guests had the
slightest idea of his person, or even made the least inquiry about
his name. Incidents of this kind are frequent; and every day teems
with fresh absurdities, which are too gross to make a thinking man
merry. [5 May; p. 57]

The focus is again defined for us at the end. Bramble is a
thinking man, one who does not simply witness but is profoundly affected by the things he sees; and such absurdities
cannot therefore cause amusement. One may take up the
other half of Mack's formulation: 'In the tragic mode, since
the meaning lies in the protagonist's consciousness of this
moment, this choice, this irreversible event for him, our consciousness must be continuous with his, and we are given a
point of view inside that consciousness'.[28] Of course Bramble is not a tragic figure; but Mack himself has only used the
term (as he says, 'for want of a better') to draw the contrast
he wishes to make—with respect to Fielding and Richardson—between two alternative points of view, and the contrast also applies here. Bramble takes his experiences
inward, they are registered and evaluated on a distinct

centre of apprehension.

The strength of Bramble's feelings is fully matched (to be accurate, one should say created) by the energy of the prose; nervous energy has been turned into words. Where Jery's description kept an even pace, Bramble's accelerates as the focus sharpens from general observation to particular instances. His state of excitement leads him to envisage sober citizens being chased from Bath to Exeter, to the mountains of Wales, and eventually 'from place to place to the very Land's End', until 'I suppose' (this very phrase identifies the source of the idea in Bramble's outraged imagination) 'they will be obliged to ship themselves to some other country'. What starts off as 'the madness of the times' becomes before the end of the tirade a 'portentous frenzy'. In the last example, the prodigious excess of the Jamaican slaver's entertainment, Bramble insists that '*not one* of his guests had the *slightest* idea of his person, or even made the *least* enquiry about his name': this use of absolute and superlative forms is typical of Smollett's style at its most emphatic.

As a concluding point of contrast between these two passages, we may observe that whereas Jery's description is spare, literal, and unadorned by figures, Bramble is driven to metaphor to convey his sense of outrage at the 'flood of luxury and extravagance', his disgust at the way Bath 'is become a mere sink of profligacy and extortion', and his contempt for one particularly extravagant 'mushroom of opulence'.

I have tried in this chapter to identify the 'separation of styles' one encounters in Smollett, and if possible to devise some convenient way of describing the different levels. And I hope that the figure of a circle will provide a useful diagram. One may imagine the comic style—the style used for energetic action, dialogue, caricature and perceived incongruity—operating on the circumference of this circle. This would conform to the conventional idea that comedy offers an 'external' view of life—and a view of life's externals, as they are registered on the senses, functioning, as it were, independently of each other, and of a central organised sensibility. It is for this reason that the circle is divided into five

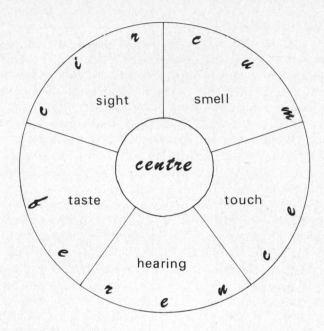

segments, one for each sense, it being part of Smollett's comic technique to describe the operation of each sense in isolation. This I shall show in the next chapter. For the present let me simply suggest that the 'farce of life' is played on the edge or circumference of our apprehension, and is celebrated by what I shall call the circumference of style.

What one might then describe as a passionate or expressive style, a style which renders an immediate involvement with experience, occupies the centre of this circle: where simple sense impressions are, as it were, digested by a moral sense, understood, fused as part of a total and recognisably human impression. Smollett wrote of the French that if one could not find cleanliness among them, much less could one expect to find 'delicacy, which is the cleanliness of the mind' (*Travels*, 5; p. 35). Here we have his own explicit fusion of the physical and moral orders, imaged in terms of each other. To revert to the conventional metaphor, the style of the centre[29] will therefore communicate an internal view of life; it represents what Mack calls the core of self-discovery rather than the curve of self-exposure.[30]

The style of the circumference relates facts, events, in a certain detached way, and deals with the 'quantity' of experience; the style of the centre attends to the complicated emotional response to these facts and events, accommodating therefore the 'quality' of experience. In the former Smollett appears to adopt the attitude of Swift's fool among knaves: 'He that can with *Epicurus*, content his Ideas with the *Films* and *Images* that fly off upon his Senses from the *Superficies* of Things'.[31] Writing in this style, Smollett deliberately restrains that curiosity which 'enters into the Depth of Things', and the events related do become (in a sense with which we could not charge Swift) a kind of speeded-up film. Here Roderick and Strap seek an interview with Mr Cringer:

When we came to Mr. Cringer's door, Strap, to give me an instance of his politeness, run to the knocker, which he employed so loud and so long, that he alarmed the whole street; and a window opening up two pair of stairs in the next house, a chamber-pot was discharged upon him so successfully that the poor barber was wet to the skin, while I, being luckily at some distance, escaped the unsavoury deluge.—In the mean time, a footman opening the door, and seeing nobody in the street but us, asked with a stern countenance, if it was I who made such a damned noise, and what I wanted.—I told him I had business with his master, whom I desired to see. Upon which, he clapt the door in my face, telling me, I must learn better manners before I could have access to his master. Vexed at this disappointment, I turned my resentment against Strap, whom I sharply reprimanded for his presumption; but he not in the least regarding what I said, wrung the urine out of his periwig, and lifting up a large stone, flung it with such force against the street door of that house from whence he had been bedewed, that the lock giving way, it flew wide open, and he took to his heels, leaving me to follow him as I could.—Indeed there was no time for deliberation; I therefore pursued him with all the speed I could exert, until we found ourselves, about the dawn, in a street we did not know. [*Random*, 14; i, 106–7]

This passage has the mechanical animation of one of those Victorian amusements where you put in a penny and at once a number of figures in a scene (a fairground, a railway station, a drawing room, a public house) whirr into simultaneous action. Strap *runs* to the knocker, we notice, and then employs it 'so loud and so long, that he alarmed the whole street'. The characteristic hyperbole includes the knocking itself and the reaction to it—at five in the morning. Of course the discharged chamber-pot soaks Strap to the skin: comic action always observes this principle of maximum efficiency. A door is opened and slammed. Strap wrings the urine out of his wig (a marvellous detail: we are getting our penny's worth) and, 'lifting up a large stone' (the use of the present participle helps to concentrate the actions, contributes to the magical simultaneity of the scene), flings it at the door 'with such force'—and such precision, once again—that 'the lock giving way, it flew wide open, and he took to his heels'. The extravagance of the action narrated is admirably supported by the controlled tempo of the prose: we have here a good example of that 'powerful adjustment of style to substance'[32] for which Stevick rightly singles Smollett out among comic writers, whose prose so often degenerates to the insipid, leaving us with only the futile gestures of unrealised comic intention. In the last sentence here Roderick observes, understandably in the circumstances, that 'there was no time for reflection': he follows Strap, and the two run until they find themselves 'about the dawn in a street we did not know'. The coin is spent; the machine is wound down.

But elsewhere in the same novel we encounter certain facts and realisations which resist the impulse towards the circumference. Then the film (to resume my earlier metaphor) is slowed down, or stopped, and we are forced to attend to the quality of the experience. We are at the centre, where we encounter 'the Sower and the Dregs' which Swift's fool leaves 'for Philosophy and Reason to lap up'.[33] The sour and the dregs are the realities of our physical and moral circumstance, which language here seeks to concentrate rather than distract from. It is in such a style that Smollett conveys Roderick's panic at his first experience of a storm at sea (chapter 28), panic which is caused by the sudden assault on a vivid imagination of various confused impressions; or his reaction to the conditions in the sick bay of the *Thunder*:

. . . when I followed him with the medicines into the sick birth
or hospital, and observed the situation of the patients, I was much
less surprised to find people die on board, than astonished to find
any body recover.—Here I saw about fifty miserable distempered
wretches, suspended in rows, so huddled one upon another, that
not more than fourteen inches space was allotted for each with his
bed and bedding; and deprived of the light of the day, as well as of
fresh air; breathing nothing but a noisome atmosphere of the mor-
bid steams exhaling from their own excrements and diseased
bodies, devoured with vermin hatched in the filth that surrounded
them, and destitute of every convenience necessary for people in
that helpless condition. [25; i, 235]

Here the senses (of sight and smell) that Smollett often used
to achieve comic distance are allowed their full cognitive
value, and operate within a complete human personality.
The result in moral terms is a compassionate response; and,
for the style, it means a less obtrusive but no less disciplined
arrangement of its materials—materials which will not speak
for themselves effectively except where promoted by
imaginative endorsement; except where the novelist
becomes, that is, a literalist of the imagination.

It is not surprising that we should have these levels of
style close together, even overlapping, in the first novel by
the Smollett who was later to produce *Humphry Clinker*. The
division of sensibility finally achieved between Bramble and
Jery is already evident in the contrasting characters of
Roderick and Strap. A particular example of the resultant
mixture of styles occurs where the two 'dive for dinner' at an
ordinary in London. A friend leads the way:

I followed his example, and descended very successfully, where
I found myself in the middle of a cook's shop, almost suffocated
with the steams of boil'd beef, and surrounded by a company of
hackney-coachmen, chairmen, draymen, and a few footmen out of
place or on board wages; who sat eating shin of beef, tripe, cow-
heel, or sausages, at separate boards, covered with cloths, which
turned my stomach.—While I stood in amaze, undetermined
whether to sit down or walk upwards again, Strap, in his descent
missing one of the steps, tumbled headlong into this infernal ordinary, and overturned the cook as she carried a porringer of soup to

one of the guests: In her fall, she dashed the whole mess against the legs of a drummer belonging to the foot guards, who happened to be in her way, and scalded him so miserably, that he started up, and danced up and down, uttering a volley of execrations that made my hair stand on end. [13; i, 102]

Strap is victim of the familiar mechanical sequence: he misses the step, overturns the cook, who scalds the drummer; and the details are concatenated to the maximum comic effect. But if we return to Roderick we notice that his own registration of the experience is quite different. And we can notice this in the first place only because we are inside him, not outside him, and therefore share his impressions. These are mainly of oppression—almost claustrophobia—and disgust. He is 'almost suffocated' in this dismal cellar, and observes the cheap dishes being eaten off boards 'covered with cloths which turned my stomach': even the internal organs involved are explicitly referred to.[34] Then Roderick has time to reflect what to do ('undetermined whether to sit down or walk upwards again'), until Strap's precipitate entrance decides things for him. Roderick responds as a human being, Strap reacts as a caricature; and the style adjusts accordingly.

It is my contention that Smollett's achievement as a novelist is founded on his ability to provide appropriate expression for the many different levels of his response to experience—levels which provide of themselves a kind of drama. Free of the formal inhibitions of his time, linguistic and stylistic, he could drive his verbal penetration to the centre; or design and decorate those astonishing verbal inventions which define the circumference of his style. In so doing he exhibits a range of style beyond any other novelist (indeed any other writer) of the period; the evidence for which is the substance of the next three chapters.

III   *Exercise*

6   *Style at the circumference*

Throughout this study I have claimed that in Smollett form is the instrument of style. I must not neglect, therefore, the formal strategy which serves the comic style; the spokes, one might say, that support the rim. Smollett's approach through externals is directed in ways that can be simply illustrated. What typically happens in the comic sequences in his novels is that the details of the situation are registered by the main character — who tends to be the agent rather than the object of the narrative comedy — sense by sense, as if to prohibit the complication of a total response. This elementary comic procedure also enables Smollett to develop the separate strands (or spokes) of each situation, outwards, in a way that heightens the incongruity of the whole.

Early in *Random* Roderick and Strap join up with the waggon making its slow way towards London, and when they try to climb aboard this vehicle meet with the displeasure of Captain Weazel. This scene offers a paradigm of many others that are to follow. Strap it is who approaches first: 'but just as he was getting in, a tremendous voice assailed his ears in these words: "God's fury! There shall no passengers come here".—The poor shaver was so disconcerted at this exclamation, which both he and I imagined proceeded from the mouth of a giant, that he descended with great velocity, and a countenance as white as paper'. However, Roderick musters his courage and climbs aboard, 'without being able to discern the faces of my fellow-travellers in the dark': Smollett deliberately restrains the comedy at the aural —and tactile—level. Strap (who is very much an object of the comedy) is jolted by the carriage, and 'pitched directly upon the stomach of the captain, who bellowed out in a most dreadful manner: "Blood and thunder! where's my sword?" '. The captain's wife then joins him in a superior discourse on their situation, which gives Roderick 'such a high notion of the captain and his lady, that I durst not venture to join the conversation'. However, 'another female voice' volunteers a broad mockery of their affectation, and then addresses itself in terms of contemptuous familiarity to a silent companion (' "Speak, you old *cent. per cent.* fornicator" '), the words 'accompanied with a hearty smack' that exacts a 'quavering' reply.

After these preliminaries Roderick falls asleep; waking when they arrive at the inn, where he has 'an opportunity of viewing the passengers in order as they entered': we move to the visual level. And even here the group is itemised, treated in order. First we have Miss Jenny, 'a brisk airy girl, about twenty years old' (the owner of the second 'female voice') and her usurer companion, who is more fully described: 'His eyes were hollow, bleared and gummy; his face was shrivelled into a thousand wrinkles, his gums were destitute of teeth, his nose sharp and drooping, his chin peeked and prominent, so that when he mumped or spoke, they approached one another like a pair of nutcrackers; he supported himself on an ivory-headed cane, and his whole figure was a just emblem of winter, famine, and avarice'. (Smollett refers to this figure as an 'emblem' in accordance with the typical comic process of abstraction, to which I shall return later.) It is the captain's appearance, however, that most astonishes Roderick:

But how was I surprized, when I beheld the formidable captain leading in his wife; in the shape of a little thin creature, about the age of forty, with a long, withered visage, very much resembling that of a baboon, through the upper part of which, two little grey eyes peeped: He wore his own hair in a queue that reached to his rump, which immoderate length, I suppose, was the occasion of a baldness that appeared on the crown of his head, when he deigned to take off his hat, which was very much of the size and cock of Pistol's—Having laid aside his great coat, I could not help admiring the extraordinary make of this man of war: he was about five feet and three inches high, sixteen inches of which went to his face and long scraggy neck; his thighs were about six inches in length, his legs resembling spindles or drumsticks, two feet and an half, and his body, which put me in mind of extension without substance, engrossed the remainder;—so that on the whole, he appeared like a spider or grasshopper erect,—and was almost a *vox & preterea nihil*.

Here we have one of Smollett's most memorable caricatures, and I shall have more to say about the style of it in a moment. For the present we may at least notice the aptness of the summary at the end: Weazel does indeed 'exist' in his voice, he is a sound; and having entertained us with the incongruity of his appearance Smollett reverts to this feature, which is very successfully exploited for the rest of this chapter and the next (11; i, 74–8).

A similar pattern is observable throughout this first novel. When Smollett turns the 'visage, voice, and gesture' of the surgeon's mate Morgan to comic effect, Roderick hears him first, and sees him afterwards, in the appropriate order: ' . . . we heard a voice on the cockpit ladder, pronounce with great vehemence, in a strange dialect, "The devil and his dam blow me from the top of Mounchdenny, if I go to him before there is something in my belly;—let his nose be as yellow as saffron, or as plue as a pell, look you, or green as a leek, 'tis all one" '. A conversation ensues, very promisingly, for half a page, and only then does Morgan actually appear: 'At the same time I saw him come into the birth. He was a short thick man, with a face garnished with pimples, a snub nose turned up at the end, an excessive wide mouth, and little fiery eyes, surrounded with skin puckered up in innumerable wrinkles' (25; i, 229–30). But Morgan's physical presence is never as fully realised in the book as his voice.

Smollett uses a similar strategy in the two chapters which relate Roderick's journey to Bath in the stagecoach with Miss Snapper, her mother and a miscellaneous group of other characters (*Random*, 53–4; ii, 181–200), chapters which take us full circle round the circumference of Smollett's style. The reader might also look at the second chapter of *Pickle*, which is literally 'invaded' by Trunnion and his associates (pp. 6–12); and the three chapters in *Fathom* which describe the hero's brief sojourn in prison (39–41; pp. 181–96), which are another sustained exercise in alternate aural and visual representation, a brilliant transcription in Smollett's most confident and assertive style.

One thing we cannot fail to notice is how often the actual organs of perception are referred to in each case: ears are 'invaded' by voices, eyes have 'remarkable objects' thrust before them. It is as if Smollett intends to separate the organ in question from any cognitive faculty, using it simply to register an event for comic effect. Ronald Paulson remarks how 'in the run-of-the-mill narrative satires of the seventeenth and eighteenth centuries, the Picaresque relationship between two people dwindled to the relationship between an eye and an object',[1] and any of the senses may be similarly isolated to provide the raw material of comedy. Because comedy works through a logical process of abstraction and simplification; the writer uses certain techniques in order to focus our attention on the particular enlarged or elaborated detail he has chosen to emphasise, and thereby to direct our response. The comic imagination operates on life as a prism does on light: it 'analyses' experience, reduces it to its constituent parts, which will then appear either grotesque or absurd.

It is clear that Smollett was conscious of this process, from comments that occur in the novels themselves. The effete Captain Whiffle inspects Roderick one sense at a time before he admits him into conversation. 'When I entered the room, I was ordered to stand by the door, until Captain Whiffle had reconnoited me at a distance, with a spy glass, who having consulted one sense in this manner, bid me advance gradually, that his nose might have intelligence, before it could be much offended' (35; i, 309–10). In a somewhat different context, Smollett describes the condition of being 'all ears' when he has the imprisoned hero of *Sir Launcelot Greaves* listen 'as if his whole soul was exerted in his sense of hearing' to the voice of Aurelia Darnel in the next cell (23; p. 191). And there is a curious passage earlier in this novel where Captain

Crowe seems to exploit the stratagem himself to effect a kind of metamorphosis before his hearers:

> As for captain Crowe, who used at such pauses to pour in a broadside of dismembered remarks, linked together like chain-shot, he spoke not a syllable for some time; but, lighting a fresh pipe at the candle, began to roll such voluminous clouds of smoke as in an instant filled the whole apartment, and rendered himself invisible to the whole company. Though he thus shrouded himself from their view, he did not long remain concealed from their hearing. They first heard a strange dissonant cackle, which the doctor knew to be a sea-laugh, and this was followed by an eager exclamation of 'rare pastime, strike my yards and top masts!—I've a good mind—why shouldn't—many a losing voyage I've—smite my taffrel but I wool—'
> By this time, he had relaxed so much in his fumigation, that the tip of his nose and one eye reappeared; and as he had drawn his wig forwards so as to cover his whole forehead, the figure that now saluted their eyes was much more ferocious and terrible than the fire-breathing chimaera of the antients. [6; p. 51]

Smollett exhibits his technique here very deliberately, as Crowe is first visible and silent, then conceals himself in clouds of smoke in order to speak, and finally reappears—in parts: 'the tip of his nose and one eye'. His body as well as his language has been dismembered in the process.

If this technique enables Smollett to exhibit his comic creations to best advantage, we need also to consider how these creations are themselves prepared for exhibition. What happens in the prismatic presentation of comic 'character' (which word, in this context, seems to require the reservation of inverted commas) is that the stuff of character is thrown out by a kind of centrifugal energy, and reveals itself in 'visage, voice, and gesture'. 'Nature sometimes makes a strange contrast between the interior workmanship and the exterior form', confesses Smollett in the *Atom*, 'but here the one reflected a true image of the other' (i, 141); comedy will normally employ characters who answer to the second description. When Fathom meets Sir Giles Squirrel in Paris he is struck by his manner, which is readily interpreted.

The baronet's disposition seemed to be cast in the true English mould. He was sour, silent and contemptuous; his very looks indicated a consciousness of superior wealth, and he never opened his mouth, except to make some dry, sarcastic, national reflection: nor was his behaviour free from that air of suspicion which a man puts on, when he believes himself in a crowd of pickpockets whom his caution and vigilance set at defiance: in a word, though his tongue was silent on the subject, his whole demeanour was continually saying, 'You are all a pack of poor, lousy rascals, who have a design upon my purse: 'tis true, I could bury your whole generation; but, I wont be bubbled, d'ye see; I am aware of your flattery, and upon my guard against all your knavish pranks; and I come into your company, for my own amusement only.' [22; p. 92]

The meanness of a moneylender who turns up in the same novel is actually conveyed by a sudden distortion of his features: 'when the merchant understood the nature of the security, his visage was involved in a most disagreeable gloom, and his eyes distorted into a most hideous obliquity of vision . . .' (44; p. 208).

The corollary of the idea that character is visible in this way, and may be defined externally, is that it will be expressed in action rather than reflection. As Albrecht Strauss has observed, 'Smollett is not the man to linger over subtle Jamesian analyses of states of feeling. Like Fielding and Defoe, he is committed to describing emotional life mainly by its external manifestations'.[2] But Smollett's 'gesture' is more extreme than that of Fielding or Defoe. Roderick's resentment is expressed by the knocking out of teeth, his love by distracted behaviour, and his jealousy by even wilder demonstrations: 'It set all my passions into a new ferment, I swore horrible oaths without meaning or application, I foamed at the mouth, kicked the chairs about the room, and play'd abundance of mad pranks that frightened my friend almost out of his senses' (58; ii, 239). Even his conversation is liable to desert the verbal for the physical level: 'To this innuendo I made no reply but by a kick on the breech, which overturned him in an instant' (44; ii, 68). On another occasion he is only restrained from kicking the master of ceremonies at Bath by the fact that his companion

(Miss Snapper) gets in first with a satisfactory verbal rejoinder (55; ii, 204).

It is in the person of Hugh Strap, Roderick's almost constant companion throughout his travels, that Smollett realises this comic gesture most consistently. Strap is the very embodiment of the comic style in Smollett; his every action is characterised by an achieved extravagance and incongruity, from the time he first recognises Roderick while he is shaving the hero on his way to London—'he discovered great emotion, and not confining his operation to my chin and upper lip, besmeared my whole face with great agitation' (8, i, 49)—to the scene at the end where Roderick meets his father in Jamaica, and his fortune and happiness are assured: 'Never was rapture more ludicrously expressed, than in the behaviour of this worthy creature, who cried, laughed, whistled, sung and danced, all in a breath' (76; ii, 336). It is Strap who tumbles into Weazel's guts in the waggon, and gets into his bed by mistake in the middle of the night (11; i, 75, 80); Strap who falls down the steps into the ordinary, while Roderick is reflecting on the unsavouriness of the place (13; i, 102); Strap who receives the 'unsavoury deluge' from a window whilst Roderick is standing 'luckily at some distance' from the discharge (14; i, 107). Roderick's misfortunes are often perceived through Strap's reaction to them, which allows for greater comic possibility. Strap is used to offer an extreme externalisation, as it were, of Roderick's own reactions; fear becomes panic, and distress despair. When they are alarmed at night by the highwayman Rifle, Strap 'crept under the bed, where he lay without sense or motion' (8; i, 54); another highwayman causes him to jump out of the waggon, and hide behind a hedge (12; i, 90). Later he is terrified by a raven, 'for his fears had magnified the creature to the bigness of a horse, and the sound of small morris bells to the clanking of chains' (13; i, 96); he is 'quite stupefied with horror' when he finds out that Roderick has fought a duel, and faints at the sight of his blood (59; ii, 253–4). He lapses into despair with equal precipitation. When Roderick is cheated at cards of all the pair possess he spends that night 'involved in doubts and perplexities'; but

when Strap hears the news 'the bason in which he was preparing the lather for my chin, dropped out of his hands, and
he remained for some time immoveable in that ludicrous
attitude, with his mouth open, and his eyes thrust forward
considerably beyond their station' (67; ii, 120, 122). Roderick
perceives Strap's 'inward affliction' when 'his visage sensi-
bly increased in longitude' after another reverse (49; ii, 142);
and on a later occasion he pauses to remark on his friend's
legible countenance: 'I never in my life saw sorrow so
extravagantly expressed in any countenance as in that of my
honest friend, which was, indeed, particularly adapted by
nature for such impressions' (61; ii, 268). This specification
has been endorsed earlier, when Roderick is recounting to
Strap the adventures he has had before meeting with him in
France.

During the recital, my friend was strongly affected, according to
the various situations described. He started with surprize, glowed
with indignation, gaped with curiosity, smiled with pleasure,
trembled with fear, and wept with sorrow, as the vicissitudes of
my life inspired these different passions; and when my story was
ended, signified his amazement on the whole, by lifting up his
eyes and hands, and protesting, that tho' I was a young man, I had
suffered more than all the blessed martyrs. [44; ii, 74]

The language of gesture reaches its most extreme here. Strap
is 'strongly affected, according to the various situations
described': his affective centre is atomised rather than
analysed by the style, which ensures that the rapidly successive emotions are not resolved into anything. The simple
demonstrative verbs ('started . . . glowed . . . gaped . . .
smiled . . . trembled . . . wept') have more to do with Smollett's excess of language than with Strap's excess of emotion.
As should be obvious to any reader, there is no question of
a relationship between Roderick and Strap, whose persistent
devotion to the hero, and unhesitating self-sacrifice in his
interest, are a simple reflex of his being. Roderick has told us
at the beginning that 'The attachment of Strap flowed from a
voluntary disinterested inclination, which had manifested
itself on many occasions in my behalf, he having once

rendered me the same service that I had offered to Gawky, by saving my life at the risk of his own; and often fathered offences I had committed, for which he suffered severely, rather than I should feel the weight of the punishment I deserved' (5; i, 25–6). The 'relationship' is a mechanical convenience, not a psychological necessity; on these terms, we should not be surprised that Roderick feels in no way bound to his self-appointed servant. Strap is restricted to the cold latitude of comedy, his orbit is out on the circumference, where he is immune through what Bergson calls 'insensibilité'[3] to any complication of feeling. Smollett was amused to record that Strap had become 'a favourite among the Ladies everywhere';[4] but he would not have understood Taine's indignation at the treatment meted out to him at the end of the novel.[5]

II

So far I have been concerned more with strategy than style, more with the alignment of comedy than its actual linguistic features; more with the spokes and bearings of the circumference than its actual composition. But I believe there is a necessary connection between the strategy I have been describing—the systematic registering of the external aspect of experience—and the style which carries it out. Only with a remarkable degree of verbal vitality and control can a writer hope to generate the kind of energy which is required to attain the orbit of caricature, and to remain, as it were, weightless in that thin air. Philip Stevick has remarked, very justly, that 'locating his energy in his variety of incidents and odd characters tells us nothing about how Smollett differs from, say, Surtees and Captain Marryat, or a considerable number of other novelists who are inventive in that sense but not really worth reading. The difference lies . . . in the remarkably articulated vehicle by which the incidents and characters are conveyed'.[6]

The obvious place to start is with Smollett's caricatures, literary creations of startling originality whose like had not appeared in English since the Elizabethan age. Martin Turnell says of characters in fiction generally that each is 'a verbal construct which has no existence outside the book';[7] the truth of this statement is nowhere more obvious than in the case of the caricature, who is conceived at and remains on the level of words, who lives only in a linguistic dimension, never challenging any response on our part beyond an appreciation of his creator's virtuosity. The first notable example we meet in Smollett is Crab, Roderick's original employer.

This member of the faculty was aged fifty, about five foot high, and ten round the belly; his face was capacious as a full moon, and much of the complexion of a mulberry: his nose, resembling a powder-horn, was swelled to an enormous size, and studded all over with carbuncles; and his little grey eyes reflected the rays in such an oblique manner, that while he looked a person full in the face, one would have imagined he was admiring the buckle of his shoe. [*Random* 7; i, 40]

What is immediately obvious is that there is no real attempt to describe here, to make us actually visualise a human figure as a result of reading the words. The caricature is pure verbal gesture, and retains a purely verbal identity. 'Five foot high, and ten round the belly' is not a satisfactory measurement but a satisfying phrase, constructed according to a self-contained mathematical logic. The moon, the mulberry and the powder-horn make no attempt to function as actual images, discovering similarity in dissimilars, but become instead obtrusive and outrageous in the degree of dissimilarity they introduce on such a poor pretext of illustration; while the specified angle of Crab's vision is one final fantastic detail that brings the structure to a satisfying climax. Forms like 'about', 'as if', 'it seemed' and 'one would have imagined' offer unlimited opportunity for the analogy to fly off into fantasy; these phrases are the typical triggers (in Smollett as well as in Dickens) for some extraordinary invention.

The caricature of Captain Weazel, which I have quoted in another connection earlier in this chapter, is of the same kind. The details do not amount to an actual description, but form part of a distinctly poetic alternative mode, offering an impressionistic verbal correlative to the comic conception in Smollett's mind. The distorted dimensions of this portrait allow Weazel seventeen inches for his body, once the head and limbs have 'engrossed the remainder': which gives to the phrase 'extension without substance' a certain plausibility. In his analysis of this description Boucé suggests that the systematic 'mensuration' of Weazel gives him 'an almost anthropometric aspect';[8] but it works more as a parody of anthropometry than the real thing. Rather than relating Weazel to average human dimensions, this description expels him from the human centre, casting him in the fixed postures and extreme expressions symptomatic of those characters who are pinned on the circumference.

It would result in needless repetition to deal exhaustively with Smollett's caricatures—quite apart from the fact that they are best encountered in their contexts, where they burst in upon the narrative with all the effect of surprise, rather than in the protective custody of criticism. But in order to place the necessary emphasis on Smollett's verbal imagination, his originality and abundance in the use of words, I shall consider one or two more examples here.[9] The curious assortment of characters Fathom meets in prison (chapters 39–41) are a gallery of caricatures. The Governor himself, Bess Beetle the maid, Captain Minikin, General Macleaver and Sir Mungo Barebones are all animations of the comic cast. Minikin is 'equally remarkable for his extraordinary figure and address'; the more developed of Smollett's caricatures, such as Weazel, Morgan, Minikin here, Sir Stentor Stile, Captain Crowe, Lieutenant Lismahago and Hawser Trunnion himself, all have voices to provide, as it were, another plane of existence, though this is still emphatically a verbal one. The figure is made ludicrous through 'an extravagant exaggeration of the mode':

. . . exclusive of the fashion of the cock, which resembled the form of a Roman galley, the brim of his hat, if properly spread, would have projected a shade sufficient to shelter a whole file of musqueteers from the heat of a summer's sun; and the heels of his shoes were so high as to raise his feet three inches at least, from the surface of the earth. [39; p. 186]

The combination of comic image and absurd extravagance in this description inevitably brings to mind Rabelais, the master of both. The monstrous descriptions in the *Gargantua* are a systematic affront—a comic outrage—to the analogical faculty proper. Consider the extraordinary accretion of ludicrous images that constitute the Anatomy of King Lent: his brain is 'of the size, colour, substance, and strength of a male flesh-worm's left ball', 'His eardrums like a whirligig . . . the back of his mouth like a porter's hod . . . His ideas like snails crawling down from strawberry plants . . . the base of his spine like a billiard table . . . His breast like a portable organ'.[10] It is is in this tradition of the parodic, detonated image that Ben Jonson compares copulation with the fat trull Ursula in *Bartholomew Fair* to 'falling into a whole shire of butter';[11] that Dickens compares the 'ragged, yellow head' of Mr Rugg to 'a worn out hearth broom', and his sister's nankeen spots to shirt buttons.[12]

And it is in this tradition that Smollett compares Weazel's legs to 'spindles or drum-sticks', and his person to 'a spider or grasshopper erect'; Minikin's voice to 'the sound of a bassoon, or the aggregate hum of a whole bee-hive'; the wrinkles on Crabshaw's cheeks to 'the seams of a regimental coat as it comes from the hands of the contractor' (*Greaves*, 2; p. 10); and even Fathom's constricted situation in the stagecoach (not only caricatures may be treated in this way) to that of 'a thin quarto between two voluminous dictionaries on a bookseller's shelf' (28; p. 130). Such images distract the reader from the subject' and compel his attention to the play of the writer's mind itself. They are a kind of intellectual free-style, a celebration of the voluntary powers of the imagination. Sir Stentor Stile, with his eccentric clothes 'rendered still more conspicuous by the behaviour of the man who owned them', and a voice 'something less melodious than the cry of mackerel or live cod' (*Fathom*, 24; p. 101); the misanthrope Ferret, with his eyes 'small and red, and so deep set in the sockets, that each appeared like the unextinguished snuff of a farthing-candle, gleaming through the horn of a dark lanthorn' (*Greaves,* 1; p. 2); the captious Lismahago, his face 'at least, half a yard in length, brown and shrivelled, with projecting cheek-bones, little grey eyes on the greenish hue, a large hook-nose, a pointed chin, a mouth from ear to ear, very ill furnished with teeth, and a high, narrow forehead, well furrowed with wrinkles' (*Clinker,* 10 July; p. 188)—all exemplify Smollett's instinct to start his figures spontaneously, out of the resources of language, rather than develop them patiently by observation and analysis. They emerge, as it were, fully fledged from the mind of their creator, and begin to speak and act in a way that is totally predictable.

But no account of Smollett's caricatures would be complete without the support of Timothy Crabshaw, Launcelot's lumpish squire, who is perhaps the most extravagant of them all.

His stature was below the middle size: he was thick, squat, and brawny, with a small protuberance on one shoulder, and a prominent belly, which, in consequence of the water he had swallowed, now strutted out beyond its usual dimensions. His forehead was remarkably convex, and so very low, that his black bushy hair descended within an inch of his nose: but this did not conceal the wrinkles of his front, which were manifold. His small glimmering eyes resembled those of the Hampshire porker, that turns up the soil with his projecting snout. His cheeks were shrivelled and puckered at the corners, like the seams of a regimental coat as it comes from the hands of the contractor: his nose bore a strong analogy in shape to a tennis-ball, and in colour to a mulberry; for all the water of the river had not been able to quench the natural fire of that feature. His upper jaw was furnished with two long white sharp-pointed teeth or fangs, such as the reader may have observed in the chaps of a wolf, or full-grown mastiff, and an anatomist would describe as a preternatural elongation of the *dentes canini.* His chin was so long, so peaked and incurvated, as to form in profile with his impending forehead the exact resemblance of a moon in the first quarter . . . [2; p. 10]

The company at the Black Lion survey Crabshaw 'with admiration', but we as readers have the advantage of them; for no such figure could exist as a visual phenomenon. He is wholly a creature of words. Everything in the description is extreme ('remarkably . . . so very . . . manifold') and even the improbable analogies are thrown into extra relief by a special emphasis: his nose bears a *'strong* analogy in shape to a tennis-ball, and in colour to a mulberry', his profile forms 'the *exact* resemblance of a moon in the first quarter'. The real strength here is in the assertion and confidence of Smollett's style, the exactness in the gauging of that specious precision which accentuates any comic gesture. There is the usual redundancy of epithet ('thick, squat, and brawny'), besides one instance where the adjectives are arranged in a progressive manner: 'so long, so peaked and incurvated', the latinate word resounding at the end. And an extra feature here is the comic periphrasis of some descriptive phrases: 'a preternatural elongation of the *dentes canini'*, 'that curvature known by the appellation of bandy legs' (this last detail comes later in the description).

These caricatures, then, live at the very circumference of style, where it takes off, relinquishes any responsibility to the real world, and creates its own curve in a condition of weightlessness. Caricature is, in fact, the nearest we can get to 'pure style'; the pure style Flaubert dreamed of when he wrote to Louise Colet, using an image which is happily consonant with my own: 'What I should like to do is to write a book about nothing, a book with no reference to anything outside itself, which would stand on its own by an inner strength of style, just as the earth holds itself without support in space'.[13]

III

I remarked earlier that the more developed of his caricatures have voices as well, and we must pass on to Smollett's dialogue for further illustration of his linguistic facility; of how his imagination functions in the crush of words, and feeds on their fields of energy. The habitual brilliance of his comic dialogue is very original in the novel; neither Defoe nor Richardson ever attempted such a thing, and even Fielding, despite his experience as a dramatist, never created dialogue so idiosyncratic. (Mrs Slipslop is, after all, a very slight example; and Fielding declines the challenge presented by his promising jailbird Blear-eyed Moll in *Amelia* with the lame excuse that her language is 'not proper to be repeated here'.[14] Smollett appears again as the honourable antecedent of Dickens in this respect; his marvellous voices adumbrate—and often provide the pattern for—such characters as Jingle, Boythorn and Micawber.

Gary Underwood devotes the larger part of his article 'Linguistic realism in *Roderick Random*'[15] to arguing that Smollett's ability to 'recreate peculiarities in the speech of his characters' is an important aspect of his realism, and one in which he is 'extremely accurate'. But this argument misses, or does not reach, the point: as Underwood himself concedes when, at the end of the article, he quotes Sumner Ives's observation that ' "the author is an artist, not a linguist or a sociologist, and his purpose is literary rather than scientific" '. One is happier, therefore, with Underwood's conclusion that these features (which represent 'something new in the English novel') are 'not just realistic idiosyncrasies; they are often comic. They are another manifestation of Smollett's genius, his ability to fuse the real with the comic and make it one.' This genius is amply demonstrated in the extravagant Welsh dialect of Morgan, which provides a rich diversion during Roderick's adventures at sea. Morgan's speech is not achieved by the facile expedient of substituting one consonant for another; Smollett endows him with that kind of verbal luxuriance, and redundancy of epithet, which are the life of a comic character. ' "Got pless my soul!" [Morgan exclaims at his captain's orders], "does he think, or conceive, or imagine, that I am a horse, or an ass, or a goat, to trudge backwards and forwards, and upwards and downwards, and by sea and by land, at his will and pleasures?" ' (25; i, 230). Morgan is in permanent and voluble dispute with his superiors. He declares to Captain Oakum that he will not be ' "a tennis-ball, nor a shittle-cock, nor a trudge, nor a scullion, to any captain under the sun" ' (30; i, 267) and protests to the effeminate Captain Whiffle that ' "I do affirm, and avouch, and maintain, with my soul, and my pody, and my plood, look you, that I have no smells about me, but such as a christian ought to have, except the effluvia of topacco, which is a cephalic, odoriferous, aromatick herb, and he is a son of a mountain-goat who says otherwise.—As for my being a monster, let that be as it is: I am as Got was pleased to create me, which, peradventure, is more that I shall aver of him who gave me that title; for I will proclaim it before the world, that he is disguised, and transfigured, and transmographied with affectation and whimsies, and that he is more like a papoon than one of the human race" ' (34; i, 308). On one occasion Smollett introduces an interesting variation by transferring the peculiarities of Morgan's dialect into indirect speech: after another contretemps with the captain he comes down to the berth, 'where finding Thomson and me at work preparing medicines, he bid us leave off our lapour and go to play, for the captain, by his sole word and power and command, had driven sickness a pegging to the tevil, and there was no more malady on poard. So saying, he drank off a gill of brandy, sighed grievously three times, poured forth an ejaculation of "Got pless my heart, liver, and lungs!" and then began to sing a Welch song with great earnestness of visage, voice, and gesture" (27; i, 247). Visage, voice and gesture: tensors of the taut circumference.

But it is certainly true that Smollett achieves his best effects, in dialogue, with his naval characters—among whom Morgan, like Roderick himself, is only an interloper. From Tom Bowling, who comes to young Roderick's rescue at the beginning of his first novel, to Sam Balderick, whom Bramble runs into in Bath in his last, these highly original characters offer Smollett a regular series of opportunities to exercise his invention. Bowling's threat to Roderick's cousin (whose hounds he has killed when they attacked him) is promise enough. ' "Lookee, brother, your dogs having boarded me without provocation, what I did was in my own defence. So you had best be civil, and let us shoot a-head, clear of you . . . Lookee, you lubberly son of a w——e, if you come athwart me, 'ware your gingerbread work—I'll be foul of your quarter, d——n me" ' (3; i, 14). And the Lieutenant animates the next three chapters, advising Roderick's grandfather that he is ' "bound for the other world, but I believe damnably ill provided for the voyage" ', scattering the 'young fry' that surround this 'old shark' with the violence of his denunciation, and consigning them eventually to 'the latitude of hell' (3, i, 18; 4, 22–3). To the end Smollett managed to invest this idiom with new energy and freshness. Balderick is 'metamorphosed into an old man, with a wooden leg and a weatherbeaten face', and his manner of address to Bramble is appropriate to his age. ' "An old friend, sure enough! (cried he, squeezing my hand, and surveying me eagerly thro' his glasses) I know the looming of the vessel, though she has been hard strained since we parted; but I can't heave up the name—" The moment I told him who I was, he exclaimed, "Ha! Matt, my old fellow cruizer, still afloat!" And, starting up, hugged me in his arms' (*Clinker*, 5 May; p. 55).

But it is Commodore Trunnion himself, after all, who provides the richest examples of Smollett's dialogue, where the exuberance and complexity of the sustained metaphoric language amount to something which many have found it more just to call poetic than comic, ultimately, in effect. There is plenty to choose from, and one must at least mention the celebrated 'ride to Church' for Trunnion's wedding (where, as Herbert Read says, 'we pass from realism to phantasy'[16]) and the commodore's subsequent account of this expedition to the Hunt (8; p. 40); but it is at the scene of Trunnion's death, in the middle of the novel, that Smollett let him speak most unforgettably. Peregrine has appeared—a pale figure beside his uncle—in tears; and Trunnion 'consoled him in these words':

"Swab the spray from your bowsprit, my good lad, and coil up your spirits. You must not let the top-lifts of your heart give way, because you see me ready to go down at these years; many a better man has foundered before he has made half my way; thof I trust, by the mercy of God, I shall be sure in port in a very few glasses, and fast moored in a most blessed riding: for my good friend Jolter hath overhauled the journal of my sins; and by the observation he hath taken of the state of my soul, I hope I shall happily conclude my voyage, and be brought up in the latitude of heaven. Here has been a doctor that wanted to stow me chock-full of physic; but, when a man's hour is come, what signifies his taking his departure with a 'pothecary's shop in his hold? Those fellows come along side of dying men, like the messengers of the admiralty with sailing orders: but, I told him as how I could slip my cable without his direction or assistance, and so he hauled of in dudgeon". [79; p. 392]

This is much more than 'jargon'; Smollett has succeeded in colouring Trunnion's whole expression with a dense network of images, until it seems almost another created language—which can then start using similes again ('like the messengers of the admiralty . . .') as if to form a double layer of analogy. A whole page of counsel to Peregrine follows, and then Smollett reverts to indirect speech for Trunnion's last words, expressing his hope 'that, for all the heavy cargo of his sins, he should be able to surmount the foothook-shrouds of despair, and get aloft to the cross-trees of God's good favour' (p. 394). Even the pedantic naval commentator who objected to the 'extravagant metaphor' of Smollett's naval idiom in general, complaining that it is often 'broken by the most violent incongruities', was prepared to applaud this death scene as beyond such literal criticism. [17] Because this is indeed poetry, *poesis*, the making of a new thing in words; and though it may be different from the explosive utterance of Weazel or Stentor Stile it is different perhaps more in degree than kind; a concentration of those techniques, operating on the verbal level, which detain a character in 'the pale of Words' in a sense rather different from that Pope intends when he uses the phrase in *The Dunciad*.[18] One of the reasons for the success of such dialogue is that it projects what Bergson called *raideur*, 'inflexibility' or comic predictability, in the form of speech.[19] Smollett actually uses this word when he says that Trunnion 'was altogether as inflexible with respect to the attitudes of his body' as he was in his patterns of speech (4; p. 17), reminding us once again how true was his instinct for the source of laughter.

IV

If caricatures talk, they also move; we can pass on now to
consider the effects Smollett attains from the description of
comic action. Bergson evades the critical problem here when
he says that 'verbal comedy should correspond, point for
point, to comedy of action and situation; and is only, one
might almost say, a projection of these at the verbal level'.[20]
Because the whole problem is, of course, *how* the verbal level
can be made to accommodate the comic gesture; how the
comic intention shall translate itself into articulation, and not
get diffused in the process. Middleton Murry said that it is a
writer's attitude that makes articulate his feeling, for 'an
emotion which has not the endorsement of an attitude has a
trick of dissolving away in the mere act of expression',[21] and
this 'attitude'—which I understand as a kind of verbal posture, a posture to one's materials continuously implied in the
words you use—is absolutely essential in comic writing.

One comes to appreciate, in reading Smollett, that the
successful creation of comic scenes requires an extreme verbal fastidiousness and an almost pedantic accuracy. The
same verbal energy is required here as elsewhere to keep the
circumference taut; the comedy is only effective where a
tight circle, not a slack loop, is its geometric image. Consider
Smollett's description of Trunnion and his companions on
their way to church, as seen by a valet who has been sent out
to look for them. 'The valet having rode something more
than a mile, espied the whole troop disposed in a long field,
crossing the road obliquely, and headed by the bridegroom
and his friend Hatchway, who finding himself hindered by a
hedge from proceeding farther in the same direction, fired a
pistol, and stood over to the other side, making an obtuse
angle with the line of his former course; and the rest of the
squadron followed his example, keeping always in the rear
of each other, like a flight of wild geese' (8; p. 36). The
identifying feature of this is its precision, which is largely
created by the incongruous use of geometric terms: the troop
is 'disposed in a long field', crosses the road 'obliquely',
Hatchway makes 'an obtuse angle with the line of his former

course'. Such language helps to sharpen the comedy, in that the disorder of the scene is paradoxically related in poised and sober prose. The term 'stood over' is used in its precise nautical sense (stand over: 'to leave one shore and sail towards another; *OED*), and the concluding simile is both graphic and apt for the occasion.

Just as the success of visual farce depends on exquisite timing, so the successful narration of a farcical episode in words depends upon exquisite verbal tact, poise; the ability to 'keep a straight face', verbally, and heighten rather than surrender the comic possibilities. The 'Feast in the Manner of the Ancients' in *Pickle* provides an interesting study in the management of a large-scale comic situation (48; pp. 233–41). Peregrine is invited to this feast, which is to be presented by the doctor whose portrait Smollett drew from Akenside, along with the doctor's friend (and adversary) Pallet, 'a French marquis, an Italian count and a German baron'—already a promising collection. The point is that the doctor is a pedant (he has been introduced a few pages previously as one 'in whose air and countenance appeared all the uncouth gravity and supercilious self-conceit of a physician piping hot from his studies' (46, p. 224)) and intends to model his dinner on the lines of an ancient banquet. At several points in the meal he pauses to describe the ingredients: ' "This here, gentlemen, is a boiled goose, served up in a sauce composed of pepper, lovage, coriander, mint, rue, anchovies and oil; I wish for your sakes, gentlemen, it was one of the geese of Ferrara, so much celebrated among the ancients for the magnitude of their livers, one of which is said to have weighed upwards of two pounds: with this food, exquisite as it was, did the tyrant Heliogabalus regale his hounds . . ." '. This kind of thing recalls another of Bergson's observations, that 'humour delights in concrete words, technical terms, precision . . . this is not simply an aspect of humour, but partakes of its very essence'.[22] The redundant detail serves as a comic surcharge.

It is the exposure of the doctor's affectation and the exaggerated reactions of his guests that occupies the centre of the stage. When they first approach the table the smell of the various preparations causes the Italian's eyes to water, 'the German's visage underwent a violent distortion of features', Peregrine has recourse to breathing only through his mouth, and 'the poor painter, running into another room, plugged his nostrils with tobacco'. But the best paragraph is probably that which describes in jealous detail how the guests endeavour to dispose themselves on the benches which their host has thoughtfully substituted for 'the exact triclinia of the ancients'. After 'a pantomime of gesticulations' Peregrine and the marquis install themselves:

The Italian being a thin, limber creature, planted himself next to Pickle, without sustaining any misfortune, but that of his stocking being torn by a ragged nail of the seat as he raised his legs on a level with the rest of his limbs. But the baron, who was neither so wieldy nor supple in his joints as his companions, flounced himself down with such precipitation, that his feet suddenly tilting up, came in furious contact with the head of the marquis, and demolished every curl in a twinkling, while his own skull, at the same instant, descended upon the side of his couch with such violence, that his periwig was struck off, and the whole room filled with pulvilio.

The Italian is deftly dealt with, and his misadventure with the ragged nail, as it were, elided by the syntax: 'without sustaining any misfortune, but . . .'—the intactness of the phrase is juxtaposed in the mind with the torn stocking, and the effect is comic. Also the deliberateness of the delineation ('on a level with the rest of his limbs') contrasts with the absurd uncertainty and tentativeness of the scene described. The baron commits a grosser blunder, which the style interprets almost as a diagram: with the balance of his feet coming up and his head going down; while the final clause, with its satisfying summary 'and the whole room was filled with pulvilio', comes rather like the last culminating line of a verse paragraph. The whole scene, we might say, has been picked clean of its comic possibilities by the fine touch of Smollett's prose.

V

Precision, then, one can safely identify as the essential characteristic of comic writing: it 'partakes of its very essence'. This is the 'firmness' that (recalling Donne's compass image) makes the circle just. This it is that generates the articulate energy which is as essential to comic prose as it is to the heroic couplet that Smollett so much admired. And I shall illustrate the special effects achieved through comic precision with a number of passages, sentences or simply phrases taken from the range of Smollett's writing which are marked and made memorable by this quality.

Roderick gives the following account of the culinary arrangements in the medical mess on board the *Thunder*. 'The cloath, consisting of a piece of old sail, was instantly laid, covered with three plates, which by the colour, I could with difficulty discern to be metal, and as many spoons of the same composition, two of which were curtailed in the handles, and the other abridged in the lip' (25; i, 234). The death of the octogenarian captain of the *Lizard* is thus narrated: 'he departed in the night, without any ceremony, which indeed was a thing he always despised . . . ' (37; ii, 2). Smollett underlines the comic element in an especially vigorous asseveration from Bowling with the ironic phrase that follows it: ' "I trust to no creed but the compass, and do unto every man as I would be done by; so that I defy the pope, the devil, and the pretender; and hope to be saved as well as another".—This association of persons gave great offence to the friar . . .' (42; ii, 50). After composing his quarrel with Rourk Oregan, Roderick examines the Irishman's pistols and finds that 'one of them had been loaded without being primed, and the other primed without a charge' (49; ii, 135). This sentence exhibits the comic mechanism of style at its simplest and most effective: the counterpoint of true absurdity.

When Peregrine quotes from Homer, in conversation with a pedantic doctor, this 'self-sufficient physician . . . looked upon his reply as a fair challenge and instantly rehearsed forty or fifty lines of the Iliad in a breath' (46; pp. 225–6). The prose here (precipitated by the word 'instantly') enacts the pedant's automatic reaction as appropriately as it registers the ludicrous hesitation of a philosopher encountered later in the novel, 'who seemed to have consulted all the barometers and thermometers that ever were invented, before he would venture to affirm that it was a chill morning' (103; p. 662), or suggests Fathom's bemusement at the deviousness of a certain lawyer, when he discovers he has 'incurred the penalty of three shillings and four-pence for every time he chanced to meet the conscientious attorney, either in the park, the coffee-house or the street, provided they had exchanged the common salutation; and he had great reason to believe the solicitor had often thrown himself in his way, with a view to swell this item of his account' (37; p. 174). In a particularly energetic phrase, the 'ragged attendant' who precedes Major Farrel in his attempt to gain entry to Renaldo's castle is described as 'extorting music from a paultry viole' (58; p. 287).

Greaves provides further examples of this stylistic virtuosity—the achieved completeness and finality of comic statement which, like any art, succeeds by announcing and at the same time fulfilling a purpose. Ferret's character is summarised in its 'three peculiarities' as follows: 'He was never seen to smile; he was never heard to speak in praise of any person whatsoever; and he was never known to give a direct answer to any question that was asked; but seemed, on all occasions, to be actuated by the most perverse spirit of contradiction' (1, p. 3). The insistent 'never' and the concluding 'on all occasions' create a comic impression through their very absoluteness; once again, it is Ferret's *inflexibility* that provides the potential for laughter. At the end of the book Ferret confesses to his imposition as a conjuror in the sharp style which is habitual to him: ' " . . . I did little or nothing but eccho back the intelligence they brought me, except prognosticating that Crabshaw would be hanged; a prediction to which I found myself so irresistibly impelled, that I am persuaded it was the real effect of inspiration" ' (chapter the last; p. 204).

Smollett is less concerned with comic effect in the *Travels*, since most of the absurdities he discovers on the Continent are of the kind that are 'too gross to make a thinking man merry', and I shall have enough to say about these in the next chapter. But the *Atom* reveals Smollett at his most brilliant and inventive, and includes some of his most finished comic fantasy, his most assured comic style. The fantasy works like yeast on what is substantially factual material, and turns the political situation in which Smollett was himself so painfully involved into the 'farce of human government' (ii, 121)—the phrase identifies the confident external view—that Smollett invented for his own satisfaction. His determination to retain a consistent ironic distance from materials that had previously engulfed him results in a kind of inversion whereby things about which he does have a passionate feeling are flung to the circumference by the dismissive energy of his style.

We have a vigorous overstatement of the incompetence of the administration under Newcastle: 'Here then was the strangest phaenomenon that ever appreared in the political world. A statesman without capacity, or the smallest tincture of human learning; a secretary who could not write; a financier who did not understand the multiplication table; and the treasurer of a vast empire who never could balance accounts with his own butler' (i, 28). We are later invited to believe that under George III 'a certain person who could not read was appointed Librarian to his imperial majesty' (ii, 90). Enduring Bute's economies, the King's household are 'not only punished in their bellies, but likewise curtailed in their clothing, and abridged in their stipends' (ii, 87): the two last being the very same verbs, and conveying the same comic attitude, that were used to describe the culinary arrangements aboard the *Thunder* in *Random*. Smollett achieves his decisiveness in part, again, from the astringent use of technical terms. Grenville is described as 'an old experienced shrewd politician, who conveyed more sense in one single sentence, than could have been distilled from all the other brains in council, had they been macerated in one alembic' (i, 66); and a financial enterprise of Pitt's evaporates into smoke 'without leaving so much as the scrapings of a crucible for a specific against the itch' (i, 181). But the most conclusive

example, where the idea is pinioned and expressed with
most exacting, most satisfying completeness, occurs where
Smollett is describing Newcastle's fatal inability to say 'no':
'He never had the courage to refuse even that which he
could not possibly grant; and at last his tongue actually for-
got how to pronounce the negative particle: but as in the
English language two negatives amount to an affirmative,
five hundred affirmatives in the mouth of Fika-Kaka did not
altogether destroy the efficacy of simple negation. A promise
five hundred times repeated, and at every repetition
confirmed by an oath, barely amounted to a computable
chance of performance' (i, 40–1). The light of pure intelligence is brilliantly refracted in the precise articulation of this
prose, which represents the style of the circumference at its
most taut and invulnerable.

One could fill a whole chapter with examples of this style
from *Clinker* in the letters of Jery Melford, whose confession
of his detached attitude I have used to define my own
approach here. Each of his twenty-eight letters is an exercise
in comic narration, always amusing, often extravagantly
funny; it is Jery's letters, as much as anything else in Smollett, which have created those 'peals of unextinguishable
laughter' of which Scott wrote.[23] But it is not enough to
appeal to the echoes of this laughter: I intend to keep a sharp
focus on the prose that occasions it.

Consider the description Jery gives of the guests who
come to Smollett's house in Chelsea for his Sunday entertainment. There is one who 'had contracted such an
antipathy to the country, that he insisted upon sitting with
his back towards the window that looked into the garden,
and when a dish of cauliflower was set upon the table, he
snuffed up volatile salts to keep him from fainting; yet this
delicate person was the son of a cottager, born under a
hedge, and had many years run wild among asses on a
common'. Smollett's ridicule of this affectation could not be
more comprehensively articulated than it is in these bathetic
biographical details. Of another (who suffers from a stutter)
the host remarks; 'this wag, after having made some abortive
attempts in plain speaking, had recourse to this defect, by

means of which he frequently extorted the laugh out of the
company, without the least expense of genius; and that
imperfection, which he had at first counterfeited, was now
become so habitual, that he could not lay it aside' (10 June; p.
125). The prose is alive with comic implication, and the
alertness is due to the use of words ('abortive attempt . . .
had recourse to . . . extorted the laugh . . . expense of
genius') capable of balancing a fine irony. I shall restrict
myself to quoting only one more paragraph: where Jery
relates the discomfiture of 'a fat-headed justice of the peace,
called Frogmore' at the hands of his host's doctor.

Divers tolerable jokes were cracked upon the justice, who ate a
most unconscionable supper, and, among other things, a large
plate of broiled mushrooms, which he had no sooner swallowed
than the doctor observed, with great gravity, that they were of the
kind called *champignons*, which in some constitutions had a
poisonous effect.—Mr. Frogmore, startled at this remark, asked, in
some confusion, why he had not been so kind as to give him that
notice sooner.—He answered, that he took it for granted, by his
eating them so heartily, that he was used to the dish; but as he
seemed to be under some apprehension, he prescribed a bumper
of plague-water, which the justice drank off immediately, and
retired to rest, not without marks of terror and disquiet. [3
October, pp. 298–9]

The prose here maintains its poise largely through the use of
indirect speech, which irons out any untoward exclamation
and emphasises the superfluous politeness of a phrase like
'been so kind as ' in deliberate contrast to the confusion of
Frogmore's state of mind. The result is the achievement of a
structure which compels us to adopt the attitude of an
amused spectator. This is what one calls 'comic distance'; the
sum of which techniques goes to create the style of the circumference, moving in its untroubled intellectual orbit.

It is interesting to consider the principle which lies behind
the typical forms and figures of language used by Smollett in
these instances, and indeed throughout his comic writing.
This might be described as the determination to construct a

curve of statement rather than to betray meaning in the bar-
renness of a straight line. The tentativeness of 'it seems',
'probably', and 'perhaps': 'it seems the hooks that supported
this swinging couch were not calculated for the addition of
weight which they were now destined to bear' (*Pickle*, 9; p.
44); the withdrawal into the passive voice: the sign of the inn
at which *Greaves* opens 'was said to exhibit the figure of a
black lion' (I, 1); the deliberate understatement of *'tolerable*
jokes', *'some* confusion'—most effectively expressed by the
figure of litotes, as when Crab's servant girl informs him that
she is pregnant and we are told that 'he was far from being
over-joyed at this proof of his vigour' (*Random*, 7; i, 46); the
self-conscious qualification of phrase (in a manner for once
reminiscent of Fielding): Mr Pickle's father-in-law, 'though
he had but little fortune to bestow upon his children, had (to
use his own phrase) replenished their veins with some of the
best blood in the county' (*Pickle*, 3; p. 13); Lydia Melford's
reference to newspapers as 'these offices of intelligence, (as
my brother calls them) . . .' (Clinker, 26 April; p. 40); the erec-
tion of an ironic frame around a word: 'that curvature known
by the appellation of bandy-legs' (*Greaves*, 2; p. 10); 'those
animals who lead raw boys about the world, under the
denomination of travelling governors' (*Pickle*, 43; p. 207); the
use of words of 'disproportionate magnitude' and pedantic
etymological accuracy: lawyer Clarke, threatened by a bully,
'bestowed such a benediction on his jaw, as he could not
receive without immediate humiliation' (*Greaves*, 13; p. 110);
the kind of 'elegant variation' so well demonstrated by Smollett's use (twice) of 'curtailed . . . and abridged . . . '; all
these are devices employed to avoid the waste of direct
statement, and allow that fermentation in the wort of words
which makes an idea potent. Think how inert Morgan's
three spoons would be if they were simply old, bent and
battered: it is precisely the phrase 'two were curtailed in the
handles, and one abridged in the lip' that promotes them to
comic properties.

Again the image of the circumference proves its aptness.
There are implications for comedy in Emily Dickinson's lines

Tell all the Truth but tell it slant—
Success in Circuit lies . . .[24]

Directness dissipates, indirectness generates energy: it is like an electrical coil, which increases the charge. Style retains a deliberate distance from the naked, inert and (most intimately) *dumb* idea, creates in the circling labour of speech the very tension by which it lives. Language itself *is* the 'beautiful circuiting' Keats described,[25] the intellectual pattern one creates and superimposes on the chaos of total experience.

It is generally true that comic writing will emphasise the form and substance of language itself, the mind's creation, against the experiential flux that seeks to challenge this and break it down. Vocabulary, syntax, rhythm, will all be exploited to achieve the necessary pattern, to cage the world securely in a comic perspective. One is used to the simpler expedients from a selection of writers: Ben Jonson giving us the addict of tobacco who 'voided a bushel of soot yesterday, upward and downward',[26] Jane Austen trapping Mr Elton 'in the same room at once with the woman he had just married, the woman he had wanted to marry, and the woman whom he had been expected to marry',[27] Dickens recalling, with typical stylistic assertiveness, 'the smallest boy I ever conversed with, carrying the largest baby I ever saw', who 'offered a supernaturally intelligent explanation' of the former whereabouts of the Marshalsea prison;[28] Henry James relying on the same inherent structures of language to discover Maisie's predicament: 'As she was condemned to know more and more, how could it logically stop before she should know Most? It came to her in fact as they sat there on the sands that she was distinctly on the road to know Everything'.[29]

Such explicit, obtrusive patterning of experience in language is, we may conclude, intrinsic to comic writing; and we may observe Smollett's systematic exploitation of verbal and syntactic pattern at its most developed in two passages that I have reserved for this purpose. The first occurs early in *Random*, where Roderick relates the injustice he suffered whilst at school.

F

I was often inhumanly scourged for crimes I did not commit, because having the character of a vagabond in the village, every piece of mischief whose author lay unknown, was charged upon me.—I have been found guilty of robbing orchards I never entered, of killing cats I never hurted, of stealing gingerbread I never touched, and of abusing old women I never saw.—Nay, a stammering carpenter had eloquence enough to persuade my master, that I fired a pistol loaded with small shot, into his window; though my landlady and the whole family bore witness, that I was a-bed fast asleep at the time when this outrage was committed.— I was flogged for having narrowly escaped drowning, by the sinking of a ferry-boat in which I was passenger.—Another time for having recovered of a bruise occasioned by a horse and cart running over me. A third time, for being bit by a baker's dog.—In short, whether I was guilty or unfortunate, the vengeance and sympathy of this arbitrary pedagogue were the same. [2; i, 9–10]

Roderick's complaint is delivered with admirable lucidity and rhetorical address; but the examples are so extreme, and so expressed, that our response is one of amusement rather than sympathy. (Smollett knew better than most writers how to animate his reader's indignation; and he also knew that this was not the way to do it.) The charges relating to orchards, cats, gingerbread and old women are made to seem doubly absurd by the way the simple fact of Roderick's innocence is, as it were, embedded in the syntax itself ('never . . . never . . ' etc.), becoming the actual burden of the iteration. The episode involving the 'stammering carpenter' is a fantasy of unlikely misfortune, tricked out in all its farcical detail—right down to the specification of the 'small shot' supposedly used in the outrage. And the ludicrous idea of receiving punishment for the defensive act of escaping drowning and for the involuntary recovering from a bruise reaches a final pitch of absurdity when punishment is extended to the wholly passive act of 'being bit by a baker's dog'. The last sentence offers to summarise these misadventures ('In short . . . '), and the way 'vengeance and sympathy' become synonymous confirms the fact of Roderick's arbitrary and indeed absurd experience.

My second example comes from *Greaves*. Sir Launcelot,

imprisoned in the private asylum, overhears a noisy altercation among the inmates.

This dialogue operated like a train upon many other inhabitants of the place: one swore he was within three vibrations of finding the longitude, when this noise confounded his calculation: a second, in broken English, complained he vas distorped in the moment of de proshection—a third, in the character of his holiness, denounced interdiction, excommunication, and anathemas; and swore by St. Peter's keys, they should howl ten thousand years in purgatory, without the benefit of a single mass. A fourth began to hollow in all the vociferation of a fox-hunter in the chace; and in an instant the whole house was in an uproar—The clamour, however, was of a short duration. The different chambers being opened successively, every individual was effectually silenced by the sound of one cabalistical word, which was no other than *waistcoat*: a charm which at once cowed the king of P——, dispossessed the fanatic, dumbfounded the mathematician, dismayed the alchemist, deposed the pope, and deprived the squire of all utterance. [23; p. 186]

Here Smollett develops a complicated antithetical movement. The first part of the paragraph is structured very simply, as a numerical list: one, a second, a third, a fourth, allowing for elaboration in the incongruous details (the alchemist with his vibrations, the 'pope' with his anathemas); while the last sentence repeats this structure—or rather dismantles it—in an accelerated rhythm, as the different categories of lunatic are successively stripped of their pretensions. The alliterative verbs are particularly well chosen, and satisfyingly progressive in signification. There is a further satisfaction in the amplitude of the final phrase, which again recalls the movement of verse rhythm or the return to the 'home' note in music.

It was Coleridge who remarked of one of Smollett's novels that it had 'no growth from within'.[30] Certainly there is no 'within' where Smollett's comedy is concerned, even where the materials it deals with might be available to different treatment. An external view of the world is the necessary condition of the comic style; all lies exposed on the spinning surface, the light circumference, the brilliant rim of the imagination.

VI

I have suggested that comic writing offers a critique of reality.[31] Humour is a province of the intellect, claimed as such by Rabelais when he prefaced the *Gargantua* with the observation

Mieulx est de ris que de larmes escripre,
Pour ce que rire est le propre de l'homme[32]

and recognised by Shaftesbury when he asserted that one test of any idea should be its ability to withstand ridicule.[33] Now one of the effects of the simplification of reality by pattern, which I have just been considering, is that it throws into relief the incongruous elements which compose our experience; and by way of conclusion to this chapter I shall look more closely at the techniques Smollett uses to precipitate this sense of incongruity.

In his *Lectures on the English Comic Writers* Hazlitt trained a light on the incongruous which will help us to understand its effect in Smollett's work. 'The essence of the laughable', he wrote, 'is the incongruous, the disconnecting one idea from another, or the jostling of one feeling against another . . . the ridiculous, which is the highest degree of the laughable, is that which is contrary not only to custom but to sense and reason, or is a voluntary departure from what we have a right to expect from those who are conscious of absurdity and propriety in words, looks, and actions.'[34]

Smollett was one so conscious. In a letter he wrote to Dr William Hunter from Nice in 1764 he mentions having seen in a peasant's stable 'a starved Ox, a Jack-ass, and a He-goat' and continues, 'I mention this assemblage because in passing thro' Burgundy I saw three animals of the same species drawing a Plough very peaceable together.'[35] The incongruity of 'this assemblage' must have impressed Smollett, since he includes both instances in the *Travels* two years

later: 'In Burgundy I saw a peasant ploughing the ground
with a jack-ass, a lean cow, and a he-goat, yoked together'
(8; p. 71); 'In the Cella Sanctior, I found a lean cow, a he-goat,
and a jack-ass; the very same conjunction of animals which I
had seen drawing a plough in Burgundy' (13; p. 124). No
comment is necessary; it is the nature of the incongruous
that it declares itself. All that is needed are the external facts
which clash in the mind to produce the desired effect. One
feels Smollett must have had these experiences in mind
when, a few years later, in the *Atom*, he made use of the
following image to expose one of Bute's political stratagems:
the idea of 'forming an administration equally composed of
the two factions, was as absurd as it would be to yoke two
stone-horses and two jack-asses in the same carriage' (ii, 70).

The perception of incongruity, then, as illustrated here, is
one of the mainsprings of the comic intelligence, and one
that we find tightly wound throughout Smollett's work. His
first novel provides many examples. It is a 'voluntary departure from what we have a right to expect' where Jackson
confesses to Roderick that 'although he had seen a great deal
of the world both at land and sea, having cruiz'd three whole
months in the channel, yet he should not be satisfied until he
had visited France' (16; i, 129). There is a similar discordance
in the details we are given of Roderick's room at the house of
the French apothecary Lavement:

. . . a back room up two pair of stairs, furnished with a pallet for
me to lie upon, a chair without a back, an earthen chamber-pot
without a handle, a bottle by way of candlestick, and a triangular
piece of glass instead of a mirrour; the rest of the ornaments having
been lately removed to one of the garrets, for the convenience of
the servant of an Irish captain, who lodged on the first floor. [18; i,
154]

It is this free play of the imagination that is put to good use
by a sailor from the *Thunder* who affronts the Welshman 'by
discovering to the people on board that Mr Morgan's wife
kept a gin-shop in Rag-Fair' and raising a laugh at his
expense (27; i, 251). Captain Oregan, from the condition of

whose pistols in a duel Smollett has already extracted some amusement, introduces Roderick to two literary compatriots of his whose appearance certainly fulfils Hazlitt's conditions: 'But it seems these literati had been very ill rewarded for their ingenious labours; for between them both there was but one shirt and half a pair of breeches' (49; ii, 138). It is the use of the word 'literati' here that ensures the effect, from its inappropriateness in such a degraded context. But perhaps the purest example of incongruity in *Random*, that which most nearly conforms to the surrealists' ideal of pure humour, occurs where Roderick informs us that on a visit to Versailles he 'had the honour of seeing his Most Christian Majesty eat a considerable quantity of olives' (44; ii, 79). The dignity of the phrase, and situation, form an extreme, one might almost say a vertiginous contrast with the triviality of the actual information imparted.

Peregrine also exploits the offensive possibilities of incongruity when imprisoned in the Bastille; his trembling tutor finds him 'whistling with great unconcern, and working with his pencil at the bare wall, on which he had delineated a ludicrous figure labelled with the name of the nobleman whom he had affronted, and a English mastiff with his leg lifted up, in the attitude of making water in his shoe' (50; p. 249). The pretensions of the company of philosophers later in the book are similarly routed when Peregrine declares that a medal they have been venerating as an antique is 'no other than the ruins of an English farthing' (103; p. 662). There are several incongruous moments in the prison chapters in *Fathom*, notably the war waged on a table-top between the king of Corsica and Major Macleaver with mussel shells, oyster shells and grey peas (39; pp. 186–7), and the fantasy of the 'duel by smoking' fought between Macleaver and Captain Minikin (41; pp. 194–5). The conclusion of the former encounter at the end of one chapter enables Smollett to begin the next as follows: 'This expedition being happily finished, general Macleaver put the whole army, navy, transports and scene of action into a canvas bag . . .' (40; p. 187), which sentence represents as comprehensive a dislocation of reality as one can perhaps imagine. *Greaves* is well provided with this dry extreme of humour through the character of Ferret. Ferret's dexterity in defending himself against Tom Clarke's chastisement with a heavy kitchen implement prompts the suggestion that 'before he plunged into the sea of politicks, he had occasionally figured in the character of that facetious droll who accompanies your itinerant physicians, under the familiar appellation of Merry-Andrew, or Jack-Pudding, and on a wooden stage entertains the populace with a solo on the salt-box, or a sonnata on the tongs and gridiron' (4; p. 30). The gratuitous details with which Smollett sketches in this improbable background are meant to suggest the critical destructiveness of Ferret's own intelligence; which is confirmed later in the novel. At one point Ferret appears as a quack doctor offering an Elixir for sale to a crowd of rustics. His rambling, three-page-long harangue is a wild mixture of asseveration and absurdity which recalls Volpone's virtuoso performance as a mountebank in Ben Jonson's play. Ferret disclaims with amazing fertility and irrelevance the successive characters of ' "a felonious dry-salter returned from exile, an hospital stump-turner, a decayed stay-maker, a bankrupt printer, or insolvent debtor, released by act of parliament" ' on the way to his climactic affirmation of the virtues of the Elixir itself, which ' "contains the essence of the alkahest, the archaeus, the catholicon, the menstruum, the sun, moon, and to sum up all in one word, is the true, genuine, unadulterated, unchangeable, immaculate and specific *chrusion pepuromenon ek puros*' " (10; pp. 79–81).

This climax of absurdity would be enough by itself; but is compounded by the fact that the real motive of Ferret's speech is an attack on the Hanoverian policy of the administration, which keeps breaking through. And indeed the anarchic humour which Ferret provides is oddly related to his political extremism; it is an intrinsic part of his criticism of the political reality of the time. (We may remember that the surrealists employed their own forms of destructive humour very deliberately in order to discredit nineteenth-century positivism and its moral, social, and political superstructure.)

The pursuit of the incongruous is, then, an essential part of Smollett's comic style. One might mention the example (still from *Greaves*) of the confused Dolly setting the kettle on the table, and the tea board on the fire (15; pp. 123–4); or the redundant particularity of Farmer Stake's deposition with regard to Crowe, that he saw him breaking the king's peace 'with a pole or weapon, value three pence' (17; p. 141); or, elsewhere, the superlative accusation made by the Atom to Peacock, that he has been in communication with witches, in particular one 'goody Thrusk at Camberwell, who undertook for three shillings and four-pence to convey you on a broomstick to Norway, where the devil was to hold a conventicle' (*Atom* i, 195).

It is a departure not only from what we expect but from what Lismahago himself expects when the girth on his saddle snaps, and his attempt at a gallant salute ends with a tumble in the dust: it is Jery, of course, who is allowed to extract the comic potential from the episode (*Clinker*, 10 July; p. 188). And one further example at least deserves to be recalled from *Clinker*: the threat of the bookseller Birkin to the unfortunate author Tim Cropdale, that he would serve a writ 'if he did not very speedily come and settle accounts with him, respecting the expense of publishing his last Ode to the king of Prussia, of which he had sold but three, and one of them was to Whitefield the methodist' (10 June; p. 128)—as if to imply, by this superfluity in the statement of account, that the last transaction was somehow invalid.

After all these examples we can be certain that it was not without mischievous intention that Smollett included the information (in the *Continuation* of his History) that in 1758 the National Debt stood at 'eighty-seven millions three hundred sixty-seven thousand two hundred and ten pounds, nineteen shillings and tenpence farthing'.[36] The process of computation provides Smollett—as it provided Rabelais and Swift—with a self-inflating, self-detonating image of the alienating effect of the mind's mechanisms in general. The incongruous humour here exposes the suspicious insensitivity of abstract formulation, and symbolic systems, to the implicity judgement of the mind at its most critical, complex and alert: the mind, that is to say, looking in from the circumference.

My discussion of Smollett's comic style has led me into what might at first seem to be inappropriately theoretical areas, towards what Moelwyn Merchant calls 'The Metaphysics of Comedy'.[37] But the implications of comedy lead us inevitably into such areas; the circumference has its bearing, ultimately, at the centre, and the fact of comedy must be related to our total experience. It is only necessary that we should keep in mind, all the time, the way this or that comic effect actually works, and not become lost in abstract considerations. It is the meticulous attention consistently apparent in his prose that enabled Smollett to attain the position he holds among the few great masters of comic statement in English.

7   *Style at the centre*

We move inwards now, from the style of the circumference
to the style of the centre; to that style which instead of dis-
tancing and dislocating reality by means of an external prismatic analysis approaches and intensifies it, *realises* reality
through a concentrated internal focus.

The centre is the centre of organised apprehension; the
core of moral response which informs a writer's possession
and transformation of his experience. It is the source of the
interest and aversion, the determination, resentment and
enthusiasm—the *life* that animates those of his creations who
are allowed to respond as complete moral beings. And the
style of the centre is the sum of expressive techniques (or
instances) that serve to focus and articulate this complex
centre of self. This is where I intend to focus my own attention: on the expressive technique involved in giving significant form to such accelerated apprehension. When David
Hannay says that 'the satirist must justify his work to posterity by his workmanship'[1] he lays the duty at the same time
upon criticism to assist in this justification by attending to
the workmanship involved; a duty which I hope to carry out
in this chapter.

II

Although the apprehension of the centre is essentially integrated, yet the style may be considered initially in two contexts; according to two orders of experience, the physical and
the moral. And so let us consider first Smollett's ability to
render physical experience. This cannot be dismissed as
mere journalistic technique (nor, perhaps, should journalistic

technique); it requires a sophisticated literary skill to create that full sense of physical circumstance that we discover so often in Smollett's work. It may seem simple to provide the specific details that such writing often involves; but in fact the judgement involved in the presentation of such details, and the demonstrative energy needed if they are not simply to encumber the style, are the marks of a gifted and experienced writer.

A scale of reference devised by W. K. Wimsatt in his essay 'The substantive level' will be useful here. Wimsatt distinguishes three main styles of description:

1 The abstract or less than specific-substantive style, e.g. *implement.*
2 The minimum concrete or specific-substantive style, e.g. *spade.*
3 The extra-concrete, the detailed, or more than specific style, e.g. *rusty garden spade.* [2]

If we apply this scale to Smollett we shall find that much of his description falls into the third category, the 'extra-concrete'. Consider this description of a hunt breakfast in *Clinker:*

The following articles formed our morning's repast: one kit of boiled eggs; a second, full of butter; a third, full of cream; an entire cheese, made of goat's milk; a large earthern pot full of honey; the best part of a ham; a cold venison pasty; a bushel of oatmeal, made in thin cakes and bannocks, with a small wheaten loaf in the middle for the strangers; a large stone bottle full of whisky, another of brandy, and a kilderkin of ale. There was a laddle chained to the cream kit, with curious wooden bickers to be filled from this reservoir. The spirits were drank out of a silver quaff, and the ale out of horns . . . [3 September; p. 243].

It is partly the vocabulary that creates the effect here, the 'kit of boiled eggs', the 'kilderkin of ale', the 'laddle', 'bannocks' and 'bickers'. But the sustained physicality of the passage is also due to those phrases which fulfil the criterion for Wimsatt's 'more than specific style': 'large earthern pot full of honey', 'cold venison pasty', 'small wheaten loaf', 'large stone bottle full of whisky'. The passage as a whole suggests a real relish in the wholesomeness of this repast; it is a confident exercise in the equivalence of *res* and *verba*.

But no one would attempt to present Smollett as a Whitmanesque celebrator of reality. Far the greater part of his descriptive writing is concerned with what offends rather than what pleases the senses; where Matthew Bramble rather than Jery Melford is its typical agent of expression. It is no accident that the former seems to be more susceptible of energetic expression for a man of Smollett's temper; the very rhetorical patterns of such prose as Swift's and Smollett's are designed for 'cutting, and opening, and mangling, and piercing' (to return to Swift's alternatives in *A Tale of a Tub*) rather than for 'creaming off nature'. Jery's account of the breakfast is from Scotland, which Smollett permits himself to describe in his last novel in a mood of self-indulgence and nostalgia; but most of his narratives are set in England, France, or further afield, where Smollett is more concerned to criticise than celebrate. It is the descriptions which occur here that express Smollett's habitual attitude, and locate the true centre of his style.

Although there is ample evidence in Smollett's earlier work of his remarkable talent for the delineation of an oppressive physical context, it is to the *Travels* and *Clinker* that we have to go for the fullest exercise of this style of animated description. I have already considered what Seccombe referred to as the 'remarkable veracity' of the *Travels* as a document, and I will now try to illustrate—with what can be only very selective examples—how the truth of Smollett's picture is relieved by style; how the details are made over to the reader in all their soiled abundance.

This is sometimes achieved by what one calls, evasively and inadequately, 'straight' description, where the details of a scene or situation are cast in a curiously sharp light. Consider this account of the *uffiziale* to whom Smollett makes a complaint after being exasperated by 'the villainy of the hostler' at an inn in Buon Convento.

I found him wrapped in an old, greasy, ragged, great-coat, sitting in a wretched apartment, without either glass, paper, or boards in the windows; and there was no sort of furniture but a couple of broken chairs and a miserable truckle-bed. He looked pale, and meagre, and had more the air of a half-starved prisoner than of a magistrate. Having heard my complaint, he came forth into a kind of outward room or bellfrey, and rung a great bell with his own hand. [29; p. 242]

The detail is closely observed here: the room, the furniture, the magistrate himself; the fact that he rings the bell 'with his own hand'. But if we ourselves observe the prose more closely we shall notice the continuous verbal emphasis with which Smollett particularises each detail, preserving in words the vitality of his own impression. One moment the emphasis is adjectival: 'an old, greasy, ragged, great-coat'; the next Smollett relies on the cumulative effect of (negated) nouns: 'without either glass, paper, or boards in the windows'. Such 'solidity of specification'[3] is always a positive feature of this style, the detail serving a very different purpose at the centre (where it concentrates our attention) to that we observed at the circumference (where it is used essentially to dislocate). Then the adjectives describing the magistrate are animated by the image of the 'half-starved prisoner', which conveys a lively idea both of the official's appearance and of Smollett's attitude towards him.

Sometimes the image is more central to the animation, as when Smollett remarks of the beds in the small cabin of the boat that transported them to France that they 'put me in mind of the holes described in some catacombs, in which the bodies of the dead were deposited, being thrust in with the feet foremost' (1; p. 6), but it is certainly true that throughout the greater part of this work the physical immediacy is achieved through simple but powerful verbal intensification. Smollett describes the Roman Campania as 'nothing but a naked withered down, desolate and dreary, almost without enclosure, corn-field, hedge, tree, shrub, house, hut, or habitation; exhibiting here and there the ruins of an ancient castellum, tomb, or temple, and in some places the remains of a Roman via' (29; p. 245). The required negative impression is positively enforced—a kind of 'darkness visible'—by the animated and abundant list of things missing, after which the adjectival qualification 'desolate and dreary' seems hardly necessary. But the best example of this kind of thing in the *Travels* is in Smollett's livid description of the 'vermin' that make life in Nice distinctly uncomfortable.

Among the inconveniences of this climate, the vermin form no inconsiderable article. Vipers and snakes are found in the mountains. Our gardens swarm with lizzards; and there are some few scorpions; but as yet I have seen but one of this species. In summer, notwithstanding all the care and precautions we can take, we are pestered with incredible swarms of flies, fleas, and bugs; but the gnats, or *couzins*, are more intolerable than all the rest. In the day-time, it is impossible to keep the flies out of your mouth, nostrils, eyes, and ears. They croud into your milk, tea, chocolate, soup, wine, and water: they soil your sugar, contaminate your victuals, and devour your fruit; they cover and defile your furniture, floors, cielings, and indeed your whole body. As soon as candles are lighted, the *couzins* begin to buz about your ears in myriads, and torment you with their stings, so that you have no rest nor respite 'till you get into bed, where you are secured by your mosquite-net. [24; pp. 198–9]

The essential characteristics we may observe here are the close substantival reference: 'mouth, nostrils, eyes, and ears . . . milk, tea, chocolate, soup, wine and water', and the ceaseless activity of the verbs: 'croud . . . soil . . . contaminate . . . devour . . . cover and defile', which combine the effect of reiteration with the progressive development of the idea. The resultant crowding of the details parallels the crowding of the insects to create a very complete impression of a physical context. But the most significant single factor is the movement that carries the description so confidently forward. The fluent, sympathetic syntax through which Smollett persuades impression and expression to cling together in this passage has grown quite away from the insensitive syntactic substructure commonly found in eighteenth-century prose. It is the kind of syntax which (as

Donald Davie has said) 'mimes an action outside the mind',[4] and which is as intimately related to the style of the centre as it would be inappropriate to the circumference.

Smollett's extreme sensitivity is the human coefficient for these passages and the many like them which will be found in the *Travels*. It is where the senses are oppressed in this way that we are made most aware of their operation on a central organism, and where the style of the centre generates, as it were under physical pressure, its expressive energy. Smollett refers more than once in the *Travels* to his dislike of crowds; he cannot support either the 'croud of company, such as pours in upon us unexpectedly at all hours' at Montpellier (10, p. 93); or 'the tumult of a populous commercial city' with which Pisa forms such an agreeable contrast (27; p. 222). It is both interesting and amusing to compare the passage from Smollett's very scientific account of the silk-worm industry in Nice, in which he attributes to the silk-worm the same exacerbated sensibilities, and extends his sympathy to an unfortunate animal trapped in circumstances so analogous to his own (22; pp. 186–7).

But Matthew Bramble is a finer organism even than a silk-worm, and it is the expression Smollett affords him of the physical oppression he experiences in Bath, London and elsewhere that provides some of the most remarkable pages in *Humphry Clinker*. Bramble confesses at the outset that 'the inconveniences which I overlooked in the high-day of health, will naturally strike with exaggerated impression on the irritable nerves of an invalid, surprised by premature old age, and shattered with long-suffering' (23 April; p. 34), but if the impression is 'exaggerated' then at least the style is well able to support the point of view; there is no tentativeness or apology in the way it operates on 'the dirt, the stench, the chilling blasts' of Bristol Hot Well (20 April; p. 24) or the 'confused heap of stones and brick' which Durham suggests to him (15 July; p. 202), and all the intervening geography which is submitted to his critical inspection.

There is no relief for Bramble, any more than there was for Smollett himself abroad; and it is the very persistence of his complaint that augments its significance and validity. Bath is become 'the very center of racket and dissipation'; 'here we have nothing but noise, tumult, and hurry; with the fatigue and slavery of maintaining a ceremonial, more stiff, formal, and oppressive, than the etiquette of a German elector'. The avenues which lead to the Square are 'mean, dirty, dangerous, and indirect', presenting a complication of hazards that Bramble goes on to enumerate (23 April; p. 34). If he tries to take the air he is immediately 'stifled with dust, or pressed to death in the midst of post-chaises, flying-machines, waggons, and coal horses'; and so 'we poor valetudinarians pant and struggle, like so many Chinese gudgeons, gasping in the bottom of a punch-bowl' (8 May; p. 64). It is relevant to recall that Smollett was a consumptive, and therefore shares with other writers who were similarly afflicted a degree of sensitivity to the physical which is generally recognised to be beyond the experience of more robust constitutions.

London is, if possible, even more oppressive than Bath, and Smollett's style rises to the occasion. Bramble's complaint centres again on the grotesque scramble to which urban life has degenerated:

In short, there is no distinction or subordination left—The different departments of life are jumbled together—The hod-carrier, the low mechanic, the tapster, the publican, the shop-keeper, the pettifogger, the citizen, and courtier, *all tread upon the kibes of one another*: actuated by the demons of profligacy and licentiousness, they are seen every where, rambling, riding, rolling, rushing, justling, mixing, bouncing, cracking, and crashing in one vile ferment of stupidity and corruption—All is tumult and hurry; one would imagine they were impelled by some disorder of the brain, that will not suffer them to be at rest. The foot-passengers run along as if they were pursued by bailiffs. The porters and chairmen trot with their burthens. People, who keep their own equipages, drive through the streets at full speed. Even citizens, physicians, and apothecaries, glide in their chariots like lightning. The hackney-coachmen make their horses smoke, and the pavement shakes under them; and I have actually seen a wagon pass through Piccadilly at the hand-gallop. In a word, the whole nation seems to be running out of their wits. [29 May; p. 88]

The factual detail on which this passage is founded—the tradesmen are identified, the different passengers particularised, and Bramble's 'I have actually seen . . .' finally focuses the account with one decisive example—is what gives substance and authority to the rush of present participles ('rambling, riding, rolling, rushing, justling, mixing, bouncing, cracking and crashing . . .') that best communicate Bramble's own distracted sense of how things are. The technique Smollett employs to achieve the desired effect of animation here is identical to that used by James Joyce in *Ulysses*, where a market scene is brought to life by 'a trampling, cackling, roaring, lowing, bleating, bellowing, rumbling, grunting, champing, chewing, of sheep and pigs and heavyhooved kine . . .'.[5] The unusual concatenation of a series of words of whatever kind (and we have seen Smollett doing this with nouns, adjectives, and different parts of verbs) results, from the very obtrusiveness of the material of language in such passages, in an effect of linguistic enforcement; it is a species of linguistic prodigality through which words are persuaded to reveal properties that tend to remain submerged in ordinary usage. When J. I. M. Stewart writes of Joyce's developing style that 'vocabulary, syntax, rhythm are now boldly varied to accentuate the contours of the underlying emotion, and Joyce is thus beginning to deploy his resources as a master of imitative form',[6] we may consider how readily such a description might be applied to the style Smollett has evolved for his own pressing purposes, 150 years previously. It is a significant artistic achievement, which, far from suggesting the 'fallacy of imitative form' of Yvor Winters's analysis,[7] actually asserts the *fact* of imitative form, the degree of syntactic flexibility that a truly expressive style will both require and justify.

There are several other passages one could take from Bramble's letters to provide further illustration of this style of concentrated rendering; for example, the letter from Bath (8 May) describing the physical ordeal of attending a ball, or the earlier letter (28 April) in which Bramble communicates his abhorrence at the thought of bathing in and drinking the Bath waters with an intensity that is quite remarkable. But I will restrict myself here to a consideration of Bramble's third letter from London (8 June), in which Smollett provides an account of the physical conditions of the capital—particularly with regard to its food—so livid and astonishing that one cannot help wondering why it is not better known as an object lesson in the capabilities of English prose in this direction: the registering of physical impressions in concrete terms. Bramble sets out with his usual reference to the body, the matrix of all sense impressions and therefore of taste. 'What kind of taste and organs must those people have, who really prefer the adulterate enjoyments of the town to the genuine pleasures of a country retreat? . . . their very organs of sense are perverted, and they become habitually lost to every relish of what is genuine and excellent in its own nature' (p. 118). Then, after first establishing his rural ideal, he goes on to elaborate on London's deficiencies. The water is as bad as in Bath:

> If I would drink water, I must quaff the maukish contents of an open aqueduct, exposed to all manner of defilement; or swallow that which comes from the river Thames, impregnated with all the filth of London and Westminster—Human excrement is the least offensive part of the concrete, which is composed of all the drugs, minerals, and poisons, used in mechanics and manufacture, enriched with the putrefying carcases of beasts and men; and mixed with the scourings of all the wash-tubs, kennels, and common sewers, within the bills of mortality. [p. 120]

The wine is 'a vile, unpalatable, and pernicious sophistication, balderdashed with cyder, corn-spirit, and the juice of sloes', the bread 'a deleterious paste, mixed up with chalk, alum, and bone-ashes; insipid to the taste, and destructive to the constitution'. Again it is the unrelenting particularity of the description that brings the facts vividly home to us: Smollett provides his resentment with all the authenticity of a catalogue. The vetegables are 'produced in an artificial soil, and taste of nothing but the dunghills, from whence they spring'. The meat is neither lamb nor mutton, but something betwixt the two, gorged in the rank fens of Lincoln and Essex, pale, coarse, and frowsy—As for the pork, it is an abominable carnivorous animal, fed with horse-flesh and distillers grains . . .

The anonymous character of the meat itself is, as it were, compensated by the verbal identification to which Smollett submits it. The fish travels upwards of a hundred miles to the markets, and is rotten before it is sold; oysters are kept live in slime pots, 'and that green colour, so much admired by the voluptuaries of this metropolis, is occasioned by the vitriolic scum, which rises on the surface of the stagnant and stinking water'.

The prose then rises to its peak in Smollett's description of that very English summer delicacy, strawberries and cream.

It must be owned, that Covent-garden affords some good fruit; which, however, is always engrossed by a few individuals of over-grown fortune, at an exorbitant price; so that little else than the refuse of the market falls to the share of the community; and that is distributed by such filthy hands, as I cannot look at without loathing. It was but yesterday that I saw a dirty barrow-bunter in the street, cleaning her dusty fruit with her own spittle; and, who knows but some fine lady of St. James's parish might admit into her delicate mouth those very cherries, which had been rolled and moistened between the filthy, and, perhaps, ulcerated chops of a St. Giles's huckster—I need not dwell upon the pallid, contaminated mash, which they call strawberries; soiled and tossed by greasy paws through twenty baskets crusted with dirt; and then presented with the worst milk, thickened with the worst flour, into a bad likeness of cream: but the milk itself should not pass unanalysed, the produce of faded cabbage-leaves and sour draff, lowered with hot water, frothed with bruised snails, carried through the streets in open pails, exposed to foul rinsings, discharged from doors and windows, spittle, snot, and tobacco-quids from foot-passengers, overflowings from mud-carts, spatterings from coach-wheels, dirt and trash chucked into it by roguish boys for the joke's-sake, the spewings of infants, who have slabbered in the tin-measure, which is thrown back in that condition among the milk, for the benefit of the next customer; and, finally, the vermin that drops from the rags of the nasty drab that vends this precious mixture, under the respectable denomination of milk-maid. [pp. 121–2]

Smollett's contempt for the depravity of London is tele-scoped in this fantasy of physical loathing, finds concrete articulation in this close, minute description of the actually disgusting. The effect is prepared for by the strong personal emphasis: 'such filthy hands, as *I cannot look at* without loath-ing', which becomes not only highly personal but also highly specific in the next sentence ('It was but yesterday that I saw . . .'). This appeal to an instance reminds us of the 'long conversation with the Doctor' on the basis of which Bramble launched his attack on the Bath waters earlier. If, as Ian Watt maintains, the importance of the novel in the eighteenth century is related to new assumptions about the uniqueness and validity of individual experience, then nowhere is indi-vidual experience—of a certain kind—more guaranteed than here.

The particularity is kept up, and supported by Smollett's ability to develop upon the immediate experience with a literal intensity as Bramble imagines 'those very cherries' being consumed by an unsuspecting customer. And we may pause to notice Smollett's superbly judged choice of words here: the 'delicate mouth' of the 'fine lady of St James's parish', identified with labial, dental, and palatal conson-ants, and short vowels, is contrasted with the 'ulcerated chops of a St Giles's huckster', in which phrase the vowels are appropriately open and coarse, and the consonants harsher, produced from further back in the mouth. Bram-ble's stated intention not to dwell on the strawberries is at least partly rhetorical, since he goes on to describe the fruit in a memorable phrase ('pallid, contaminated mash') that calls the name itself into question, and then gives a vivid picture of how it is handled. The verb 'soiled' gains an extra emphasis from its position before 'tossed', suggesting that the function of contaminating the strawberries takes prece-dence over the apparent purpose of transporting them. And the adjectival qualification continues at the 'super-specific' level with 'greasy paws' and 'twenty baskets crusted with dirt'—where in less strenuous writing we might simply have had 'baskets', or even the more remote 'containers'.

After this Smollett directs his extraordinary intensity of observation to the milk, and drives towards the climax of the passage with the promise that this 'should not pass un-anlaysed'. And indeed it does not; the milk seems to curdle before our eyes as the physical reality of the liquid itself and the circumstances of its vending are precipitated in an astonishing way by the density and sheer power of the prose. One need not dwell here on the way each noun is once again galvanised by an adjective or adjectival phrase, or the way each disgusting additive is duly traced back to a specific source; although I must remark that the verbal nouns ('rinsings', 'overflowings', 'spatterings', 'spewings') are very unusual in the plural form, and testify to the urgency of Smollett's need to express the relevant meaning. But let us turn our attention to the syntactical structure of this long sentence, which is almost overturned by the jostle of the detail it includes. The sentence is sustained not by any lucid and balanced arrangement—any 'sweet falling of the clauses' would be out of place here—but by the successive iteration of offences (like the returning waves of his own nausea) with which Bramble completes his demonstration. Smollett has used only a succession of commas throughout the sentence, as far as 'the next customer'; he then gathers himself (or Bramble) with a semi-colon, and pumps the last detail into the passage—'the vermin that drops from the rags of the nasty drab'—with a heavy monosyllabic emphasis, slowed down to accumulate the maximum expressive effect, and to load every syllable with its share of insistent meaning. It is as if Bramble is trying to shake himself free of this filth by containing it so adequately in words; there is something in the broad 'a' sounds that has the very quiver of revulsion. The slight encroachment of irony towards the end ('for the benefit of the next customer', 'under the respectable denomination of milk-maid') cannot alter the tone of the passage, which remains a miracle of passionate particularity and enacted meaning, exhibiting language at its most fruit-fully obedient to the imagination—indeed, as *part* of the imagination, a true root of cognisance.

What is the status of such description? This is an interesting and possibly inexhaustible question, and one which—if
only because it is so often evaded—I must take up for a
moment here. It was a commonplace of eighteenth-century
criticism to distinguish between description and expression,
as if it had never occurred to anyone to imagine that the two
might be compatible. Steele had argued about the relative
virtues of approaching passion internally or externally (in
the drama) in these terms:

> The way of common writers in this kind is rather the description
> than the expression of sorrow. There is no medium in these
> attempts, and you must go to the very bottom of the heart, or it is
> all mere language; and the writer of such lines is no more a poet,
> than a man is a physician for knowing the names of distempers,
> without the causes of them.[8]

Description is 'mere language'. The disparagement is
interesting, and seems to imply that expression, if achieved,
will be something other than 'mere language', and not
amenable to critical discussion. Likewise Burke distinguishes
in his *Enquiry* between what he calls a 'clear expression' and
a 'strong expression':

> The former regards the understanding; the latter belongs to the
> passions. The one describes a thing as it is; the other describes it as
> it is felt . . . We yield to sympathy, what we refuse to description.
> The truth is, all verbal description, merely as naked description,
> though never so exact, conveys so poor and insufficient an idea of
> the thing described, that it could scarcely have the smallest effect,
> if the speaker did not call in to his aid those modes of speech that
> mark a strong and lively feeling in himself.[9]

It is obvious that Smollett's prose bridges the gap which is
differently described here—a gap which might ultimately (if
not very usefully) be seen to open between the overworked
concepts objective and subjective in criticism. His prose does
not fit either of Burke's categories, since it succeeds in combining both clarity *and* strength; we yield to sympathy *and*

description; Smollett's exact and 'naked description' is given a posture, an attitude, by the kind of rhetorical heightening Burke considered necessary for the proper effectiveness of prose. And to revert to Steele's terms: Smollett is both the physician who knows the names of distempers and also the poet who goes 'to the very bottom of the heart'—with nothing more than 'mere language' as his means of access.

The combination of these qualities is no doubt a rare thing. How rare we may easily appreciate if we compare any other representative descriptions of Bath or London at the time with what we get in *Clinker*. For example, compare Smollett's description of Vauxhall Gardens in Bramble's letter dated 29 May (p. 89) with Goldsmith's satire on Vauxhall in his *Citizen of the World*:[10] the one typically forceful and concrete, the other disappointingly generalised and abstract. There is a total contrast of urgency and purpose between the two.

But there lurks a more fundamental difficulty than can be coped with by such an assertion. There is a suspicious tendency for criticism when faced with prose which does, demonstrably, combine the two qualities of description and expression to ignore the actual words in which this is achieved—the 'mere language'—and attend to the 'things' themselves. (This is exactly what Locke warned against in his *Essay*, the mistaking of words for things; though whereas Locke was defending the thing against the word I find it necessary here to defend the word against the thing.) In this way the essential critical process is neatly elided. An anonymous early critic of Chaucer gave way to this temptation when he wrote:

> His langage was so fayr and pertynente
> It semeth unto mannys heerynge
> Not only the worde, but verely the thynge.[11]

This popular but ultimately misleading parallel—a parallel in which one term effectively swallows the other—is utilised by an early critic of the *Travels*, who says that Smollett 'mentions some nasty customs of both the French and Italians

with such energy of description as excite [*sic*] a nausea equal
to what could have been raised by the real presence of the
objects described'.[12]

Now it is true that Bramble himself makes comparable
observations while writing his letters. On one occasion he
says, 'I have written till my fingers are crampt, and my
nausea begins to return' (23 April; p. 37)—the nausea he has
felt at the grossness of society at Bath; and when writing of
the Harrogate water he protests, 'I can hardly mention it
without puking' (26 June; p. 163). But whereas this is accept-
able from Bramble himself, who is able to recall the actual
experience, it is inconsistent from us as readers, whose only
experience of *this* phenomenon is in *these* words. If we focus
on 'the thynge' rather than 'the worde', or 'the real presence
of the objects described' rather than the description, then we
are in effect ignoring *this* experience (of words) and transferring our attention—however unconsciously—to some other
analogous experience (of things), which must remain a
seductive irrelevance.

Of course I am not arguing that we can 'experience' words
without the experiences through which we learn, originally,
what they mean. There is no language without a context;
without life. But words do not surrender themselves, as we
read, to our memory of like events any more than they first
offer themselves to the writer as a simple by-product of his
own experience. The language remains; it retains, as created
symbol, the significance which cannot inhere (for any except
its participators) in the original event. And here I would like
to quote what W. K. Wimsatt has to say about the ontological
status of poetry in an essay from *The Verbal Icon*: words
which apply to verbal composition of any kind. Wimsatt is
trying to disentangle literature from false and distracting
parallels with the other arts:

From such notions proceed at the level of theory the various
injustices to the medium, the invalid analogies, the metaphoric
fallacies, and at the level of practice the imbecilities of verbal
medium, to which we have alluded in our brief historical survey. It
is necessary to expose oneself to the charge of being paradoxical.

For poetry approximates the intuitive sensuous condition of paint and music not by being less verbal, less characteristic of verbal expression, but actually by being more than usually verbal, by being hyperverbal. Poetry achieves concreteness, particularity, and something like sensuous shape not by irrelevance of local texture, in its meter or in its images . . . but by extra relevance or hyperrelevance, the interrelational density of words taken in their fullest, most inclusive and symbolic character. A verbal composition, through being supercharged with significance, takes on something like the character of a stone statue or a porcelain vase. Through its meaning or meanings the poem *is*. It has an iconic solidity.[13]

This, then, is how the concreteness and particularity of Smollett's style might be properly recognised; not in the 'things' it deals with, but in its 'more than usually verbal', its 'hyperverbal', texture: in the words taken (as Smollett certainly offered them) in 'their fullest, most inclusive and symbolic character'.

III

So far in this chapter I have examined only physical description, which might be considered among the simpler functions of prose, even if it is also true that some of the most complex critical questions arise in this area. But if, as we have seen, intense apprehension of the physical excites Smollett's prose to new descriptive and expressive possibilities, it is nevertheless situations of more explicit moral import that provide its typical impetus. (I am aware that in creating this distinction I am temporarily distorting the picture, or at least selecting my own perspective on Smollett's prose; but this is simply for the purpose of arrangement, and these categories will be seen to flow into each other before the end.)

It is the political and domestic situation in France that occasions some of Smollett's most emphatic moral statements in his early novels. It is in the following terms that Roderick registers his disgust at the devotion of a French soldier to the service of an absolute monarch:

When I looked upon the contemptible object that pronounced these words, I was amazed at the infatuation that possessed him; and could not help expressing my astonishment at the absurdity of a rational being, who thinks himself highly honoured in being permitted to encounter abject poverty, oppression, famine, disease, mutilation, and evident death, merely to gratify the vicious ambition of a prince, by whom his sufferings were disregarded, and his name utterly unknown. [43; ii, 61–2]

It is significant that Roderick 'could not help expressing' his feelings on this subject, in very positive terms (whose rhetorical pattern is reflected in the indirect version given here); the compulsion is, of course, Smollett's own, and such passages as this help to fulfil his declared intention (in the preface) to incite 'that generous indignation which ought to animate the reader against the sordid and vicious disposition of the world'.

There is an inevitable incongruity in the fact that his second and more disreputable hero is allowed to be equally sensitive in this area. No sooner has Smollett transported Peregrine to France than he shows him to be 'amazed as well as disgusted' at the ignorant patiality of his tutor for that country, and lets him deliver a sustained and impassioned attack on the oppression of the ordinary people by the aristocratic class (41; p. 198). The accurate observation and precise information on which this attack is founded afford the raw material of moral protest, but it is once again the distinctive movement of the prose that works on this material, and 'animates' the strong feeling that lies behind it.

Those passages in *Fathom* and *Greaves* which fight clear of a narrative encumbrance which in no sense 'contains' them do so again by reason of their rhetorical effectiveness, their undeniable adequacy as embodiments of a vigorous moral attitude. (Some of these I have already cited when considering the formal properties of the novels themselves, in chapter three.) In such passages Smollett is writing from the centre, confiding in his reader those 'crusty humours, which, by retention, would grow intolerably acrimonious'. We are not surprised, therefore, at the intrusion of the first

person singular, as when Smollett observes of the paradoxical success of the quack Joshua Ward that it might by 'some
modern moralists, be ascribed to the innate virtue and
generosity of the human heart, which naturally espouses the
cause that needs protection: But I, whose notions of human
excellence are not quite so sublime, am apt to believe it is
owing to that spirit of self-conceit and contradiction, which
is, at least, as universal, if not as natural, as the moral sense
so warmly contended for by those ideal philosophers'
(*Fathom*, 53; p. 263). And in *Greaves* it is clearly Smollett
himself, undistracted by the persona of his quixotic hero,
who reviles 'the crazed Tory and the bigot Whig' in the
celebrated election chapter (chapter 9), who attacks the evils
of the private asylum (23, p. 190), and inveighs—through
Ferret this time—against the imbecility of the Hanoverian
policies of George II (2, p. 15).

The centre asserts its gravitational pull even in the *Atom*.
Here it is the expressive power of Smollett's imagery which
enables certain attitudes to evade the ironic strategy of the
narrative as a whole. The pathetic Newcastle earns no significant image; he is unqualifiably comic (as indeed he is in
his reapearance in *Clinker*). But Anson's vanity provokes
Smollett to see him 'selfish, inelegant, arrogant, and
uncouth', as 'a Lapland idol of ice, adorned with a profusion
of brass leaf and trinkets of pewter' (i, 53–4). The lawyers
Hardwicke and Mansfield are even more severely treated.
The former has a mean, legalistic mind that obliterates all the
possibilities of life, and Smollett cuts him down again with
negatives ('he had neither genius to enlighten his understanding, sentiment to elevate his mind, nor courage to surmount the petty enclosures of ordinary practice'); 'he knew
not the use of wealth', says Smollett, 'and therefore did not
use it at all'; finally annihilating him as 'neither better nor
worse than a strong box for the convenience and advantage
of his heir' (i, 46–7). Mansfield is more formidable. The Atom
has circulated through his body, where 'I found the brain so
full and compact, that there was not room for another particle of matter. But instead of a heart, he had a membranous
sac, or hollow viscus, cold and callous, the habitation of

sneaking caution, servile flattery, griping avarice, creeping malice, and treacherous deceit' (i, 162). The adjective is no mere 'essential epithet' here, but does genuinely bring the quality it defines into sharper moral relief. Hanover itself—the cause of all the trouble—is 'a pernicious excrescence, which, like an ulcerated tumour, exhausted the juices of the body by which it was fed'. Finally, Bute's Cabinet consists of 'sauntering, strolling, vagrant and ridiculous politicians. Their schemes were absurd, and their deliberations were like the sketches of anarchy' (i, 68); which dense metaphorical phrase is comparable to Dryden's conception of the 'shapeless lump, like Anarchy' in *Absalom and Achitophel*.[14]

There is one particular idea recurring in the *Atom*—indeed, it is a theme of the work—which always tightens the sinews of Smollett's style, and thus claims its central significance. This is the idea that all human actions are in a sense equivocal, equally dependent on an indifferent informing energy:

> The same ambition can destroy or save,
> And makes a patriot as it makes a knave.[15]

It is a relativistic notion from which it is possible to draw demoralising conclusions (as Swift does in *A Tale of a Tub*), though it can also be used (as it is on the other hand by Pope in his *Essay on Man*) simply to clear the ground for a restatement of basic moral positions. But whatever purpose it serves, the idea is the result of penetrating moral consideration, the kind of thing that stimulates the style of the centre; and here is Smollett's version.

> We at different times behold the same spirit hunted down in a hare, and cried up in an Hector; fawning in a prostitute, and bribing in a minister; breaking forth in a whistle at the plough, and in a sermon from the pulpit; impelling a hog to the stye, and a counsellor to the cabinet; prompting a shoe-boy to filch, and a patriot to harangue; squinting in a goat, and smiling in a matron. [i, 23]

This is a transference to the moral sphere of the idea the *Atom* has outlined earlier in a physical context, that 'Of the

same shape, substance, and quality are the component particles, that harden in rock, and flow in water; that blacken in
the negro, and brighten in the diamond; that exhale from a
rose, and steam from a dunghill' (i, 3).

Images like these are like shafts to the centre, direct witness to the strength of Smollett's feeling and agents of its
expression. But even they are not essential. Such feeling can
erupt in different ways, and the remarkable thing about the
Travels (that 'study in calculated depreciation', as Seccombe
justly called it) is the way Smollett for the most part disdains
figurative language, and sustains his attack on the French
and Italians with the infinite resource of his supremely
emphatic statement alone; which simply sets out to acceler-
ate our sense of things 'as they are'. The same technique that
enabled him to bring alive their physical reality serves to
convey the moral experience of his travels abroad; the
'literalist of the imagination' can work in the moral as well as
the material world. All kinds of injustice are resented with
characteristic vigour in the *Travels*, from the unfair practices
of tradesmen—'One would imagine the French were still at
war with the English, for they pillage them without mercy'
(1, p. 8)—and the 'scandalous imposition' of the royal posts
(8, p. 69) to the demoralising partiality of French law and
the degeneracy of duelling. Smollett quotes an example of
the former (4, pp. 26–7) which recalls those instances of
arbitrariness which so offended Peregrine; and spends a
whole letter exposing 'the absurd and pernicious custom of
duelling' which concludes with the grotesque exploit of Vil-
liers, Duke of Buckingham, who, 'not content with having
debauched the countess of Shrewsbury and publishing her
shame', provoked the earl to combat, killed him, and then,
'elated with his exploit, set out immediately for the earl's
seat at Cliefden, where he lay with his wife, after having
boasted of the murder of her husband, whose blood he
shewed her upon his sword, as a trophy of his prowess' (15;
pp. 139–41). The bare details of such a story are image
enough, without any other enforcement, of the moral
depravity which is Smollett's consistent target in this work.

But it is for the French character itself, male and female,

that Smollett reserves the compliment of his most concentrated contempt. The denigration is once again securely founded on close detail: the *noblesse* of Boulogne 'allow their country houses to go to decay, and their gardens and fields to waste; and reside in dark holes in the Upper Town of Boulogne without light, air, or convenience. There they starve within doors, that they may have wherewithal to purchase fine cloaths, and appear dressed once a day in church, or on the rampart. They have no education, no taste for reading, no housewifery, nor indeed any earthly occupation, but that of dressing their hair, and adorning their bodies. They hate walking, and would never go abroad, if they were not stimulated by the vanity of being seen'. This kind of observation and relation provides the basis for Smollett's summary: 'I know not a more insignificant set of mortals than the noblesse of Boulogne; helpless in themselves, and useless to the community; without dignity, sense, or sentiment; contemptible from pride, and ridiculous from vanity' (4; pp. 27–8). The right to make such a decisive statement is asserted by the way it is made—a justification which Smollett regularly provides for his assaults.

There is a powerful rhythmic impetus in a later passage where Smollett has shifted his attention to the Italian women whose customs he has been observing in Florence and learning about from Goldoni's comedies. 'For my part,' declares Smollett, 'I would rather be condemned for life to the gallies, then exercise the office of a cicisbeo, exposed to the intolerable caprices and dangerous resentment of an Italian virago. I pretend not to judge of the national character, from my own observation: but, if the portraits drawn by Goldoni in his Comedies are taken from nature, I would not hesitate to pronounce the Italian women the most haughty, insolent, capricious, and revengeful females on the face of the earth' (27; p. 231). With the hint of the last phrase, is it not reasonable to find in the rhythm of this sentence the ghost of a celebrated denunciation from Smollett's acknowledged master, Swift? ' . . . I cannot but conclude the Bulk of your Natives, to be the most pernicious Race of little odious Vermin that Nature ever suffered to crawl upon the Surface of the Earth'.[16] The measure of the announced 'conclusion' or 'pronouncement', the subject, the actual terms of the description (in which the metre—as one might almost call it—is identical) and the distinctive concluding phrase amount to a resemblance that is too close to be fortuitous. Just as Johnson when he wrote the line 'They mount, they shine, evaporate, and fall'[17] must have been thinking of Pope's 'In vain! they gaze, turn giddy, rave, and die',[18] so Smollett may well have written this with the rhythm of Swift's sentence echoing in his mind.

We have already seen what is most characteristic of Bramble's expression in *Clinker*. The moral, for him, seems to be adequately expressed in the physical; there is no need for further comment. But there are a number of personal portraits to which Bramble brings his decisive powers of judgement and expression. Mr Pimpernel the attorney 'is not only a sordid miser in his disposition, but his avarice is mingled with a spirit of despotism, which is truly diabolical—He is a brutal husband, an unnatural parent, a harsh master, an oppressive landlord, a litigious neighbour, and a partial magistrate' (26 June; p. 171): it is noticeable how Smollett harnesses his adjectives each to a particular noun, to prevent any degeneration to the merely expletive. And his analysis of Mrs Baynard's character, similarly, *is* an analysis, not simply the expression of undifferentiated dislike. Her vanity is 'not that species which arises from self-conceit of superior accomplishments, but that which is of a bastard and idiot nature, excited by shew and ostentation, which implies not even the least consciousness of any personal merit'; her extravagance ensures that 'every article of house-keeping, even the most inconsiderable, was brought from the next market town, at the distance of five miles, and thither they sent a courier every morning to fetch hot rolls for breakfast' (30 September; pp. 287, 292). Indeed, her character appears most palpably in the survey of the despoiled estate (it is significant that Bramble says of his friend Baynard that 'the detail which he gave me of his affairs, filled me at once with grief and indignation': p. 292) and in the description of her frigid hospitality, where the moral and physical response become inseparable. This forms the third of my categories, which may be conveniently introduced here.

IV

I have found it convenient thus far to maintain a distinction, in considering Smollett's prose, according to whether he is concerned with physical phenomena or moral experience. This is, however, an artificial distinction, adapted as much (I hope) in my reader's interest as my own, to create one of those 'Divisions in Authors' without which, says Fielding, a volume 'resembles the opening of Wilds or Seas, which tires the Eye and fatigues the Spirit when entered upon'.[19] But I do also believe that some light may thereby have been thrown on Smollett's habits of thought and expression; and that we shall be able to observe an acceleration of energy in his combination of the two subjects: the turbulent place where two currents run together.

Because, of course, the currents do run together. It was a habit of thought which the eighteenth century had inherited to see physical form as a figuring forth of moral reality, and it became part of the strategy of Augustan satire in particular to emphasise the connection. The second book of *The Dunciad* and the fourth book of *Gulliver's Travels* are typical examples (in their different ways) of how the relation was developed; and almost any of the satirical portraits in Dryden and Swift and Pope—and Churchill and Wolcot—will bear witness to its telling effect. But as we would expect, when Smollett implicitly identifies the physical and the moral sense in his writing it is no mere observance of convention. The relation was a matter of profound instinct with him, as we know from the evidence of his own temperament. Smollett was unusually conscious of the 'subtile knot' uniting mind and body, and alludes to it frequently both in the *Travels* and in *Clinker*, where Bramble bears witness continually to the physiological ingredients of moral feeling.

Smollett had an intimate sense, then, of the rightness of this relation; it was a matter of poetic truth to him, something he had 'proved upon the pulse', and something which

lay at the root of his fertile analogical faculty. It waits like a
tight spring at the very centre of his style, ready to release its
impetus and urge his prose to a climax of irresistible statement. Such statement occurs already in his first novel. The
'History of Miss Williams' concludes with a merciless simplification of the prostitute's progress:

'I have often seen (said she) while I strolled about the streets at
mid-night, a number of naked wretches reduced to rags and filth,
huddled together like swine, in the corner of a dark alley; some of
whom, but eighteen months before, I had known the favourites of
the town, rolling in affluence, and glittering in all the pomp of
equipage and dress.'—And indeed the gradation is easily conceived; the most fashionable woman of the town is as liable to
contagion, as one in a much humbler sphere; she infects her
admirers, her situation is publick, she is avoided, neglected,
unable to support her usual appearance, which however she
strives to maintain as long as possible; her credit fails, she is
obliged to retrench and become a night-walker, her malady gains
ground, she tampers with her constitution and ruins it; her complexion fades, she grows nauseous to every body, finds herself
reduced to a starving condition, is tempted to pick pockets, is
detected, committed to Newgate, where she remains in a miserable
condition, 'till she is discharged because the plaintiff appears not to
prosecute her. No body will afford her lodging, the symptoms of
her distemper are grown outrageous, she sues to be admitted into
a hospital, where she is cured at the expence of her nose; she is
turned out naked into the streets, depends upon the addresses of
the canaille, is fain to allay the rage of hunger and cold with gin,
degenerates into a state of brutal insensibility, rots and dies upon a
dunghill. [23; i, 216–7]

I describe this as 'merciless' because the emotion which lies
behind this revelation is that anger which refuses to compromise itself as mere compassion; there is an obvious fasci-
nation at the brutal facts of prostitution here which will not
be distracted by moral platitudes. Smollett relies upon a
stark relation of the facts themselves to articulate the moral
attitude. Such writing does not serve a 'moral attitude' in
any conventional sense (we may notice that Smollett does
not try to apportion blame) but simply—what is the most

moral of all our acts—an act of imagination; which from its very intensity disallows all 'refuge from moral cognition'.

The 'facts themselves ' are at once simplified and accelerated; syntactical organisation (as in Swift's catalogues) is reduced to a minimum, as the impetus of the passage—reflecting the fearful inevitability of the prostitute's fate—proceeds uninterrupted by clausal dependance. Even the customary pronoun is often omitted before the successive verbs that drive the woman to her destruction. The energy is all a matter of verbs, moving in the bare context of her existence; the passive form 'is avoided . . . is obliged . . . is detected . . . is charged . . . is cured . . . is turned out' giving way in the end to the more expressive active voice: 'degenerates . . . rots and dies'. And the unexpected order of these last two verbs is a final grotesque effect: the prostitute rots physically (as well as morally) *before* she dies.[20]

If we return to *Clinker*, and Mrs Baynard, we can see how Bramble's wholehearted contempt for this worthless woman is once again sharply focused by its visible effects, which are related with an unrelenting demonstrativeness. Baynard's estate is despoiled as a result of her ignorance, and Bramble's indignation is conveyed in the details he gives of it. 'The tall oaks that shaded the avenue, had been cut down, and the iron gates at the end of it removed, together with the high wall that surrounded the court yard . . . As for the garden, which was well stocked with the best fruit which England could produce, there is not now the least vestige remaining of trees, walls, or hedges—Nothing appears but a naked circus of loose sand, with a dry bason and a leaden triton in the middle.'[21] This she later converts to a lake: 'the bottom of the bason, however, was so ill secured, that it would not hold the water, which strained through the earth, and made a bog of the whole plantation' (30 September; pp. 285–6, 292).

This image of futile activity is paralleled by the life Baynard is obliged to lead: 'he is hurried about in a perpetual tumult, amidst a mob of beings pleased with rattles, baubles, and gew-gaws, so void of sense and distinction, that even the most acute philosophy would find it a very hard task to discover for what wise purpose of providence they were created—Friendship is not to be found; nor can the amusements for which he sighs be enjoyed within the rotation of absurdity, to which he is doomed for life' (pp. 289–90). The particularised 'mob', and the appeal to the 'wise purpose of providence' (the same authority Smollett invoked to account for the rare Frenchman of worth) lead up to the fine phrase that summarises his situation, as a 'rotation of absurdity'.

But it is the dinner that occasions the most successful essay in disparagement. The duties of hospitality are performed as a disgusting pantomime:

At dinner, the lady maintained the same ungracious indifference, never speaking but in whispers to her aunt; and as to the repast, it was made up of a parcel of kickshaws, contrived by a French cook, without one substantial article adapted to the satisfaction of an English appetite. The pottage was little better than bread soaked in dishwashings, lukewarm. The ragouts looked as if they had been once eaten and half digested: the fricassees were involved in a nasty yellow poultice; and the rotis wre scorched and stinking, for the honour of the fumet. The desert consisted of faded fruit and iced froth, a good emblem of our landlady's character; the table-beer was sour, the water foul, and the wine vapid; but there was a parade of plate and china, and a powdered lacquey stood behind every chair, except those of the master and mistress of the house, who were served by two valets dressed like gentlemen. [p. 295]

The effectiveness of this passage is founded (as so often in Smollett) in the simultaneous accuracy and expressiveness of the words themselves, which are then accentuated by the distinctive phrasing and rhythm. 'Kickshaw' (derived from the French *quelque-chose*) is as contemptuous in its sound and signification as the diminutive 'parcel' that qualifies it; the 'nasty yellow poultice' is a concentrated image of disgust, and the 'faded fruit and iced froth' of derision. Each noun is specifically qualified: 'the table-beer was sour, the water foul, the wine vapid'; it is the uncompromising particularity of Smollett's prose that rightly earns our confidence and admiration. In proposing that the dessert is 'a good emblem

of our landlady's character' Bramble himself endorses the
point I am making. The details throughout this letter are
charged with significance, and act both as images for her and
as 'objective correlatives' for the intense indignation her
destructive vanity arouses in a man like Bramble, whose
complicated strands of thought and feeling go to create what
Smollett would himself understand by a fully human
response.

The theme of Bramble's most consistent moral complaint
throughout *Clinker*, his hatred of the mob and lamentation
for the ruins of good order, always occasions the same concentration of response in Smollett's prose. I have already
looked at one passage taken up with this theme—that where
Bramble attacks the 'luxury and extravagance' of Bath—in
chapter five. The metaphors Smollett uses here ('flood of
luxury and extravagance', 'sink of profligacy and extortion',
'mushroom of opulence') as well as the definitive phrases
('the very rabble and refuse of mankind') function by making
the physical term—flood, sink, mushroom, refuse—active
and meaningful in the moral sphere. This transfer of terms to
achieve more emphatic statement occurs earlier when Bramble complains of 'the general tide of luxury, which hath
overspread the nation, and swept away all, even the very
dregs of the people. Every upstart of fortune, harnessed in
the trappings of the mode, presents himself at Bath, as in the
very focus of observation . . .' (23 April; p. 36). The metaphor
'harnessed in the trappings of the mode' recalls Smollett's
earlier use of *le mythe animal*, which is developed later in this
same letter where Bramble observes how 'Even the wives
and daughters of low tradesmen, who, like shovel-nosed
sharks, prey upon the blubber of those uncouth whales of
fortune, are infected with the same rage of displaying their
importance; and the slightest indisposition serves them for a
pretext to insist upon being conveyed to Bath, where they
may hobble country-dances and cotillons among lordlings,
'squires, counsellors, and clergy'. This brings us back to the
pervasive image of the crowd, which is equally available to
physical or moral emphasis.

Such is the composition of what is called the fashionable company at Bath; where a very inconsiderable proportion of genteel
people are lost in a mob of impudent plebeians, who have neither
understanding nor judgment, nor the least idea of propriety and
decorum; and seem to enjoy nothing so much as an opportunity of
insulting their betters . . . This, I own, is a subject on which I
cannot write with any degree of patience; for the mob is a monster
I never could abide, either in its head, tail, midriff, or members: I
detest the whole of it, as a mass of ignorance, presumption, malice,
and brutality; and, in this term of reprobation, I include, without
respect of rank, station, or quality, all those of both sexes, who
affect its manners, and court its society. [p. 37]

This is one point at which Bramble's 'nausea begins to
return' as he writes; Smollett lets the complication of offence
here operate physically on the sensitive character he has set
on to observe it.

If *Clinker* provides, in Bramble's letters, examples of the
style of the centre at its most fused and final, we may return
to the *Travels* for evidence of how this fusion takes place, and
to consider some further examples with which this exercise
will be concluded. It was in the *Travels* that Smollett finally
harnessed together the different capabilities of his central
style—for physical description, and moral statement—to
achieve that unexampled vigour so characteristic of his later
work. The concerted attack on French manners in the fifth
letter begins with the observation that 'If there is no cleanliness among these people, much less shall we find delicacy,
which is the cleanliness of the mind' (p. 35). The phrase
'cleanliness of the mind' makes quite explicit the way Smollett understood the physical senses and the moral sense to be
related. Lower down he writes of 'those usages which cannot fail giving disgust to the organs and senses of all mankind', and the word 'senses' here—more internal than
'organs'—must mean the organised response of the senses,
the sensibility. (One is bound to reflect that Shaftesbury's
metaphoric term 'moral sense' does allow for such an
interdependence between two of Pascal's 'orders'—an interdependence which is partly Philip Stevick's subject in his
entertaining article 'The Augustan nose'.)[22]

Certainly in the observations that follow the detail is heightened by the shocked sensibility which registers it—and renders it in prose which is at the same time emphatic and flexible, an instrument of expression finely adjusted to its purpose.

A true-bred Frenchman dips his fingers, imbrowned with snuff, into his plate filled with ragout: between every three mouthfuls, he produces his snuff-box, and takes a fresh pinch, with the most graceful gesticulations; then he displays his handkerchief, which may be termed the *flag of abomination*, and, in the use of both, scatters his favours among those who have the happiness to sit near him. It must be owned, however, that a Frenchman will not drink out of a tankard, in which, perhaps, a dozen of filthy mouths have slabbered, as is the custom in England. Here every individual has his own gobelet, which stands before him, and he helps himself occasionally with wine, or water, or both, which likewise stand upon the table. But I know no custom more beastly than that of using water-glasses, in which polite company spirt, and squirt, and spue the filthy scourings of their gums, under the eyes of each other. I knew a lover cured of his passion, by seeing this nasty cascade discharged from the mouth of his mistress. [p. 36]

The iterative verbs 'spirt, squirt, and spue' are a good example of the intensification in language of an impression registered with excitement; the mutual support in sound and sense (both progressive) creates an extra dimension of meaning. And the phrase 'nasty cascade' creates a comparable echo to the sense, with its broad 'a' sounds, making the lips quiver with revulsion; almost as if the force-fed language retches at the detail it is charged with.

Later, in Nice, Smollett is shocked by the degenerate morals of the *noblesse*, particularly the overt taking of a mistress by the husband and a *cicisbeo* by the wife after the Italian fashion; and he articulates his feelings by creating an image from his own observation which puts these scandalous activities in an appropriate physical context. 'Just without one of our gates, you will find them seated in ditches on the highway side, serenaded with the croaking of frogs, and the bells and braying of mules and asses continually passing in a

perpetual cloud of dust' (17; p. 154). Such a description—-
which becomes, as I say, an image—reminds us of the
reason for the effectiveness of Smollett's aspersion of the
French and Italians throughout this work: that it is rooted in
the actual, supported in its expression always by some relevant designation. When, for example, he wishes to castigate
the 'absurd luxury' of the French army he informs us that 'a
French general in the field is always attended by thirty or
forty cooks', and goes on to specify how 'when don Philip,
and the maréchal duke de Belleisle, had their quarters at
Nice, there were fifty scullions constantly employed in the
great square in plucking poultry' (36; p. 310). The simple
detail in such an observation is persuaded to function as the
actual agent of expression; there is an articulate tension in
the prose between fact and reaction. Smollett never 'blunders round about a meaning'[23] in the way he also (as an
admirer of Pope) would have despised, because of this very
instinct to locate his attitude in powerfully projected
actualities.

The most consistent opportunity Smollett has to identify
the two central incitements of his style is provided by the
inns of both France and Italy. Here 'abundance of dirt, and
the most flagrant imposition' manifest themselves together,
and Smollett's commentary on his accommodation abroad
exposes the degraded physical and moral standards he
encountered with unrelenting vividness and particularity.
His troubles begin in fact while he is still in England, on the
Dover road, which is 'the worst road in England, with
respect to the conveniences of travelling'. 'The chambers are
in general cold and comfortless, the beds paultry, the cookery execrable, the wine poison, the attendance bad, the pub-
licans insolent, and the bills extortion; there is not a drop of
tolerable malt liquor to be had from London to Dover' (1; p.
2).[24] Each noun is struck as a single emphatic note, and these
notes then submit to the harmonising effect of the last
extended clause. The cabin on the boat that transports him
and his party to France is similarly uninviting: 'the beds put
me in mind of the holes described in some catacombs, in
which the bodies of the dead were deposited, being thrust in

with feet foremost; there was no getting into them but end-
ways, and indeed they seemed so dirty, that nothing but
extreme necessity could have obliged me to use them' (p. 6).
And once he is in France the routine of disappointment is
quickly established. 'We found good accommodation at
Montreuil and Amiens; but in every other place where we
stopped, we met with abundance of dirt, and the most
flagrant imposition' (6; p. 44). At Joinville Smollett 'was
scandalously imposed upon, and even abused by a virago of
a landlady' (8; p. 73); at Montpellier the best inn in the town
turns out to be 'a most wretched hovel, the habitation of
darkness, dirt and imposition' (10; p. 91). At Brignolles he is
'obliged to quarrel with the landlady' because he 'was not
disposed to eat stinking fish, with ragouts of eggs and
onions' on a *jour maigre* (a fast day, when Catholics abstained
from meat); the next day, at 'a wretched town called Muy,
where we dined, I had a warm dispute with our landlord'
which ends with a threat of 'manual chastisement' and a visit
to the local magistrate (12; pp. 108–9). Smollett includes a
summary of his experiences with French inns in his last letter, and one cannot imagine that the prospective travellers to
whom it was addressed found it very encouraging reading.
'Through the whole south of France, except in large cities,
the inns are cold, damp, dark, dismal, and dirty; the landlords equally disobliging and rapacious; the servants aukward, sluttish, and slothful; and the postilions lazy, loung-
ing, greedy, and impertinent. If you chide them for linger-
ing, they will continue to delay you the longer: if you chas-
tise them with sword, cane, cudgel, or horse-whip, they will
either disappear entirely, and leave you without resource; or
they will find means to take vengeance by overturning your
carriage.' One is forced to admit that Smollett conducted his
research into the different possibilities with unusual determination. The only positive advice he can offer the traveller
is that he should allow himself 'to become the dupe of
imposition, and stimulate their efforts by extraordinary
gratifications' (41; pp. 340–1).

But the situation is even worse in Italy. The eleven letters
that cover Smollett's two-month journey down through

Florence to Rome and back are given a unity (one might almost say) by the motif of the uninhabitable inn, and by the reiterated execration of landlords. 'We ascended by a dark, narrow, steep stair, into a kind of public room, with a long table and benches, so dirty and miserable, that it would disgrace the worst hedge ale-house in England': this in what purports to be 'the best auberge in the whole Riviera of Genoa'. They take rooms here, however, and 'in that where I lay, there was just room for two beds, without curtains or bedstead, an old rotten table covered with dried figs, and a couple of crazy chairs. The walls had been once whitewashed: but were now hung with cobwebs, and speckled with dirt of all sorts; and I believe the brick-floor had not been swept for half a century' (25; p. 207). Smollett claims a couple of paragraphs later that Italy 'is the native country of hyperbole'; one is tempted to observe that he himself seems, not without provocation, to have contracted the national characteristic. After an indescribable supper at another inn he wakes up with 'above a dozen large bugs' crawling on his body, and spends the rest of the night wrapped in his greatcoat on top of a chest (25; p. 211).

At Capo di Levanti the 'landlord was a butcher, and had very much the looks of an assassin. His wife was a great masculine virago, who had all the air of having frequented the slaughter-house'—which incidentally brings a 'very offensive smell' to pervade the place. Smollett is glad to escape with his throat uncut (26; p. 219). At the post-house in Lerici 'the accommodation is intolerable': Smollett's party is 'almost poisoned at supper', and he himself finishes up once more on an improvised bed for the night (p. 220). They move inland. 'Of Sienna I can say nothing from my own observation, but that we were indifferently lodged in a house that stunk like a privy, and fared wretchedly at supper.' On the heels of this comes another vigorous dispute, and another visit to an equally disreputable magistrate (29; pp. 241–2). The inn at Radicofani is 'very large, very cold, and uncomfortable' (p. 243). 'I must tell you,' Smollett says of another adventure, 'that for a dinner and a supper, which even hunger could not tempt us to eat, and a night's lodging

in three truckle beds, I paid eighty pauls, amounting to forty
shillings sterling' (34; p. 293). Camoccia offers 'a miserable
cabaret, where we were fain to cook our own supper, and lay
in a musty chamber, which had never known a fire . . . and
where we ran the risque of being devoured by rats' (p. 296).
There is worse to come.

But all the nights we had hitherto passed were comfortable in
comparison to this, which we suffered at a small village, the name
of which I do not remember. The house was dismal and dirty
beyond all description; the bed-cloaths filthy enough to turn the
stomach of a muleteer; and the victuals cooked in such a manner,
that even a Hottentot could not have beheld them without loath-
ing. We had sheets of our own, which were spread upon a mat-
trass, and here I took my repose wrapped in a greatcoat, if that
could be called repose which was interrupted by the innumerable
stings of vermin. In the morning, I was seized with a dangerous fit
of hooping-cough, which terrified my wife, alarmed my people,
and brought the whole community into the house. [p. 297]

The superlatives pursue each other as Smollett goes on to
describe a house at Massa as 'in all respects one of the worst
we had yet entered' and record a forced return to another
lodging 'where we had been shamefully fleeced by the landlord, who, nevertheless, was not such an exorbitant knave as
the post-master, whose house I would advise all travellers to
avoid' (35; p. 303). At Finale they lodge in 'a very dismal
habitation' where 'the master of the house was a surly assassin, and his cameriere or waiter, stark-staring mad'; and at
their next port of call, predictably, 'we found the post-house
even worse than that of Finale'—this being the one where
lay the girl 'quite covered with the confluent small-pox . . .
who smelled so strong as to perfume the whole house' (pp.
305–6).
   One can discover a calculated imaginative acceleration in
Smollett's discovery of his misfortunes. Imposition becomes
extortion, vermin graduate from bugs to rats, dirt gives way
to smell; the smell of a slaughterhouse, the stink of a privy,
and finally the pervading odour of disease. Attendants
degenerate from the inattentive to the disobedient, the

obstructive, and the 'stark-staring mad'. One magistrate looks like a tailor, the next like 'a half-starved prisoner'; if one landlord has 'the looks of an assassin', then the next will be 'a surly assassin' without qualification. There is no bad that cannot be followed by a worse, no worse that will not be quickly superseded by a worst, no worst but will yield to futher extremes under the pressure of his erupting emphasis. Smollett presents himself arguing and threatening his way through France and Italy, till at the end we have a picture of him waiting for his bill 'with my sword in one hand and my cane in the other' (35; p. 305).

This complicated catalogue of ill usage reaches its climax in a summary he makes of his entertainment in Italy.

. . . as for the public houses, they are in all respects the most execrable that ever I entered. I will venture to say that a common prisoner in the Marshalsea or King's-Bench is more cleanly and commodiously lodged than we were in many places on this road. The houses are abominably nasty, and generally destitute of provision: when eatables were found, we were almost poisoned by their cookery: their beds were without curtains or bedstead, and their windows without glass; and for this sort of entertainment we payed as much as if we had been genteelly lodged, and sumptuously treated. I repeat it again; of all the people I ever knew, the Italians are the most villainously rapacious. [34; pp. 291–2]

'I repeat it again': the repetition is all part of the cumulative effect, part of the pull that draws this prose to the centre, part of the projection of his own powerful feelings in language that distinguishes Smollett's prose from the common level of competent expression which was the best the eighteenth century had (or thought it should have) to offer.

Commenting on Smollett's peculiar contribution to travel literature in his book *The Grand Tour in the Eighteenth Century,* W. E. Mead remarked very justly that 'One might easily gather from his pages a choice collection of vituperative adjectives, usually in the superlative degree, for he taxes the resources of language to express his disgust at the treatment he received from scoundrels of every sort'.[25] Mead is inclined to reprove him for this, but it seems to me that we have more to be grateful for in the way Smollett 'taxes the resources of language' than we would have had from a plainer and more judicial account. It was not in Smollett's nature, fortunately, to be moderate. We can be sure he would have repudiated the stylistic advice given by his more sober compatriot Hume to Gibbon: that he should 'reduce superlatives and soften positives'[26] in his writing. Smollett's whole nature directed him towards extremes rather than away from them and encouraged—or necessitated—that sharply defined contour of style for which his writing is so remarkable.

8   *The romantic style*

Considering the effects of Johnson's prose on the later eighteenth century, W. K. Wimsatt notes how outside his own circle 'the influence of Johnson is diffused and mingled with similar forces or shaded by the various motives that were working toward romantic prose'.[1] What I want to establish in this chapter is that these 'motives' are powerfully present in Smollett, and need to be recognised in any account of his prose style.

To begin with, it is surely relevant to remember that Smollett was the only one of the major eighteenth-century novelists who thought of himself seriously as a poet, and was recognised as such by his contemporaries. His first literary endeavour was a verse tragedy, *The Regicide*, written in 1739 when he was eighteen. He carried the play with him when he went to London later that year, dreaming of fame as a dramatist, and wasted a lot of energy and goodwill trying to get it performed. But although the play miscarried, Smollett persevered with his poetic ambitions. His first published works were poems: 'The Tears of Scotland', a protest poem on the atrocities committed by Cumberland's troops after Culloden, which became very well known;[2] and the two verse satires *Advice* and *Reproof*. And the significant thing is that, unlike Fielding, who gaily repented of his youthful poetic pretensions,[3] Smollett then continued to write poems—albeit few—throughout his career. Some of these (like the 'Ode to Leven Water') he inserted in his novels; some were set to music and achieved a degree of popularity as songs.[4] At one time negotiations were apparently in hand for Smollett to write a libretto for Handel, but this unfortunately came to nothing.[5] Curiously enough,

Smollett's last (posthumous) publication was also a poem, the celebrated 'Ode to Independence'.

Robert Burns himself was inspired by what he called 'these glorious verses'[6] of Smollett's, and we can get some idea of how highly Smollett was regarded as a poet from the very enthusiastic remarks with which Alexander Chalmers introduces him in his *Works of the English Poets:* 'although his pieces are few, they must be allowed to confer a very high rank'; the 'Ode to Independence' shows 'the inspiration of real genius, free from all artificial aid, or meretricious ornament'; this poem and 'The Tears of Scotland' 'are equal to the highest efforts in the pathetic and sublime'.[7] Goldsmith was one of the earliest writers to perceive that novelists might be what he called 'poets in disguise', and he actually cites Smollett as a writer whose prose work offered him more scope for the expression of his 'real genius' as a poet than could the writing of occasional poems.[8] And as well as recalling the views of Godwin and Hazlitt on Smollett's power of expression, to which I have referred earlier, we might here add the testimony of a mid-nineteenth-century critic, David Masson, who in an early and often rewarding book on the English novel discriminated between the styles of Fielding and Smollett in a way that is exactly consistent with my own analysis.

There is . . . a rhetorical strength of language in Smollett which Fielding rarely exhibits; a power of melodramatic effect to which Fielding does not pretend; and a greater constitutional tendency to the sombre and the terrible. There was potentially more of the poet in Smollett than in Fielding; and there are more passages in his writings approaching nearer, both in feeling and rhythm, to lyric beauty.[9]

I shall be considering some such passages in a moment, in an attempt to justify Masson's adventurous criticism. The alternative to the images that fly off from the superficies of things need not be all sour and dregs; and it is with some account of the permeation of Smollett's style by the new mood and movement we associate with romanticism that I will conclude this study.

II

It would be appropriate to look first at some of the experimental stylistic effects in *Fathom*, since some of these at least have always commanded a footnote in the literary histories. *Fathom* has often been cited as an early example of the Gothic mode in fiction, containing (in 1753) elements that were to be more systematically exploited by the opportunist Walpole in *The Castle of Otranto*—itself regarded as some kind of harbinger—twelve years later. These include the episode in which Fathom is benighted in 'a forest far from the habitations of men' and narrowly escapes assassination in a cottage where he takes refuge (chapters 20 and 21), the account of the seduction of Celinda—achieved to the accompaniment of an Aeolian harp—(chapter 34), and the two scenes towards the end where Renaldo conducts his 'rites of sorrow' at Monimia's tomb before she is restored to him (chapters 62 and 63).

In the first instance Smollett makes some attempt to enter sympathetically into Fathom's disturbed state of mind:

> the darkness of the night, the silence and solitude of the place, the indistinct images of the trees that appeared on every side, 'stretching their extravagant arms athwart the gloom,' conspired with the dejection of spirits occasioned by his loss to disturb his fancy, and raise strange phantoms in his imagination.

He goes on to describe the inevitable storm: 'the Heavens contracted a more dreary aspect, the lightning began to gleam, the thunder to roll, and the tempest raising its voice to a tremendous roar, descended in a torrent of rain' (pp. 83–4). Celinda falls victim to Fathom's stratagems on account of her 'remarkable spirit of credulity and superstitious fear', which he stimulates with the aid of an Aeolian harp.

> Some years ago, a twelve-stringed instrument was contrived by a very ingenious musician, by whom it was aptly intitled the harp of Aeolus, because, being properly applied to a stream of air, it produces a wild, irregular variety of harmonious sounds, that seem to be the effect of inchantment, and wonderfully dispose the mind for the most romantic situations. [pp. 158, 160–1]

And the study of Renaldo's emotions repeats the formula
Smollett has used for Fathom: 'the soul of Melvile was
wound up to the highest pitch of enthusiastic sorrow. The
uncommon darkness of the night, the solemn silence, and
lonely situation of the place, conspired with the occasion of
his coming, and the dismal images of his fancy, to produce a
real rapture of gloomy expectation'. Smollett brings to bear
all the predictable ingredients of Gothic horror as Renaldo
enters the church: 'The clock struck twelve, the owl
screeched from the ruined battlement' (p. 317).

But these are simply stage sets for what is really a new
landscape of the mind, and it would be a mistake to see in
them the sole evidence for Smollett's expression of a new
sensibility. What is more significant is the sympathetic
inflexion of his prose in these scenes; and in other episodes,
observations and images that occur throughout the novel,
attended by no Gothic paraphernalia. Smollett describes the
solemn declaration of fidelity which the corrupted maid
Teresa extracts from Fathom as a 'certain sign that there are
some remains of religion left in the human mind, even after
every moral sentiment hath abandoned it; and that the most
execrable ruffian finds means to quiet the suggestions of his
conscience, by some reversionary hope of heaven's forgiveness' (7; pp. 30–1). This, it seems to me, is different in kind
from the standard novelistic observations 'upon the instability of human affairs, the treachery of the world, and the
temerity of youth' which Smollett deliberately disowns in
Pickle (105; p. 682). The recognisable syntactic balance is
qualified by the content, which, as it were, stands out
against the declarative temptations of the style, resists the
'neat, aphoristic finish'[10] which is often regarded as characteristic of the eighteenth-century novelists' commentary on
human behaviour. The 'some remains' and 'some . . . hope'
introduce a significant tentativeness, while the rhythm and
alliteration of the last phrase—'some reversionary hope of
heaven's forgiveness'— actually attempt to register the complexity and contradiction inherent in moral feeling. This kind
of thing contrasts markedly with the bland reflections which
we often encounter in the fiction of the time: passive

iterations of conventional syntax as well as conventional morality.

There is a comparable sentence in the Celinda section which exhibits this sensitive strain in Smollett's style more clearly. Fathom does not enjoy his success with tranquillity, on account of Celinda's remorse: 'For the seeds of virtue are seldom destroyed at once: even amidst the rank productions of vice, they regerminate to a sort of imperfect vegetation, like some scattered hyacinths shooting up among the weeds of a ruined garden, that testify the former culture and amenity of the soil' (p. 164). Here it is the development of the image rather than the syntax that conducts the sense; the image which functions more as an experiment than a deposition, inviting rather than insisting upon our response. The phrase 'a sort of imperfect vegetation' illustrates once again Smollett's effort to make the image genuinely expressive of the moral situation described. We can say of such a style that it enables him to break through the formula and reach back to the true form of feeling.

The idea of subtle gradation is essential to any sensitive account of the emotions. To recognise the possible extremes, we might contrast Fielding's summary account of Blifil's moral progression by the end of *Tom Jones* ('in short, he was now as remarkably mean as he had been before remarkably wicked')[11] with George Eliot's study of Dorothea Brooke's developing awareness of her position after her marriage to Casaubon, which will not submit to being given 'in short' at all.[12] I am not, of course, suggesting that Smollett has more in common with George Eliot than he has with Fielding; I simply wish to draw attention to a new shoot of style which is developing in this direction, a shoot on which the sensitive image is the unfolding flower.

Matthew Arnold insisted on the importance of movement in creating the authenticity or 'high seriousness' of verse, and his observation might equally well be applied to prose, where the movement will often attain greater complexity. Nothing destroys feeling more than obtrusively mechanistic movement, as Jane Austen intuitively recognised when ridiculing affected emotionalism in her very early work: 'It was too pathetic for the feelings of Sophia and myself—We fainted alternately upon a Sofa'.[13] Later on, she learnt equally well how to communicate genuine emotion through allowing the movement of her prose to mime the feeling in a more intimate way. When Anne Elliott meets Captain Wentworth by accident in Bath she is assailed by 'all the overpowering, blinding, bewildering first effects of strong surprise',[14] and the insistence of the three adjectives (a rare effect with her) seems to share the compulsion of the feeling itself. But to revert to *Fathom*; the movement co-operates very expressively with the image when Smollett alludes to Renaldo's melancholy recollection of Monimia in these terms: 'his imagination was incessantly infected with something that chilled his nerves, and saddened his heart, recurring, with quick succession, like the unwearied wave that beats upon the bleak, inhospitable Greenland shore' (57; p. 282). And there is an even more deliberate example in this novel of Smollett's ability to persuade his prose into more expressive postures. I have already referred to the Aeolian harp which Fathom used to heighten Celinda's fear. Smollett does not leave us to take the success of Fathom's stratagem on trust; he accepts the challenge of describing the effect of the music.

The soft and tender notes of peace and love were swelled up with the most delicate and insensible transition, into a loud hymn of triumph and exultation, joined by the deep-toned organ, and a full choir of voices, which gradually decayed upon the ear, until it died away, in distant sound, as if a flight of angels had raised the song in their ascent to Heaven. Yet the chords hardly ceased to vibrate after the expiration of this overture, which ushered in a composition in the same pathetic stile; and this again was succeeded by a third, almost without pause or intermission, as if the artist's hand had been indefatigable, and the theme never to be exhausted.

These two sentences seek to imitate rather than simply describe the music. The first parallels the musical idea in words which swell to 'loud', 'deep', 'full', and then subside to 'distant sound'; whilst the idea is echoed or recapitulated by the sympathetic image of the 'flight of angels' at the end.

And the iterative movement of the second sentence ('the same' . . . 'this again') has an insistent, fugual character well adapted to suggest the 'theme never to be exhausted' with which the passage concludes.

The experimental use of this style in *Fathom* was not immediately followed up. Smollett wrote no fiction for seven years; and even then the prevailing ironic atmosphere of *Greaves* was not hospitable to poetry. But the *Travels* offered Smollett an ideal opportunity to carry his exploration of style further, as might be judged from what I have said above (chapter 3) about the experimental nature of this work in various directions. The responsive note is always latent in the *Travels* and should be seen as the complement rather than the converse of its defamatory spirit; Smollett could appreciate beauty as well as ugliness, and was capable of enthusiastic approval as well as articulate disgust. We have seen examples of this responsiveness already in his art criticism, which certainly conducts him towards a greater degree of tentativeness in his use of both vocabulary and syntax; and it is also evident in his descriptions of scenery (in the course of which it may be significant that he uses the epithet 'romantic' itself no fewer than eleven times). [15]

Consider this passage, a description of the Capo di Noli, which Smollett passed on his journey by sea from Nice to Genoa:

In the evening we reached the Capo di Noli, counted very dangerous in blowing weather. It is a very high perpendicular rock or mountain washed by the sea, which has eaten into it in divers places, so as to form a great number of caverns. It extends about a couple of miles, and in some parts is indented into little creeks or bays, where there is a narrow margin of sandy beach between it and the water. When the wind is high, no feluca will attempt to pass it; even in a moderate breeze, the waves dashing against the rocks and caverns, which echo with the sound, make such an awful noise, and at the same time occasion such a rough sea, as one cannot hear, and see, and feel, without a secret horror. [25; pp. 209–10]

Smollett uses the same technique of emphasis here as we

noticed in the example from Jane Austen above; the three verbs 'hear, and see, and feel' set up an impending rhythm which is fulfilled by the 'secret horror'. And in the following description of a cataract on the river Nera the prose again develops a sympathetic movement in which the different details Smollett wishes to combine are held in syntactic suspension until their release together in the last phrase:

Such a body of water rushing down the mountain; the smoak, vapour, and thick white mist which it raises; the double rainbow which these particles continually exhibit while the sun shines; the deafening sound of the cataract; the vicinity of a great number of other stupendous rocks and precipices, with the dashing, boiling, and foaming of the two rivers below, produce altogether an object of tremendous sublimity . . . [34; p. 293]

In an early letter Smollett had dwelt on the 'romantic appearance' of the trees on the mountain of Esterelles (12; p. 111). On his return from Italy he discovered that the pines had been set on fire by vandals; his response to this outrage is fully communicated by the poetic image the burnt trees suggest to him.

The mountains of Esterelles, which in one of my former letters I described as a most romantic and noble plantation of ever-greens, trees, shrubs, and aromatic plants, is at present quite desolate. Last summer, some execrable villains set fire to the pines, when the wind was high. It continued burning for several months, and the conflagration extended above ten leagues, consuming an incredible quantity of timber. The ground is now naked on each side of the road, or occupied by the black trunks of the trees, which have been scorched without falling. They stand as so many monuments of the judgment of heaven, filling the mind with horror and compassion. I could hardly refrain from shedding tears at this dismal spectacle, when I recalled the idea of what it was about eighteen months ago. [39; p. 325]

Smollett was not so readily tearful as Sterne, and we can detect in the rhythm as well as recognise in the statement itself the strength of his feelings on this occasion.

The expansive note is even sounded in one image in the *Atom*, where Newcastle's satellites are described as forming round him 'a kind of luminous belt as pale and comfortless as the ring of Saturn, the most distant, cold, and baleful of all the planets' (i, 44). When we remember the context we must admit that the final effect of the analogy is ironic rather than poetic; but this does not prejudice the authenticity of the movement and the poetic suggestion of the words themselves. (Did not Pope reserve his most beautiful couplet for *The Dunciad?*)[16]

Humphry Clinker, as always, is the likeliest place to look for experiments in style, and the romantic imagination makes a special contribution to the novel's stylistic variety. This is not simply a matter of Wilson's love letter to Lydia, genuinely expressive though it is. 'While you stay in this place, I shall continually hover about your lodgings, as the parted soul is said to linger about the grave where its mortal consort lies' (31 March; p. 16): the words 'linger', 'hover' set up a definite trochaic rhythm which cannot be simply accidental. Nor does it depend upon Lydia's wondering letters on Bath and London, although Smollett does certainly capture the young girl's naive enthusiasm very well. Bath appears to her as 'an earthly paradise'; its new buildings 'look like so many enchanted castles raised on hanging terraces' (26 April; p. 39). In London she finds that 'the imagination is quite confounded with splendour and variety', and her excitement is conveyed in fanciful images. The three bridges over the Thames 'seem to be the work of giants'; 'Ranelagh looks like the inchanted palace of a genie'; and her party embarks for Vauxhall 'in a wherry, so light and slender, that we looked like so many fairies sailing in a nut-shell' (31 May; pp. 91–2). Lydia's relation of her dream (10 June; p. 135) is further evidence of Smollett's interest in overwrought psychological states, though in this instance there is no marked sympathetic inflexion in the prose.

Nor am I appealing simply to the fact that Jery's habitual ironic attitude softens in Scotland to one of generous appreciation, though this is in itself remarkable. He offers us an enthusiastic description of hunting in 'the lonely hills of

H

Morven, where Fingal and his heroes enjoyed the same pas-
time: I feel an enthusiastic pleasure when I survey the brown
heath that Ossian wont to tread; and hear the wind whistle
through the bending grass—When I enter our landlord's
hall, I look for the suspended harp of that divine bard, and
listen in hopes of hearing the aerial sound of his respected
spirit' (3 September; p. 240).

No: more convincing than all the other evidence in the
novel is the conversion of Jery's crusty uncle himself. It is the
permeation of Matthew Bramble's temper—and hence his
style—with this new mood that represents Smollett's final
endorsement of it. We might expect something like this in
the Scottish sequence, once Bramble has declared himself to
have 'a sort of national attachment to this part of Scotland'
(28 August; p. 247), and his response to the Highlands and
the Hebrides is indeed unreservedly romantic. 'This country
is amazingly wild, especially towards the mountains, which
are heaped upon the backs of one another, making a most
stupendous appearance of savage nature, with hardly any
signs of cultivation, or even of population. All is sublimity,
silence, and solitude . . . ' (Once again the intensity of the
impression is enforced with a triple emphasis.) This terrain
also 'affords one of the most ravishing prospects of the
whole world; I mean the appearance of the Hebrides, or
Western Islands, to the number of three hundred, scattered
as far as the eye can reach, in the most agreeable confusion'
(6 September; pp. 252–3).

But Bramble can be tempted into a more fanciful style even
in England, as when he considers the scale of the Assembly
Room at Harrogate: 'the grandeur of the fane gives a diminutive effect to the little painted divinities that are adored in it,
and the company, on a ball-night, must look like an assembly of fantastic fairies, revelling by moonlight among the
columns of a Grecian temple' (4 July; p. 181). There is at least
as much enjoyment as criticism contained in this observation, as is clear from the way Smollett lets Bramble assent
imaginatively to the fanciful idea the scene suggests to him.
And to confirm what I said earlier about the crucial place of
movement (or 'instress'?) in providing this new inscape of

prose, I should like to conclude this section by quoting a passage which occurs much earlier in the novel, in Bath, where for a self-indulgent moment Bramble reflects on his meeting with several old and now decrepit friends.

It was a renovation of youth; a kind of resuscitation of the dead, that realized those interesting dreams, in which we sometimes retrieve our antient friends from the grave. Perhaps my enjoyment was not the less pleasing for being mixed with a strain of melancholy, produced by the remembrance of past scenes, that conjured up the ideas of some enduring connexions, which the hand of Death has actually dissolved. [5 May; p. 56]

Bramble brings us much closer to the reality of sensitive human feeling here than any formula could do; the dream of his friends being retrieved from the grave is far more moving (for example) than the melodramatic resurrection of Monimia in Fathom. The tentativeness of his words, within the overall lyrical movement, helps to communicate the complex emotion to which Bramble confesses on this occasion; 'a kind of ', 'mixed with a strain of', 'sometimes', 'some', 'perhaps'—the writing itself carries a recognition that certain feelings are too subtle to be adequately described in a few ready-made phrases, and will only yield their true quality to a more patient and exploratory use of language.

III

I hope I have said, and shown, enough to allow my claim that Smollett was as alert as Collins, Gray and the Warton brothers; Edward Young, Richard Hurd or Daniel Webb, to the new influences that were to undermine Augustan criteria in both prose and verse before the end of the century. It remains to make one last point about Smollett's style here; one that applies, however, to all its different dispositions.

This is its reliance on imagery. Let me say at once that I do not intend to offer further illustration of Smollett's use of imagery at this late stage; it is sufficiently evident in everything I have quoted throughout this study. I simply wish to make some concluding and necessarily general observations about the place of imagery in determining the character of Smollett's style. It is the *fact* of the imagery I wish to isolate for a moment; a fact that informs, allows and strengthens all levels of this style, and sets it apart once again from the recognised eighteenth-century norms.

Because the analogical faculty, like the style it serves, is also a 'gift of heaven', which will always mark off the born writer from the diligent practitioner of his craft. Aristotle was very explicit about this in the *Poetics*: 'but far the most important thing to master is the use of metaphor. This is the one thing that cannot be learnt from anyone else, and it is the mark of great natural ability, for the ability to use metaphor well implies a perception of resemblances.'[17] On another occasion Aristotle actually specified that metaphor was more important for the prose writer than the poet, 'in as much as prose depends on fewer resources than verse';[18] and so there can be no doubt of the relevance of this discrimination for my purposes.

If we take a last look at the two writers who have completed my critical triangle, we see immediately how they contrast with Smollett in this important respect. Fielding was not noticeably possessed of the gift of image, and appears to have been very reluctant to cultivate what he did have. All he 'learnt from anyone else' was the habit of mistrusting it; he was one of those (many) writers of the time who could hardly make a comparison at all without looking back over one shoulder at Locke.[19] The fact that so many of his images tend to be mock-heroic underlines Fielding's basically ironic attitude to analogy, and his very typical wariness of the opportunities it provided for falsification.

Johnson, on the other hand, is frequently cited as an example of a writer who relied on imagery very extensively.[20] 'His mind was so full of imagery,' says Boswell, 'that he might have been perpetually a poet.'[21] And we remember that Imlac tells the Prince in *Rasselas* how he 'ranged mountains and deserts for images and resemblances . . . for every idea is useful for the inforcement or decoration of moral or religious truth'.[22] It is the very functionalism of Johnson's images, however, that makes one reluctant to use the term 'imagery' to describe them. Wimsatt concedes that 'the "imagery" of Johnson's writing is imagery only in the most diluted sense', and goes on to suggest that 'we must understand the term in another sense, that of simply non-literal expression'.[23] This is surely the case. Johnson's images (in his prose) do not deepen or complicate the sense in any way; they only clarify it by the use of essentially passive examples. His images are simple mechanisms.

It is revealing to consider 'a beautiful image' which Johnson cited from Bacon, proving the superiority of argument to testimony: 'testimony is like an arrow shot from a long bow; the force of it depends on the strength of the hand that draws it. Argument is like an arrow from a crossbow, which has equal force though shot by a child'.[24] The beauty of this image, for Johnson, lies in its fulfilment of a function; it illustrates an idea. And I might use the terms of this very image to illustrate the essential difference, as I see it, between the imagery of Johnson and Smollett. Smollett's images are shot from a longbow, and Johnson's from a crossbow: with the relative strengths and weaknesses implied. (And no one would dispute that the longbow is the more romantic weapon.)

Everywhere in Smollett, and in every way, the genius for comparison serves his turn. It can function equally, though differently, both at the circumference and at the centre. What happens in the comic image—as we observed in several instances in chapter six—is that the analogical process itself is distorted, turned inside out, so that the image highlights the evident discordance between the two things compared rather than (what is its usual role) obliterating this in a momentary identification. But the image comes into its own at the centre. It is at the centre that the image assumes its highest function, relating and organising, *creating;* focusing Smollett's whole experience, bringing his whole personality to bear on the expression of a single idea. It is here that the image *'fuses'* its elements, as Coleridge was to say, 'by that synthetic and magical power to which we have exclusively appropriated the name of imagination'.[25]

My last chapter is full of such instances, and I will introduce only two further examples here. Bramble writes of York Minster that 'the long slender spire puts one in mind of a criminal impaled, with a sharp stake rising up through his shoulder' (*Clinker*, 4 July; p. 181). Here an architectural fact is translated to a surprising poetic statement; the visual experience is precipitated by the vigour of Bramble's response to provide a vividly impressionistic image. The compression, the charge of energy, the imaginative freedom and confidence, are qualities that put us in mind of Dickens: the Dickens who is the greatest image-maker in English prose. And Smollett's longbow finds out its target with destructive accuracy in an extraordinary idea that he develops in the *Atom* to express his contempt for the Duke of Cumberland— 'Butcher' Cumberland of Culloden. His theme is Cumberland's intelligence:

> his intellects were so extraordinary and extensive, that he seemed to sentimentize at every pore, and to have the faculty of thinking diffused all over his frame, even to his fingers ends; or, as the Latins call it *ad unguem*; nay, so wonderful was his organical conformation, that, in the opinion of many Japonese philosophers, his whole body was enveloped in a kind of poultice of brain, and that if he had lost his head in battle, the damage with regard to his power of reflection would have been scarce perceptible. [i, 57–8]

Smollett has evidently taken a hint here from Pope's 'smart and agonize at evry pore',[26] though the word 'sentimentize' appears to be a scornful invention of his own. But what distinguishes this from many another ironic portrait is the startling phrase 'a kind of poultice of brain', the fused image that raises the idea to a higher level of intensity altogether. This is a perfect example of the image which does not merely clarify but intensifies: the kind of image for which one would range mountains and deserts in vain, but which will always be available, on the right impulse, to the right imagination.

IV

I will repeat my main argument for the last time: only that criticism which is founded in criticism of style will ever be able to perceive the real value of Smollett as a writer. And I will refer once again to Hawkesworth's remark on the *Atom*, as the sanest short criticism on any of his works: 'nothing could bear less resemblance to it, than a concise epitome of the events, taken out of the terms in which they are related'.

It is a curious fact that a good deal of the criticism which takes another point of departure includes in its argument for moral or structural coherence the claim that this has 'gone unobserved' (or some such phrase) before. Now it seems to me that what has gone unobserved by generations of readers for two hundred years is very probably not there anyway; and so what is advanced as a claim to originality in such criticism should actually be conceded as a confession of irrelevance. This simple argument by itself is enough to invalidate many factitious theses constructed on Smollett's work, and to make room for the more innocent critical perspective I have myself proposed.

I have not sought to raise any superstructure of my own on Smollett's work because I do not believe it needs any. But such are the ambitions of criticism that sometimes we need to point out the obvious. John Danby concludes his study of *King Lear* with the reminder that Shakespeare's deepest meanings are to be found 'where they should be in successful art—on the surface'.[27] And I cannot conclude this book in any better way than by reminding the reader that Smollett's 'deepest meanings' will be found on the surface too; on the endlessly interesting surface of his style.

Notes

I have used abbreviations when referring to the following works:

Boege: Fred W. Boege, *Smollett's Reputation as a Novelist* (Princeton, N. J., 1947).
Boucé: Paul-Gabriel Boucé, *Les Romans de Smollett: étude critique* (Paris, 1971).
Hannay: David Hannay, *Life of Smollett* (1887).
Kahrl: George M. Kahrl, *Tobias Smollett: Traveler–Novelist* (Chicago, 1945).
Knapp: Lewis M. Knapp, *Tobias Smollett, Doctor of Men and Manners* (Princeton, N. J., 1949).
Letters: The Letters of Tobias Smollett, ed. Lewis M. Knapp (Oxford, 1970).
Martz: Louis L. Martz, *The Later Career of Tobias Smollett*, (New Haven, Conn., 1942).
Paulson: Ronald Paulson, *Satire and the Novel in Eighteenth-century England* (New Haven, Conn., 1967).
Watt: Ian Watt, *The Rise of the Novel* (1957; Harmondsworth, 1963).

Titles of scholarly journals are abbreviated according to the usual (MLA) conventions. The place of publication is London, except where otherwise stated.

Preface

[1] Smollett's complete works have been published four times this century: ed. Henley and Seccombe (1899–1901); ed. Saintsbury (1899–1903); ed. Maynadier (New York, 1902); and in the Shakespeare Head edition (Oxford, 1925–26).
[2] 1907.
[3] *Letters of Tobias Smollett*, ed. E. S. Noyes (Cambridge, Mass., 1926).
[4] *Letters of Tobias George Smollett: a Supplement to the Noyes Collection*, ed. Francesco Cordasco (Madrid, 1950). See *PQ*, xxx (1951), 290–1; and xxxi (1952), 299–300.
[5] *Tobias Smollett, Doctor of Men and Manners* (Princeton, N. J., 1949).
[6] *Smollett's Reputation as a Novelist* (Princeton, N. J., 1947).
[7] See entries in Bibliography, IV.

8 Lawrence, 1956.
9 See the works by Buck, Wierstra, Joliat and Jones, in Bibliography, IV.
10 See the works by Martz and Kahrl in Bibliography, IV.
11 See 'Note on texts' (p. xii) for details of these editions. The *Travels* is also due to appear in the companion Oxford English Memoirs and Travels series.
12 No further details of publication are available at the time of going to press.
13 Oxford, 1970.
14 See Bibliography, IV, i, ii and iii, for details.
15 Boege, p. 48.
16 See the articles by Strauss, Stevick and Underwood in Bibliography, IV, iii; and also Boucé Part III, chapter 3, 'Aspects stylistiques'.
17 The most recent is that by C. J. Rawson, in the *Sphere History of Literature in the English Language, 4: Dryden to Johnson*, ed. Roger Lonsdale (1971) , 259–95.
18 See Boege, chapter 4, 'At the height of fame, 1801–32'.
19 Lionel Stevenson, *The English Novel: a Panorama* (Boston, Mass., 1960), p. 99.
20 See the works by Alter, Giddings and Spector in Bibliography, IV; and (in contrast) the articles by G. S. Rousseau, 'Smollett and the picaresque: some questions about a label', *Studies in Burke*, xii (1971), 1886–1904; and P-G. Boucé, 'Smollett's pseudo-picaresque', *Studies in Burke*, xiv (1972), 73–9.
21 A review of Spector's *Tobias George Smollett*, Korte's Smollett bibliography, and Knapp's *Letters of Tobias Smollett*, in *ECS*, iv (1970–71), 336–42.
22 An abridged version of Paul Boucé's work has recently been published in English translation: *The Novels of Tobias Smollett* (Longmans, 1976).
23 *Tristram Shandy*, III, chapter 12; ed. Graham Petrie (Harmondsworth, 1967), p. 192.
24 *Life of Smollett* (1887), p. 70.
25 My thesis, ' "Form" and "essence" in Smollett: a study of his work in relation to eighteenth-century criticism and aesthetics', was accepted by London university in 1966.

Chapter one

1 Page vii. Subsequent references to this edition will be included in the text.
2 See Martz, p. 15; Knapp, p. 313; A. R. Humphreys, 'Fielding and Smollett', in *The Pelican Guide to English Literature, 4: Dryden to Johnson*, ed. Boris Ford (Harmondsworth, 1957), pp. 315, 330–1; Robert Giddings, *The Tradition of Smollett* (1967), pp. 71–91; Boucé, p. 315.
3 *The English Humourists of the Eighteenth Century* (1851); in *Works* (1898), vii, 576.

⁴ 'Fielding and Smollett', in *Sphere History of Literature in the English Language, 4: Dryden to Johnson*, ed. Roger Lonsdale (1971), p. 295.

⁵ Watt, p. 302. A more extreme version is provided by Hippolyte Taine, who describes Smollett as 'a literal copyist of life' who, 'being mediocre . . . chalks out the figures insipidly, prosaically, without transforming them by the illumination of genius' (*History of English Literature*, 1863–64; trans. H. van Laun, 1871, ii, 176).

⁶ *The Republic*, trans. A. D. Lindsay (1954), p. 311.

⁷ The reader will find a fuller treatment of this argument in my *Realism* (1970).

⁸ Preface to Shakespeare; in *Johnson: Prose and Poetry*, ed. Mona Wilson (1963), p, 494. All references to Johnson's writings will be to this edition, except where otherwise indicated.

⁹ *Rambler*, 25; *Idler*, 84. All references to Johnson's periodical essays, and to the other essayists of the period, are to the edition prepared by the Rev. L. T. Berguer: *The British Essayists* (45 vols: 1823).

¹⁰ *The Art of the Novel* (1934), p. 259.

¹¹ *The Critical Review, or Annals of Literature* (1756–90); xvii (1764), 298. The reviews of the time provide a good deal of very interesting material for the study of contemporary attitudes to fiction. One such study is J. B. Heidler, *A History, 1700–1800, of English Criticism of Prose Fiction* (Illinois, 1928).

¹² ii (1756), 357.

¹³ See Derek Roper, 'Smollett's "Four Gentlemen": the first contributors to the *Critical Review*', RES, n.s., x (1959), 38–44.

¹⁴ Blake, 'The Marriage of Heaven and Hell'; *Complete Writings*, ed. Geoffrey Keynes (1966), p.152.

¹⁵ 'A sort of a Song', *The Collected Later Poems* (1965), p. 7.

¹⁶ *Opus Posthumous* (New York, 1957), p. 294.

¹⁷ In the original version of her 'Poetry', which is to be found in the notes to her *Complete Poems* (1968), pp. 266–7.

¹⁸ xxxii (1771), 81–2, 88.

¹⁹ Prefaced to his edition of *The Works of Tobias Smollett* (Edinburgh, 1870), i, 22.

²⁰ *Ibid.*, i, 30.

²¹ 'An eighteenth-century saga', *Gentlemen's Magazine*, cclxxx (1896), 453, 458.

²² *Letters*, p. 69.

²³ No. 3, 12 June 1762.

²⁴ *A Continuation of the Complete History* (1760–61, 1765); i, v.

²⁵ 1756; i, i.

²⁶ Quoted by E. H. Carr, *What is History?* (1961), p. 10.

²⁷ *Adventurer*, 4, 18 November 1752. This is an interesting essay on the novel in which Hawkesworth defends the form against the restriction of literal truth with the argument that 'though there is not a natural, there is at least a kind of moral probability preserved' in it.

²⁸ See Knapp, pp. 230–3.

[29] *Letters*, p. 103.
[30] *Poetry and Prose*, pp. 501–2.
[31] *Dunciad, I, 110.* All references to Pope's poems are to the one-volume edition of the Twickenham text, ed. John Butt (1965).
[32] *Cf.* this preface to a recent (first) novel, *Vacation*, by Alan Sheridan: 'The events described here took place in the first week of October, 1967. I first learnt of them some two months later, when, in rather strange circumstances, the documents on which this book is based came into my hands . . . .' (Quoted in a review in *The Guardian*, 11 October 1972.)
[33] Kahrl, p. 34.
[34] 1766; ii, 265–96. Seccombe omits the register of the weather in his edition.
[35] *Life of Johnson*, ed. R. W. Chapman (1953), p. 997: 17 May 1778. All subsequent references will be to this edition, with date of entry.
[36] For details of Smollett's revision of the text of the *Travels* see Seccombe's introduction, pp. xxii–iv; and my article 'Unpublished additions to Smollett's *Travels*', *Notes and Queries*, n.s., xiv (1967), 187–9.
[37] Kahrl, p. 113. *Cf.* also the article by John F. Sena, 'Smollett's Persona and the melancholy traveller', *ECS*, i (1968), 353–69; and R. D. Spector's essay 'Smollett's Traveler', in *Tobias Smollett: Essays presented to Lewis M. Knapp*, ed. G. S. Rousseau and P-G. Boucé (New York, 1971), pp. 231–46.
[38] *The Gentleman's Guide in His Tour through France. Wrote by an Officer* (fourth edn., enlarged, 1770), pp. 15–16.
[39] *Letters*, p. 125.
[40] *The Art of the Novel*, pp. 115–6, 231.
[41] Quoted by Knapp, p. 235 n.
[42] Knapp, p. 234.
[43] *Life of Johnson*, p. 904: 3 April 1778. Philip Thicknesse published two trivial books with the apparent intention of contradicting Smollett at every turn; and (as comparison with the *Travels* will show) could not even achieve this degraded objective.
[44] *Tobias Smollett* (New York, 1968), p. 71.
[45] T. S. Eliot's phrase, used to describe the comic world of Ben Jonson (*Selected Essays*, third edn., 1951, p. 159).
[46] For further consideration of this subject see Martz, Part II, chapters 4–7; Kahrl, chapters 5, 10; and Boucé, Part III, chapter 1. Also the essays by G. M. Kahrl ('Smollett as caricaturist') and Byron Gassman ('The economy of *Humphry Clinker'*) in *Tobias Smollett: Essays presented to Lewis M. Knapp*.
[47] Knapp, p. 38.

Chapter two

[1] See, for example, Richardson on *Pickle* (quoted by McKillop, *The Early Masters of English Fiction*, p. 180), and Griffiths on *Fathom* in *The Monthly Review* (1749–80), viii (1753), 203.

² See, for example, Fanny Burney, *Early Diary*, ed. Ellis (1889), ii, 231; and Mrs Barbauld, *The British Novelists*, xxx, v. Both these examples are quoted by Boege, pp. 50, 75.

³ Rufus Putney initiated the dubious moral revaluation of Smollett with his essay 'The plan of *Peregrine Pickle*', *PMLA*, 1x (1945), 1051–65. See also M. A. Goldberg, *Smollett and the Scottish School* (Albuquerque, N. M., 1959); Donald Bruce, *Radical Doctor Smollett* (1964); Robert Giddings, *The Tradition of Smollett* (1967); R. D. Spector, *Tobias Smollett* (1968).

⁴ xv, 551–2.

⁵ 'Verses on the Death of Dr. Swift', ll. 313–4; *Poetical Works*, ed. Herbert Davis (1967), p. 506.

⁶ 'A Defence of Poetry', in *English Critical Essays, Nineteenth Century*, ed. E. D. Jones (1916), p. 132.

⁷ *The Advancement of Learning* (1605); ed. Thomas Markby (1856), p. 82.

⁸ *Letters on Chivalry and Romance* (1762); xii, p. 114. *Cf.* the argument of Robert Scholes's *The Fabulators* (New York, 1967), which also uses Spenser as an example.

⁹ *History of English Literature*, trans. H. Van Laun (1871), ii, 365.

¹⁰ Robert Giddings, *The Tradition of Smollett* (1967), pp. 97, 141.

¹¹ *To the Palace of Wisdom* (New York, 1964; 1965 edn.), p. 193.

¹² 'Morality and the novel', *Phoenix*, ed. E. D. McDonald (1936), p. 528.

¹³ XV, ch. 1; ed. R. P. C. Mutter (Harmondsworth, 1966), p. 695. All references to *Tom Jones* will be to this edition.

¹⁴ *Advice* (1746), ll. 131–2.

¹⁵ *Reproof* (1747), ll. 95–6, 28, 132.

¹⁶ P. K. Elkin's recent book *The Augustan Defence of Satire* (Oxford, 1973) provides an excellent account of the subject. See especially ch. 5, 'Core of the defence: the moral function', and ch. 10, 'Conclusion: inadequacy of the defence'. It is a little surprising, however, that Smollett is not once mentioned in Elkin's book, not even in the few pages devoted to satire in the novel.

¹⁷ *Jonathan Swift* (Cambridge, 1969), p. 159.

¹⁸ *Poems and Fables*, ed. James Kinsley (1962), p. 189. All references to Dryden's poems will be to this edition.

¹⁹ See n. 5, above.

²⁰ 23 March 1728; *Letters of Alexander Pope*, selected by John Butt (1960), p. 204.

²¹ 9 October 1729; *ibid.*, p. 217.

²² *Gulliver's Travels and Selected Writings in Prose and Verse*, ed. John Hayward (1949), p. 6.

²³ No. 191, 26 August 1756.

²⁴ *To the Palace of Wisdom*, p. 16.

²⁵ *Letters*, pp. 188, 38.

²⁶ 'Epistle to Dr Arbuthnot', ll. 305–10.

²⁷ 'But General Satire in Times of General Vice has no force, and is no Punishment: People have ceas'd to be ashamed of it when so many are join'd with them; and tis only by hunting One or two from the Herd that

any Examples can be made . . . if some are hung up, or pilloryed, it may prevent others. And in my low station, with no other power than this, I hope to deter, if not to reform'. (Letter to Arbuthnot, 2 August 1734; *Letters*, p. 275.)

[28] *Tatler*, 242, 26 October 1710.
[29] *Lady Chatterley's Lover* (1928; Harmondsworth, 1960), p. 38.
[30] *Poems and Fables*, p. 188.
[31] 29 September 1725; *Correspondence of Jonathan Swift*, ed. Harold Williams (Oxford, 1963), iii, 102.
[32] 16 November 1726; *Letters*, p. 197.
[33] *The Augustan Defence of Satire*, p. 86.
[34] *A History, 1700–1800, of English Criticism of Prose Fiction* (Illinois, 1928), p. 90 n.
[35] *Cf.* Swift: 'Like the ever-laughing Sage/In a Jest I spend my Rage;/(Tho' it must be understood/I would hang them if I cou'd)'. 'Epistle to a Lady'; *Poetical Works*, ed. Herbert Davis (1967), p. 566.
[36] Line 208.
[37] *The Listener*, lxxxii (1969), p. 303.
[38] See 'Smollett's self-portrait in *The Expedition of Humphry Clinker*', in *The Age of Johnson: Essays presented to C. B. Tinker* (New Haven, Conn., 1949), pp. 149–58.
[39] *Tobias Smollett: Selected Writings* (1950), p. 11. *Cf.* Walter Raleigh on Carlyle: 'A certain exercise of contempt was necessary to [his] mind, to keep it in health' (*Six Essays on Johnson*, Oxford, 1910; p. 140).
[40] *A Short View of the Immorality and Profaneness of the English Stage* (1968), pp. 70–1.
[41] *The Rhetorical World of Augustan Humanism* (1965), p. 233.
[42] *Life of Smollett*, p. 51.

Chapter three

[1] See the critical works by Herbert, Hannay, Saintsbury, Cross, Baker and Watt, as listed in the Bibliography.
[2] See especially the article by Rufus Putney, 'The plan of *Peregrine Pickle*', *PMLA*, lx (1945), 1051–65; and the critical works by Donovan, Paulson, Spector and Boucé, as listed in the Bibliography. See also M. A. Goldberg, *Smollett and the Scottish School* (Albuquerque, N. M., 1959); P. M. Griffith, 'Fire-scenes in *Clarissa* and Smollett's *Humphry Clinker*', *Tulane Studies in English*, xi (1961), 39–50; James L. Clifford, introduction to *Peregrine Pickle* (1964); Robert Giddings, *The Tradition of Smollett* (1967); Tuvia Bloch, 'Smollett's quest for form', *MP*, lxv (1967), 103–13; John M. Warner, 'Smollett's development as a novelist', *Novel*, v (1972), 148–62.
[3] Paulson, p. 49.
[4] *Letters to Dorothy Wellesly* (1964), p. 194.
[5] Preface to Shakespeare; *Prose and Poetry*, p. 501.
[6] 'Explication as criticism', *The Verbal Icon* (Kentucky, 1954), pp. 235–51.
[7] *Ibid.*, pp. 238–9.

[8] This question is interestingly discussed by John Bayley in an article in the *TLS* (27 July 1973). Arguing that what we call 'unity' may often be an illusion—and represent simply a judgement of value—Mr Bayley goes on to suggest that it might 'be more helpful to praise the symptoms of disunity', since the novel is a product 'not of a single unit of conflict and disorder, but of competing purposes and incompatible kinds of fulfilment' (p. 853).

[9] In *Imagined Worlds*, ed. Maynard Mack and Ian Gregor (1968), pp. 91–110.

[10] Page 94.

[11] *Cf.* the essay by Martin Battestin, '*Tom Jones*: the argument of design', in *The Augustan Milieu: Essays presented to Louis A. Landa*, ed. H. K. Miller, E. Rothstein and G. S. Rousseau (Oxford, 1970), 289–319. Battestin argues that 'meaning and even the shape of the action are in large part determined by certain extrinsic, non-organic principles', by 'some ulterior, abstract intention of the author' (p. 302). See also Douglas Brooks, *Number and Pattern in the Eighteenth-century Novel* (1973): Dr Brooks argues that Smollett, too, used structure to support theme in his novels, especially in *Humphry Clinker*, where he finds evidence of 'strict numerological decorum' (p. 157).

[12] 'A Dialogue between the Soul and Body'; *Poems of Andrew Marvell*, ed. Hugh Macdonald (1952), p. 16.

[13] 'Annotations to Sir Joshua Reynolds's Discourses'; *Complete Writings*, p. 451.

[14] *The Shaping Vision*, p. 90.

[15] 1722; ed. G. A. Starr (1971), p. 3.

[16] 'On the Art of Poetry', trans. T. S. Dorsch; *Classical Literary Criticism* (Harmondsworth, 1965), pp. 42–3.

[17] Examples occur on pp. 73, 107, 181, 243.

[18] viii (1753), 206. It is worth recalling that this review was written before Griffiths's antagonism to Smollett erupted, on the launching of Smollett's rival *Critical Review* in 1756.

[19] *Letters*, p. 58.

[20] J. B. Heidler, *A History, 1700–1800, of English Criticism of Prose Fiction* (Illinois, 1928), pp. 116–7.

[21] xiii (1762), 427–8.

[22] xxi (1766), 406.

[23] *A Sentimental Journey*, ed. Ian Jack (1968), pp. xiii, 28–9.

[24] See James R. Foster, 'Smollett and the *Atom*', *PMLA*, lxviii (1953), 1032–46. Considering the evidence, Foster's claim that it is 'reasonably safe' to conclude that Smollett wrote the *Atom* is not nearly positive enough.

[25] G. P. Elliott, 'A defence of fiction', *Hudson Review*, xvi (1963), 34.

[26] xxi (1766), 406.

[27] xl (1769), 441.

[28] 'On Smollett's language: a paragraph in *Ferdinand Count Fathom*', in *English Institute Essays* (1958), pp. 53–4.

[29] Douglas Brooks concedes that his account of *Clinker* in terms of architectural metaphor ignores 'much of the novel's thematic complexity and richness'; and his criticism is most convincing where he passes beyond both this metaphor, and numerological analysis, to consider the function of imagery in the novel (*Number and Pattern in the Eighteenth-century Novel*, pp. 151–8).

[30] *Rambler*, 156, 14 September 1751.

[31] *Rambler*, 125, 28 May 1751.

[32] In *Essays in the History of Ideas* (Baltimore, Md., 1948), pp. 69–77.

[33] *Lives of the Novelists* (Paris, 1825), i, 113.

[34] viii (1759), 147.

[35] *Lives of the Novelists*, i, 153.

[36] *Lectures on the English Comic Writers* (1819); *Works*, ed. Howe (1930–34), vi, 117.

[37] 1797; p. 467.

[38] See, for example, his observations on the Pont du Gard and La Maison Carrée (6, p. 45; 10, pp. 84, 90), in contrast to domestic architecture in Nice (10, p. 87) and various churches in Genoa (26, p. 217; 28, pp. 239–40) and Rome (31, pp. 264–7).

[39] ii, 226, 228.

[40] *The Works of M. de Voltaire. Translated from the French with Notes, Historical and Critical. By Dr Smollet* [sic], *and Others*. Twenty-five vols., 1761; i, iii.

[41] Martz also points out that much of the more formal criticism in the *Travels* is adapted from earlier writers. Smollett's enthusiastic description of the Maison Carrée, for example, is translated almost word for word from Abbé Valette de Travessac's *Abrégé de l'Histoire de la Ville de Nismes*, a work published six years before his own (Martz, pp. 82–3).

[42] Blake, 'The Marriage of Heaven and Hell'; *Complete Writings*, p. 152.

[43] *Ibid.*, p. 621.

Chapter four

[1] 'Language, 1660–1784', in *The Pelican Guide to English Literature, 4: From Dryden to Johnson*, ed. Boris Ford (Harmondsworth, 1957), pp. 125–6.

[2] *Of Dramatic Poesy and Other Critical Essays*, ed. George Watson (1962); ii, 152.

[3] Quoted by Collins, *From Dryden to Johnson*, p. 127.

[4] *The Rhetorical World of Augustan Humanism* (1965), p. 139.

[5] References are to the first edition (1690), by chapter and section.

[6] Page 237.

[7] *Poetry and Prose*, pp. 319–21.

[8] *Ibid., pp.* 304–5.

[9] 'An Essay on Criticism', ll. 482–3.

[10] *Poetry and Prose*, pp. 129–30.

[11] *Ibid.*, p. 322.

[12] The evidence will be found both in the Preface to Shakespeare and

throughout Johnson's notes on the plays. Compare Dryden's account of Shakespeare's language in his preface to *Troilus and Cressida* of 1679, 'The Grounds of Criticism in Tragedy'. Dryden maintains that Shakespeare 'often obscures his meaning with his words', and if he were 'stripped of all the bombast in his passions, and dressed in the most vulgar words, we should find the beauties of his thoughts remaining'. (*Of Dramatic Poesy and Other Critical Essays*, ed. George Watson, 1962, i, 257–9.) George Steiner has recently remarked, 'Why the eighteenth century should have been so largely indifferent to the linguistic structures underlying literature is a problem which . . . has been little looked into.' (*Extraterritorial*, 1972; p. 131.)

13 *Poetry and Prose*, p. 909.
14 *Henry Fielding and the Language of Irony* (Chicago, 1968), p. 43.
15 Book XII, chapter 11 (p. 588).
16 James R. Sutherland and Ian Watt, *Restoration and Augustan Prose* (Los Angeles, 1956), p. 28.
17 IV, 6 (p. 167).
18 XI, 4 (p. 519).
19 *Henry Fielding and the Language of Irony*, pp. 6, 3.
20 VI, 5 (p. 313); XVIII, 3 (p. 820); VIII, 2 (pp. 367–8).
21 V, 12 (p. 247).
22 *Spectator*, 297, 9 February 1712.
23 VII, 13 (p. 349).
24 W. B. Yeats, 'Ego Dominus Tuus'; *Collected Poems* (1950), p. 180. Walter Jackson Bate writes of the 'remorseless deepening of self-consciousness' and the accompanying lack of self-confidence in eighteenth-century poetry. (*The Burden of the Past and the English Poet*, 1971, p. 4 and *passim*.) I would argue that the same process is taking place in the novel, with Fielding the most obvious example.
25 G. G. Sedgewick; quoted by Hatfield, p. 154.
26 1797; p. 462.
27 See also the discussion of Fielding's style by Henry Knight Miller in his *Essays on Fielding's Miscellanies* (Princeton, N. J., 1961). Miller notes the typical complexity of Fielding's syntax, and also his 'strong inclination to the parenthesis'—observations which would seem to provide evidence to support my own view of this style.
28 'In the destructive element immerse': Stern's incitement to the hero in *Lord Jim*, chapter 20 (Harmondsworth, 1949, p. 164).
29 Quoted by Robert Graves in the introduction to his translation of the work (Harmondsworth, 1950), p. 7.
30 *Anatomy of Criticism*, p. 266.
31 The phrase reads 'shameful rascal or shameful villain' in the original, but this must surely be a printer's error; only if the second 'shameful' reads 'shameless' does the example illustrate Smollett's point. I am grateful to Dr J. J. Anderson for suggesting this emendation.
32 *John Locke and English Literature of the Eighteenth Century* (New Haven, Conn., 1936), p. 115.

33 17 January 1740.
34 *The Death of the Moth and other Essays* (1942; Harmondsworth, 1961, p. 176).
35 Boucé, p. 394.
36 *The Uncanny Scot* (1968), p. 165.
37 *How are Verses Made?*, trans. G. M. Hyde (1970), p. 19.
38 *The Uncanny Scot*, p. 166.
39 *Prose and Poetry*, p. 306.
40 *Grub Street: Studies in a Subculture* (1972), p. 11.
41 Quoted by G. L. Brook, *The Language of Dickens* (1970), p. 211.
42 Boucé, p. 297.
43 'Stylistic energy in the early Smollett', *SP*, lxiv (1967), p. 716.
44 *Charles Dickens and Appropriate Language* (Durham, N. C., 1959), p. 7.
45 'The Second Part of Absalom and Achitophel', ll. 496–7.
46 Boucé, p. 394.
47 This critical omission is really rather surprising, especially when we consider how freely Dickens himself acknowledged his debt to Smollett. George Saintsbury referred to Dickens at the turn of the century as 'Smollett's great imitator' (*Prefaces and Essays*, 1933, p. 76), but the details—and the implications—of this imitation have never been fully worked out. The little-known monograph *Smollett and Dickens* by F. D. Wierstra published in 1928 represents the most serious attempt; from the evidence of numerous verbal (and other) parallels Wierstra argues that 'Dickens's debt to Smollett must be considerable' (p. 114). But most critics of Dickens—even those who deal specifically with his style—give Smollett at best a passing mention. In a jealous note on 'Dickens and Smollett' in *Dickens the Novelist* (1970; pp. 30–3) Q. D. and F. R. Leavis pointedly contrast Smollett's 'brutal humour' with Dickens's 'profounder genius', whilst ignoring the true nature of Smollett's influence on Dickens, which is most evident at the verbal level. *Cf.* the more general observation by Oliver Elton that Smollett's 'far-reaching influence on the English novel has always been recognized, but is not yet fully explored' (*A Survey of English Literature, 1730–1780*, 1928, i, 216).
48 *Charles Dickens and Appropriate Language*, p. 6.
49 This generally neglected aspect of Smollett's work has, however, attracted the attention of some writers. V. S. Pritchett was the first critic (so far as I know) to adopt a positive attitude towards it, making the significant comparison between Smollett and Joyce (in 'The Shocking Surgeon', *The Living Novel*, 1946; 1960 edn., pp. 35–6). The comparison is intriguingly developed by Giorgio Melchiori in his chapter 'Joyce and the tradition of the novel' from *The Tightrope Walkers* (1956). Hugh Macdiarmid also refers to Smollett's anticipation of Joyce (*The Uncanny Scot*, p. 165). Paul Boucé provides a useful discussion of Smollett's own debt to Shakespeare in this respect, and notices the existence of these effects earlier in Smollett's work as well (*Les Romans de Smollett*, pp. 374 ff). The reader might like to consider two letters which are included in *Random* (16; i, 128) and *Pickle* (45; p. 219), which will certainly sustain the kind of

analysis I attempt here. See also J. Arthur Boggs, 'A Win Jenkins lexicon', *Bulletin of the New York Public Libraries*, lxviii (1965), pp. 323–30.

50 To avoid undue disfigurement of the text I shall give only page references to the quotations that follow.

51 *The Tightrope Walkers*, p. 48.

52 *Ibid.*, p. 48.

53 *Seven Types of Ambiguity* (1930; Harmondsworth, 1961), p. 71.

54 'Fielding and Smollett', in *Sphere History of Literature in the English Language, 4: Dryden to Johnson*, ed. Roger Lonsdale (1971), p. 295.

55 Denis Donoghue, *Jonathan Swift* (Cambridge, 1969), p. 125.

56 *Dublin's Joyce* (1955), p. 301.

57 'The Marriage of Heaven and Hell'; *Complete Writings*, p. 151; 'Jerusalem'; *ibid.*, p. 621.

58 *Love's Labour's Lost*, V, i, 33–6.

Chapter five

1 See Denis Donoghue, *Jonathan Swift*, chapter 4, 'Words'.

2 Steele, *Guardian*, 60, 20 May 1713.

3 In *Gulliver's Travels and Selected Writings in Prose and Verse*, ed. John Hayward (1949), pp. 401–4.

4 Quoted by A. S. Collins, 'Language, 1660–1784', in *The Pelican Guide to English Literature, 4: From Dryden to Johnson*, ed. Boris Ford (Harmondsworth, 1957), pp. 127–8.

5 *Life of Johnson*, pp. 158–9; 1750.

6 *Ibid.*, pp. 909, 913; 7 April 1778.

7 Preface to Sarah Fielding's *Familiar Letters* (1747), i, x.

8 1744; ed. Malcolm Kersall (1969), p.8.

9 See Boucé, p. 394.

10 ix (1760), pp. 177–8. For details of Smollett's involvement with the *Critical Review* see Knapp, pp. 170–82, and the article by Derek Roper. 'Smollett's "Four Gentlemen": the first contributors to the *Critical Review*', *RES*, n.s., x, (1959), 38–44.

11 *The Art of the Novel* (1934), p. 345. Smollett may have taken a hint from Steele here: 'by the least transposition, that assemblage of words which is called a style, becomes utterly annihilated' (*Guardian*, 60, 20 May 1713).

12 *Critical*, i (1756), 226–39. (See also the article by Roper, above.)

13 *The Prose Style of Samuel Johnson*, p. 89.

14 See the essay 'Psychology and literature' in *Modern Man in Search of a Soul* (1933).

15 'For me writing—*the only possible writing*—is just simply the conversion of nervous force into phrases'. (Letter to H. G. Wells, 30 November 1903; *Life and Letters*; ed. G. Jean-Aubry, New York, 1957, i, 321.)

16 Hugh MacDiarmid, *The Uncanny Scot*, pp. 125–6.

17 *Collected Essays, Journalism, and Letters* (Harmondsworth, 1970), iii, 283.

18 Hannay, p. 160.

19 Knapp, pp. 303–6.
20 Boucé, pp. 70–90.
21 *Ibid.*, p. 428.
22 *The Standard Edition of the Complete Psychological Works of Sigmund Freud*, ed. J. Strachey (1953–73), ix, 150.
23 'Smollett's self-portrait in *Humphry Clinker*', in *The Age of Johnson: Essays presented to C. B. Tinker*, ed. F. W. Hilles (New Haven, Conn., 1949), p. 154.
24 W. K. Wimsatt uses the phrase, to describe the prose style of Hazlitt (with its 'large planes of meaning' and 'variegated details') in contrast to that of Johnson (*The Prose Style of Samuel Johnson*, p. 48).
25 T. S. Eliot, 'Portrait of a Lady', III.
26 '*Joseph Andrews* and *Pamela*', in *Fielding: a Collection of Critical Essays*, ed. Ronald Paulson (Englewood Cliffs, N. J., 1962, pp. 52–8); p. 57.
27 Preface to *Joseph Andrews* (1742; ed. Douglas Brooks, 1970), p. 6.
28 '*Joseph Andrews* and *Pamela*', p. 57.
29 I make no reference here to Arnold's 'prose of the centre' as defined in his essay 'The literary influence of academies' (1864). The centre invoked by Arnold is the 'centre of good taste', the 'centre of information' (immediately, the French Academy) which provides the 'classical prose, prose of the centre' in which the English are noticeably wanting (*Essays in Criticism*, ed. Kenneth Allott, 1964; pp. 47–9).
30 '*Joseph Andrews* and *Pamela*', p. 57.
31 *A Tale of a Tub*, sect. IX; ed. A. C. Guthkelch and D. N. Smith (Oxford, 1958); p. 174.
32 'Stylistic energy in the early Smollett'; *SP*, lxiv (1967), 719.
33 *A Tale of a Tub*, p. 174.
34 *Cf.* the article by Philip Stevick, 'The Augustan nose', *University of Toronto Quarterly*, xxxiv (1965), 110–17.

Chapter six

1 *The Fictions of Satire* (Baltimore, Md., 1967), p. 175.
2 *English Institute Essays* (1958), p. 28.
3 *Le Rire* (1900; PUF edn., 1940), p. 3.
4 *Letters*, p. 8.
5 'Roderick oppresses the faithful Strap, and ends by marrying him to a prostitute' (*History of English Literature*, 1863–64; trans. H. van Laun, 1871, ii, 178).
6 'Stylistic energy in the early Smollett', *SP*, lxiv (1967), 719.
7 *The Novel in France* (1950), p. 6.
8 Boucé, p. 399.
9 W. B. Piper has written very interestingly on the 'brilliant, obtrusive presence' of what he calls the 'grotesques' in Smollett's novels: see 'The large diffused picture of life in Smollett's early novels', *SP*, lx (1963), 45.
10 *Gargantua and Pantagruel*, Book IV, chapters 30–32; trans. J. M. Cohen (Harmondsworth, 1955), pp. 513–9.

[11] II, v; ed. Edward B. Partridge (1964), p. 58.

[12] *Little Dorrit*, chapter 25; Oxford Illustrated Dickens edn. (1953), p. 297.

[13] *Correspondence* (Paris, 1926–33); ii, 345–6.

[14] 1751; I, chapter 3 (i, 19).

[15] *JEGP*, lxix (1970), 32–40.

[16] *Reason and Romanticism* (1926), p. 199.

[17] William N. Glascock, *Naval Sketch Book* (1834), pp. 124–5, 139–40.

[18] IV, 160.

[19] *Le Rire*, pp. 7–17 and *passim*.

[20] *Ibid.*, pp. 84–5.

[21] *The Problem of Style* (1922), p. 46.

[22] *Le Rire*, pp. 97–8.

[23] *Lives of the Novelists*, i, 155.

[24] *The Complete Poems of Emily Dickinson*, ed. Thomas H. Johnson (1970), p. 506.

[25] Letter to Reynolds, 19 February 1818; *Letters of John Keats*, selected by Frederick Page (1954), p. 79.

[26] *Every Man in his Humour*, III, ii; ed. J. W. Lever (1971), p. 149.

[27] *Emma*, chapter 32; *Works*, ed. R. W. Chapman, iv, 271.

[28] *Little Dorrit*, preface, p. xvii.

[29] *What Maisie Knew*, chapter 26 (Harmondsworth, 1966), p. 195.

[30] Quoted by Boege, p. 82.

[31] *Cf.* Boucé: 'the comic element in Smollett's novels seems to be the most serious, or at least the most lasting expression, of a fundamental sanity' (p. 388).

[32] Ed. Pierre Michel (Paris, 1965), p. 23.

[33] This argument is developed in Shaftesbury's 'Letter concerning enthusiasm', included in his *Characteristics of Men, Manners, Opinions and Times* (1711).

[34] 'Lectures on the English comic writers' (1819; *Works*, 1930, vi, 7).

[35] *Letters*, p. 124.

[36] *Continuation of the Complete History of England* (1760–61; 1765), ii, 196.

[37] *Comedy* (1972), p. 79.

Chapter seven

[1] Hannay, p. 51.

[2] *The Verbal Icon*, p. 138.

[3] Henry James remarked that 'solidity of specification' was 'the supreme virtue of a novel': 'The art of fiction', in *Selected Literary Criticism*, ed. Morris Shapira (Harmondsworth, 1968), pp. 86–7.

[4] *Articulate Energy* (1955), p. 85.

[5] 1922; 1960, p. 380.

[6] *James Joyce* (1960), p. 19.

[7] *The Function of Criticism* (1962), p. 54.

[8] *Tatler*, 47, 28 July 1709.

[9] *A Philosophical Enquiry into the Origin of our Ideas of the Sublime and*

Beautiful (1757; second edn., 1759), pp. 339–40.

10 Letter 71; *Collected Works of Oliver Goldsmith*, ed. Arthur Friedman (Oxford, 1966), ii, 293–8.

11 *Book of Courtesy* (1477); in *Geoffrey Chaucer: a Critical Anthology*, ed. J. A. Burrow (Harmondsworth, 1969), p. 44.

12 *The Works of Tobias Smollett, M. D.*, ed. J. Moore (1797), i, clxix.

13 Page 231.

14 Part One, l. 172.

15 Pope, *Essay on Man*, II, 201–2.

16 Swift, *Gulliver's Travels*, II, chapter 6; ed. Hayward (1949), p. 130.

17 'The Vanity of Human Wishes', l. 76.

18 *The Dunciad*, IV, 648.

19 *Joseph Andrews*, II chapter 1; ed. Douglas Brooks (1970), p. 79.

20 There is contemporary testimony to the power of this passage in that Edward Cobden, Archdeacon of London, quoted it in full in a sermon 'A Persuasive to Chastity', subsequently printed in the *Gentleman's Magazine* (xix, 1749, 125–6).

21 Smollett is surely recalling details from Pope's Epistle to Burlington here: where 'The thriving plants ignoble broomsticks made./Now sweep those Alleys they were born to shade'; where 'Cupids squirt' in front of the house, and 'gaping Tritons spew to wash your face' (ll. 89–168).

22 *University of Toronto Quarterly*, xxxiv (1965), 110–17.

23 'Epistle to Dr Arbuthnot', l. 186.

24 It is possible that Dickens may have had Smollett's misfortunes in mind when he described the similarly inauspicious first stage of Mr Dorrit's travels. 'The whole business of the human race, between London and Dover, being spoliation, Mr Dorrit was waylaid at Dartford, pillaged at Gravesend, rifled at Rochester, fleeced at Sittingbourne, and sacked at Canterbury'. (*Little Dorrit*, Book Second, chapter 18; Oxford Illustrated Dickens, 1953, p. 634.)

25 *The Grand Tour in the Eighteenth Century* (Boston, Mass., 1914), p. 112.

26 Quoted in a review of *The English Essays of Edward Gibbon*, ed. Patricia B. Craddock, in the *TLS*, 1 June 1973 (p. 613).

Chapter eight

1 *The Prose Style of Samuel Johnson*, p. 140.

2 See Knapp, pp. 58–61.

3 'The Poetical Pieces which compose the First Part of the First Volume, were most of them written when I was very young, and are indeed Productions of the Heart rather than of the Head.' (Preface to *Miscellanies*, 1743; ed. Henry Knight Miller, Oxford, 1972, I, 3.)

4 See Howard S. Buck, *Smollett as Poet*, (New Haven, Conn., 1927), pp. 41–8.

5 See Knapp, pp. 87–91.

6 *Letters of Robert Burns*, ed. J. de Lancey Ferguson, 1931, i, 244. (See Boege, pp. 54–5.)

7 1810; xv, 552–3.
8 Letter 40; *Collected Works*, ed. Arthur Friedman, ii, 171. Howard S. Buck
   puts forward this view in his short but useful study *Smollett as Poet*,
   undertaken he says, not 'to rehabilitate Smollett as a poet' but 'with the
   conviction that a fuller knowledge of these matters was indispensable to
   an understanding of Smollett the man and the novelist' (pp. xii, xiv).
   Buck makes some distinctly interesting comments on Smollett's poetic
   use of language, and I would certainly endorse his challenging and
   perhaps unexpected conclusion: 'The fact that he possessed in some
   degree the poetical temperament, and used it in his novels, is, in a
   word, their saving grace. For without it, what would they be? In his
   prose fiction . . . it was the poet that was in him that is the leaven of the
   lump' (p. 84).
9 *British Novelists and their Styles* (1859), p. 144.
10 Irma Z. Sherwood, 'The novelists as commentators', in *The Age of Johnson: Essays presented to C. B. Tinker*, ed. F. W. Hilles (New Haven, Conn.,
   1949), p. 113.
11 Book XVIII, chapter 11; p. 861.
12 *Middlemarch*, chapter 42.
13 'Love and Freindship', Letter the eighth; *The Works of Jane Austen*, ed. R.
   W. Chapman (1923–54), vi, 86.
14 *Persuasion*, chapter 19; *Works*, ed. R. W. Chapman, v, 175.
15 Page references only: pp. 18, 69, 78 (twice), 111, 125, 206, 226, 243, 292,
   325.
16 To the lines: 'Lo! where Maeotis sleeps, and hardly flows/The Freezing
   Tanais thro' a waste of snows' (III, 87–8) James Sutherland appends
   Johnson's comment: 'I have been told that the couplet by which he
   declared his own ear to be most gratified was this' *The Dunciad* (1943), p.
   156.
17 Chapter 22; in *Classical Literary Criticism*, trans. T. S. Dorsch (Harmondsworth, 1965), p. 65.
18 *Rhetoric*, trans. R. C. Jebb (Cambridge, 1909), p. 149.
19 Twice in *Tom Jones* Fielding recalls Locke's example of the blind man
   who identified scarlet with the sound of a trumpet: IV, chapter 1 (p.
   152), and VI, chapter 1 (p. 253). In the latter instance Fielding remarks
   ironically to the reader that 'love probably may, in your opinion, very
   greatly resemble a dish of soup, or a sir-loin of roast-beef'.
20 For example by Paul Fussell, *The Rhetoric of Augustan Humanism*
   (Oxford, 1965), chapter 7.
21 *Life of Johnson*, p. 1401: 1784.
22 Chapter 10; *Poetry and Prose*, pp. 409–10.
23 *The Prose Style of Samuel Johnson*, p. 65.
24 *Life of Johnson*, p. 1283: 30 May 1784.
25 *Biographia Literaria*, chapter 14; ed. George Watson (1956), p. 174.
26 *Essay on Man*, I, 198.
27 *Shakespeare's Doctrine of Nature* (1948), p. 224.

Bibliography

The bibliography is divided for convenience into four sections: I, Smollett; II, Bibliography of Smollett; III, Biography of Smollett; IV, Selected criticism of Smollett. Within each section the arrangement is chronological. The place of publication is London, except where otherwise stated.

I Smollett

(i) Single works, in order of publication:

Advice: a Satire, 1746.
Reproof: a Satire, 1747.
The Adventures of Roderick Random, 1748.
The Regicide: or, James the First of Scotland, 1749.
The Adventures of Peregrine Pickle, 1751.
A Faithful Narrative of the Base and Inhuman Arts that were Lately Practised upon the Brain of Habbakkuk Hilding, 1752.
An Essay on the External Use of Water, 1752.
The Adventures of Ferdinand Count Fathom, 1753.
The Reprisal: or, the Tars of Old England, 1757.
A Complete History of England from the Descent of Julius Caesar to the Treaty of Aix la Chapelle, 1757–58.
The Adventures of Sir Launcelot Greaves, 1762 (first published in *The British Magazine*, i, ii, 1760–61).
A Continuation of the Complete History, 1760–61, 1765.
Travels Through France and Italy, 1766.
The History and Adventures of an Atom, 1769. (The first edition was deliberately misdated 1749.)
The Expedition of Humphry Clinker, 1771.
Ode to Independence, Glasgow, 1773.

(ii) Works translated or edited by Smollett:

Le Sage, *The Adventures of Gil Blas*, 1749.
Cervantes, *The History and Adventures of Don Quixote*, 1755.
The Critical Review: or, Annals of Literature, 1756–90. (Smollett was editor-in-chief from 1756 to 1763, and an occasional contributor thereafter.)
A Compendium of Authentic and Entertaining Voyages, 1756. (For a study of Smollett's editorial methods in this work see Martz, pp. 23–9. Smollett himself contributed 'An Account of the Expedition Against Carthagene', v, 313–42.)

The British Magazine, 1760–7. (Smollett was active on *The British Magazine* from 1760 to 1763. See Martz, pp. 6, 178–80.)
The Works of M. de Voltaire, 1761.
The Briton, 1762–63. (The single essays of which this paper was composed were mostly Smollett's own work.)
The Present State of All Nations, 1768–69. (The extent of Smollett's contribution to this work is discussed by Martz, pp. 104–6.)
Smollett also contributed to *The Monthly Review*. See B. C. Nangle, *The Monthly Review. Indexes of Contributors and Articles*, Oxford, 1934.

(iii) Letters:
The Letters of Tobias Smollett, ed. Lewis M. Knapp, Oxford, 1970.

II Bibliography of Smollett

A bibliography by John P. Anderson is included at the end of David Hannay's *Life of Smollett* (1887), pp. i–x.
Francesco Cordasco, *Smollett Criticism, 1770–1924: a Bibliography, Enumerative and Annotative* (Long Island, 1948).
—*Smollett Criticism, 1925–1945: a Compilation* (Long Island, 1947).
Donald M. Korte, *An Annotated Bibliography of Smollett Scholarship, 1946–68* (Ontario, 1969).
For corrections and additions to the above see Boucé, pp. 454–6.
There is also a useful bibliography in R. D. Spector, *Tobias Smollett* (New York, 1968), pp. 161–7.
See also *The New Cambridge Bibliography of English Literature*, ed. George Watson, vol. 2: *1660–1800* (Cambridge, 1971), and *The English Novel*, ed. A. E. Dyson (1974), both of which contain bibliographical sections on Smollett by Lewis M. Knapp.

III Biography of Smollett

David Hannay, *Life of Smollett* (1887).
Lewis M. Knapp, *Tobias Smollett, Doctor of Men and Manners* Princeton, N.J., 1949).
See also Paul-Gabriel Boucé, *Les Romans de Smollett: étude critique* (Paris, 1971); 'Première Partie: de Smollett à ses romans'.

IV Selected criticism of Smollett

(i) Books devoted to Smollett:

Arnold Whitridge, *Tobias Smollett: a Study of his Miscellaneous Works* (published by the author, 1925).
Howard S. Buck, *A Study in Smollett, Chiefly 'Peregrine Pickle'* (New Haven, Conn., 1925).
—*Smollett as Poet* (New Haven, 1927).
F. W. Wierstra, *Smollett and Dickens*, (Den Helder, 1928).
Eugène Joliat, *Smollett et la France* (Paris, 1935).

Claude E. Jones, *Smollett Studies* (Los Angeles, 1942).
Louis L. Martz, *The Later Career of Tobias Smollett* (New Haven, Conn., 1942).
George M. Kahrl, *Tobias Smollett, Traveler–Novelist* (Chicago, 1945).
Fred W. Boege, *Smollett's Reputation as a Novelist* (Princeton, N.J., 1947).
Laurence Brander, *Tobias Smollett*, British Council pamphlet, 1951.
M. A. Goldberg, *Smollett and the Scottish School* (Albuquerque, N.M., 1959).
Donald Bruce, *Radical Doctor Smollett* (1964).
Robert Giddings, *The Tradition of Smollett* (1967).
R. D. Spector, *Tobias Smollett* (New York, 1968).
Paul-Gabriel Boucé, *Les Romans de Smollett: étude critique* (Paris, 1971).
—English translation (abridged) *The Novels of Tobias Smollett* (1976).
G. S. Rousseau and P.-G. Boucé (eds.), *Tobias Smollett: Essays presented to Lewis M. Knapp* (New York, 1971).

(ii) Books with chapters or sections on Smollett:

William Hazlitt, *Lectures on the English Comic Writers* (1819; in *Works*, ed. Howe, 1930–34, vi).
Walter Scott, *Lives of the Novelists* (Paris, 1825).
W. M. Thackeray, *The English Humourists of the Eighteenth Century* (1851; in *Works*, 1898).
David Masson, *British Novelists and their Styles* (Cambridge, 1859).
Wilbur L. Cross, *The Development of the English Novel* (1899).
George Saintsbury *The Peace of the Augustans* (1916).
—*Prefaces and Introductions* (1933).
Herbert Read, *Reason and Romanticism* (1926).
E. A. Baker, *History of the English Novel* (1930).
V. S. Pritchett, *The Living Novel* (1946).
A. D. McKillop, *The Early Masters of English Fiction* (Lawrence, 1956).
Giorgio Melchiori, *The Tightrope Walkers* (1956).
Robert Alter, *Rogue's Progress* (Cambridge, Mass., 1964).
R. A. Donovan, *The Shaping Vision* (Ithaca, N.Y., 1966).
Ronald Paulson, *Satire and the Novel in Eighteenth-century England* (New Haven, Conn., 1967).
Douglas Brooks, *Number and Pattern in the Eighteenth-century Novel* (1973).
Pat Rogers, *The Augustan Vision* (1974).
Thomas R. Preston, *Not in Timon's Manner: Feeling, Misanthropy and Satire in Eighteenth Century England* (Alabama, 1975).

(iii) Essays:

David Herbert, introduction to *The Works of Tobias Smollett*, (Edinburgh, 1870), i, 5–40.
J. A. Nicklin, 'An eighteenth-century saga', *Gentleman's Magazine*, cclxxx (1896), 453–8.
Thomas Seccombe, introduction to *Travels Through France and Italy* (1907), pp. v–lx.

George Orwell, 'Scotland's best novelist', *Tribune*, 22 September 1944; in *Collected Essays, Journalism and Letters* (Harmondsworth, 1970), iii, 282–6.

Rufus Putney, 'The plan of Peregrine Pickle', *PMLA*, lx (1945), 1051–65.

L. M. Knapp, 'Smollett's self-portrait in *Humphry Clinker*', in *The Age of Johnson: Essays presented to C. B. Tinker*, ed. F. W. Hilles (New Haven, Conn., 1949), pp. 149–58.

James R. Foster, 'Smollett and the *Atom*', *PMLA*, lxviii (1953), 1032–46.

A. R. Humphreys, 'Fielding and Smollett', in *The Pelican Guide to English Literature, 4: Dryden to Johnson*, ed. Boris Ford (Harmondsworth, 1957), 313–32.

Albrecht B. Strauss, 'On Smollett's language: a paragraph in *Ferdinand Count Fathom*', *English Institute Essays* (1958), pp. 25–54.

Derek Roper, 'Smollett's "Four Gentlemen": the first contributors to the *Critical Review*', *RES*, x (1959), 38–44.

Sheridan Baker, '*Humphry Clinker* as comic romance', *Papers of the Michigan Academy of Science, Arts and Letters*, lxvi (1961), 645–54; reprinted in R. D. Spector (ed.), *Essays on the Eighteenth-century Novel* (Bloomington, Ind., 1964).

Byron Gassman, 'The *Briton* and *Humphry Clinker*', *SEL*, iii (1963), 397–414.

William B. Piper, 'The large diffused picture of life in Smollett's early novels', *SP*, lx (1963), 45–56.

Thomas R. Preston, 'Smollett and the benevolent misanthrope type', *PMLA*, lxxix (1964), 51–7.

Tuvia Bloch, 'Smollett's quest for form', *MP*, lxv (1967), 103–13.

Philip Stevick, 'Stylistic energy in the early Smollett', *SP*, lxiv (1967), 712–9.

John F. Sena, 'Smollett's persona and the melancholy traveller', *ECS*, i (1968), 358–69.

Gary N. Underwood, 'Linguistic realism in *Roderick Random*', *JEGP*, lxix (1970), 32–40.

C. J. Rawson, 'Fielding and Smollett', in *Sphere History of Literature in the English Language, 4: Dryden to Johnson*, ed. Roger Lonsdale (1971), 259–95.

John M. Warner, 'Smollett's development as a novelist', *Novel*, iv (1972), 148–61.

Index